PHP
Essentials

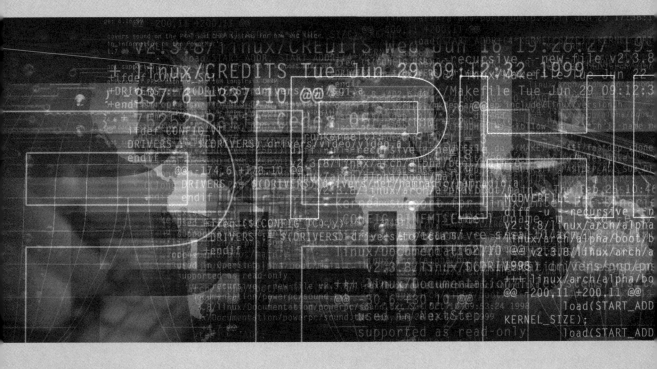

PHP
Essentials

Julie Meloni

Premier
Press

ISBN: 1-931841-34-9

Library of Congress Catalog Card Number: 2003101207

Printed in the United States of America

03 04 05 06 07 BH 10 9 8 7 6 5 4 3 2 1

Premier Press, a division of Course Technology
25 Thomson Place
Boston, MA 02210

Publisher
Stacy L. Hiquet

Senior Marketing Manager
Martine Edwards

Marketing Manager
Heather Hurley

Manager of Editorial Services
Heather Talbot

Acquisitions Editor
Todd Jenson

Project Editor
Estelle Manticas

Technical Reviewer
Michelle Jones

Copy Editor
Estelle Manticas

Interior Layout
Marian Hartsough

Cover Designer
Mike Tanamachi

Indexer
Sharon Shock

Proofreader
Sean Medlock

Acknowledgments

Thanks as always to the PHP Group, Zend Technologies, the Apache Software Foundation and MySQL AB for creating and maintaining such wonderful and accessible products for all users.

Thanks to every single PHP user and developer, because without you, I wouldn't have anything to write about.

Enormous thanks to everyone at i2i Interactive, for their never-ending support and encouragement.

About the Author

JULIE MELONI is the technical director for i2i Interactive, a multimedia company located in Los Altos, California. She's been developing Web-based applications since the Web first saw the light of day and remembers the excitement surrounding the first GUI Web browser. She is the author of several books and articles on Web-based programming languages and database topics, and you can find translations of her work in many different languages, including Chinese, Danish, Finnish, Italian, Portuguese, Polish and even Serbian.

Contents at a Glance

Contents

Introduction

If you compare this book to most of the other books on PHP, you'll quickly notice that this book is much smaller than those thousand-page behemoths. The relative smallness of this book is intentional—I've found it's easier to learn from a book you can actually hold!

That being said, plenty of topics that are covered in those lengthier books are not covered in this book. This book offers, as its title, says the *essential* information. In other words, information that will provide a solid foundation for the additional topics you will find in longer, more advanced books.

A main characteristic of this book, besides teaching the fundamentals, is that you don't have to be a computer scientist or programmer to learn from it. If you *are* a computer scientist or programmer already, you may not like the rather prosaic nature of the explanations and instructions in this book. Ultimately, I wanted to write a book that someone could take off the shelf, skim through, and say, "Hey, this PHP thing looks like a neat language, and ever-so-easy to learn!" Because it is!

If you've been programming with PHP since the beginning of time, there's probably not much you can get out of this book, except to hand it to your boss and say, "Look! Another book on what a wonderful language this is. Can we please stop using ASP/Cold Fusion/Java/Perl/C++ and migrate to PHP? " But if you've just dabbled with PHP or have never seen a PHP script, I am certain this book will be of some use to you.

Supplemental Web Site

Additional information for this book (and for other books I've written) can be found at http://www.thickbook.com/. At this site you can download all the code samples in this book, as well additional tutorials and notifications of any errors in the book. You can also use the site to get help with any problems you may have with the examples.

Getting Started with PHP

Whether you're a first-time programmer or you have a few years of Web application development under your belt, you'll find something useful in this book. Hopefully, what you'll find is a simple "learn-by-example" path to developing successful dynamic Web sites.

Unlike the Web itself, this book is fairly linear. You'll start by installing the software needed to use PHP, and then you'll gradually move into "Hello World!" scripts and eventually create shopping carts and other database-driven applications.

If you have an account with an Internet Service Provider who has enabled the use of PHP for all users on the server, you can skip ahead to Chapter 2. But as you can install freely available Web servers, PHP, and a databsse or two on your own machine—with a little poking and prodding—I recommend you do so. It's a great way to learn the "guts" of the tools you'll be using.

What Is PHP?

PHP is a server-side scripting language. When your Web browser accesses a URL, it is making a request to a Web server. If you are requesting a PHP page, something like http://www.yourcompany.com/home.php, the Web server wakes up the PHP parsing engine and says, "Hey! You've got to do something before I send a result back to this person's Web browser." The PHP parsing engine runs through the PHP code found in the home.php file and returns the resulting output. This output is passed back to the Web server as the HTML code in the document, which in turn is passed on to your browser, which displays it to you.

A Brief History of PHP

In 1994, an incredibly forward-thinking man named Rasmus Lerdorf developed a set of tools that used a parsing engine to interpret a few macros here and there. They were not extravagant: a guest book, a counter, and some other "home page" elements that were cool when the Web was in its infancy. He eventually combined these tools with a form interpretation (FI) package he had written, added some database support, and released what was known as PHP/FI.

Then, in the spirit of Open Source software development, developers all over the world began contributing to PHP/FI. By 1997, more than 50,000 Web sites were using PHP/FI to accomplish different tasks—connecting to a database, displaying dynamic content, and so on.

At that point, the development process really started becoming a team effort. With primary assistance from developers Zeev Suraski and Andi Gutmans, the version 3.0 parser was created. The final release of PHP3 occurred in June of 1998, when it was upgraded to include support for multiple platforms (it's not just for Linux anymore!) and Web servers, numerous databases, and SNMP (Simple Network Management Protocol) and IMAP (Internet Message Access Protocol).

After PHP 3.0 was released, the aforementioned Suraski and Gutmans began to develop a super-fast engine to replace the core elements of PHP, and in mid-1999 the Zend Engine was born. PHP 4.0 was based on this engine, and was released in the Spring of 2000. This release was a watershed for PHP—the vast amount of new featues and incresed performance results now found in PHP 4.0 made it a viable tool for advanced Web application development. The current version is PHP 4.3, which you'll learn to install in Chapter 1, "Getting Started with PHP."

In the three years between the appearance, in early 2000, of the first edition of this book and this newest edition, PHP usage has exploded. Companies like Amazon.com and Yahoo! use PHP in various areas of their Web sites. That's definitely high praise! The most recent survey from Netcraft (http://www.netcraft.com/) show PHP is installed on over 9.5 million domains. It is commonplace for Internet Service Providers to offer PHP and MySQL in even the most basic (or free!) hosting packages, and PHP source code is shipped with most Linux distributions.

Additionally, there are hundreds of books which address PHP development in some way—a marked increase from the five or so which were available when the first edition of this book was published. The tens of thousands of developers who use and contribute to PHP have made this simple language near-revolutionary, and those numbers continue to grow.

What Does PHP Do?

PHP does anything you want, except sit on its head and spin. Actually, with a little on-the-fly image manipulation and Dynamic HTML, it can probably do that, too.

According to the PHP Manual, "The goal of the language is to allow Web developers to write dynamically generated pages quickly."

The list below show some common uses of PHP. This is by no means a complete list, and doesn't indicate any of the more advanced functionality that developers use in large applications; it's just an idea of the items that your average developer may use on a daily basis.

♦ Perform system functions: create, open, read from, write to, and close files on your system, execute system commands, create directories, and modify permissions.

♦ Gather data from forms: save the data to a file, send data via e-mail, return manipulated data to the user.

♦ Access databases and generate content on-the-fly, or create a Web interface for adding, deleting, and modifying elements within your database.

♦ Set cookies and access cookie variables.

♦ Use PHP user authentication to restrict access to sections of your Web site.

♦ Create images on-the-fly.

♦ Encrypt data.

A Note Regarding Open Source Development

Open Source software must follow these criteria (they are available in detail at http://www.opensource.org/):

♦ Free redistribution.

♦ The program must include source code and must allow distribution in source code as well as compiled form.

♦ The license must allow modifications and derived works.

♦ Integrity of the author's source code.

♦ No discrimination against persons or groups.

♦ No discrimination against fields of endeavor.

♦ Distribution of license.

♦ License must not be specific to a product.

♦ License must not contaminate other software.

PHP is a fine example of Open Source development and distribution. Other examples include the following:

- **Apache.** The Web Server of choice for more than 4.8 million Web sites.
- **Linux.** The operating system of choice for more people than Microsoft would have you think.
- **BIND.** The software providing Domain Name Services to the Internet—all of it.
- **Sendmail.** The most widely-used software for transporting e-mail from sender to recipient.

Synonymous with "Open Source" is "volunteerism." Developers contributing to Open Source software don't directly make money from doing so. Wherever possible, contribute to your favorite Open Source organization, be it the PHP Group or someone else. Give back some time by answering questions, helping with documentation, contributing code where possible, or even making a monetary donation. The cost of equipment, connectivity, tools, and, most importantly, brainpower is absorbed directly by the volunteer developer, so that you and I have a freely (and widely) available piece of software.

Is PHP Right for Me?

Only you can decide if PHP should be your language of choice, whether you're developing sites for personal or commercial use on a small or large scale. I can only tell you that in the commercial realm, I've worked with all the popular server-side scripting languages—Active Server Pages (ASP), ColdFusion, Java Server Pages (JSP), Perl, and PHP—on numerous platforms and various Web servers, with various degrees of success. PHP is the right choice for me: it's flexible, fast, and simplistic in its requirements yet powerful in its output.

Before deciding whether to use PHP in a large-scale or commercial environment, consider your answers to the following questions:

- Will you always use the same Web server hardware and software? If not, look for something cross-platform and available for multiple Web servers: PHP.
- Will you always have the exact same development team, comprised entirely of ASP (or ColdFusion) developers? Or will you use whoever is

available, thus necessitating a language that is easy to learn and syntactically similar to C and Perl? If you have reason to believe that your ASP or ColdFusion developers might drop off the face of the earth, don't use those tools; use PHP.

◆ Are memory and server load an issue? If so, don't use bloated third-party software that leaks precious memory; use PHP.

There are plenty of other questions to ask yourself when making a decision regarding a development language, and in short I can only say "Try it, you'll like it!"

Chapter 1

**Getting Started
with PHP**

This chapter will walk you through the basics of getting PHP and a Web server up and running on your system, and will show you how to add database support as well. You may or may not need to read this entire chapter—if you don't plan to install Microsoft IIS, then, don't worry about reading that section.

No matter what section or sections you choose to read, please pay close attention to the instructions given. The installation is not difficult, but it is important to follow the steps closely. Missing one instruction will result in frustration on your part and angry e-mails in my inbox, both of which I'd like to avoid!

Installing a Web Server

In this section, you'll learn to install Apache on Linux/UNIX or Windows, and you'll also learn the basics of getting and installing other Web servers, such as Microsoft IIS. Personally, I never install anything other than Apache, even if it's on my personal Windows machines. But if you want to install Microsoft IIS or another Web server, feel free! Some other Web servers will be discussed at the end of this section.

Throughout the Apache installation sections, the instructions assume you know the basics of administering either Linux/UNIX or Windows. If you don't know anything about the command line, or have never logged on as Administrator to a Windows machine, you should take a step back and brush up on your system administrator skills before continuing.

Working with Apache

The Apache Web server is an open-source project produced and maintained by the Apache Software Foundation. Since 1996, Apache has been the most popular Web server in use on the Internet—quite a run! Apache currently holds over 60 percent of the Web server market share, and there are no signs of it relinquishing its stronghold.

The current version of the Apache server is 2.0.44, which is the version used as the basis for the installation instructions in this chapter. Should you purchase this book and find the current version is different, first try the instructions as written here, and then check for updated instructions at this book's Web site, http://www.thickbook.com/. Unless something drastic has happened to the Apache source code (or this book is years out of date), the installation instructions in this book will work despite minor version changes.

When working with Apache, you have two options for installation: building from source or installing from a pre-compiled binary. Building from source gives you the greatest flexibility, as it enables you to remove modules you don't need and extend the server with third-party modules. Additionally, building from source enables you to easily upgrade to the latest versions and quickly apply security patches, whereas updated versions from vendors can take days or weeks to appear.

Pre-compiled binary installations are available from third-party vendors and can also be downloaded from the Apache Software Foundation Web site. This installation method provides a simple way to install Apache for users with limited system administration knowledge or with no special configuration needs.

In the following sections, you'll use the build-from-source method for installation on Linux/UNIX and the pre-compiled installation method (in this case, using an Installer) for Windows systems.

Installing and Configuring Apache on Linux/UNIX

In this section, you'll install a fresh build of Apache 2.0 on Linux/UNIX. The official Apache download page is located at http://httpd.apache.org/download.cgi, and it will always clearly indicate the most recent version of Apache for your platform.

The Apache source distribution files are first packed with the tar utility and then compressed, either with the gzip tool or the compress utility. Download the .tar.gz version if you have the gunzip utility installed in your system, and download the tar.Z file if gunzip is not present in your system.

The file you want to download will be named something like httpd-2.0.*version*.tar.gz or httpd-2.0.*version*.tar.Z, where *version* is the most recent release version of Apache. For example, Apache version 2.0.44 is downloaded as a file named httpd-2.0.44.tar.gz or httpd-2.0.44.tar.Z. Whichever file you download, put it in directory reserved for source files, such as /usr/src/ or /usr/local/src/.

Now, let's get on with the installing. If you downloaded the tarball compressed with gzip, uncompress and unpack the software by typing the following command at the prompt (#):

```
# gunzip < httpd-2.0*.tar.gz | tar xvf -
```

If you downloaded the tarball compressed with compress (tar.Z suffix), type the following command at the prompt (#):

```
# cat httpd-2.0*.tar.Z | uncompress | tar xvf -
```

Whichever method you used, you should now have a structure of directories, with the top-level directory named httpd-2.0.*version*. Change your current directory to this top-level directory to prepare for configuring the software. For example:

```
# cd httpd-2.0.44
```

With the Apache distribution unpacked, you can now configure a basic version of the server and start it up. You'll make some modifications later when you install PHP, but first things first!

By running the configure script in the top-level distribution directory, you can add and remove functionality from Apache. By default, Apache is compiled with a set of standard modules that are compiled statically. However, in preparation for the PHP installation later in the chapter, you need to ensure that the mod_so module is compiled into Apache. This module, named for the Unix shared object (*.so) format, enables the use of dynamic modules such as PHP with Apache. To configure Apache to install itself in a specific location (in this case /usr/local/apache2/) and to enable the use of mod_so, issue the following command at the prompt:

```
# ./configure --prefix=/usr/local/apache2 --enable-module=so
```

The configure script will run, determining the location of libraries, compile-time options, platform-specific differences, and so on, and will end up creating a set of makefiles. If everything goes well after running the configure script, you will see a set of messages related to the different checks just performed, and you will be returned to the prompt.

```
...
creating test/Makefile
```

```
config.status: creating docs/conf/httpd-std.conf
config.status: creating include/ap_config_layout.h
config.status: creating support/apxs
config.status: creating support/apachectl
config.status: creating support/dbmmanage
config.status: creating support/envvars-std
config.status: creating support/log_server_status
config.status: creating support/logresolve.pl
config.status: creating support/phf_abuse_log.cgi
config.status: creating support/split-logfile
config.status: creating build/rules.mk
config.status: creating include/ap_config_auto.h
config.status: executing default commands
#
```

If the configure script fails, you will see warnings that will allow you to track down additional software, such as compilers or libraries, that must be installed. After you install any missing software, you can try the configure command again, after deleting the config.log and config.status files from the top-level directory.

Assuming that all went smoothly with the configure script, simply type make at the prompt in order to build Apache. You will see several messages indicating the progress of the compilation, and you will end up back at the prompt. When compilation is complete, you can install Apache by typing make install at the prompt. The makefiles will install files and directories, and return you to the prompt:

```
...
Installing header files
Installing man pages and online manual
mkdir /usr/local/apache2/man
mkdir /usr/local/apache2/man/man1
mkdir /usr/local/apache2/man/man8
mkdir /usr/local/apache2/manual
Installing build system files
make[1]: Leaving directory `/usr/local/bin/httpd-2.0.44'
#
```

The Apache distribution files should now be in the /usr/local/apache2 directory, as specified by the `--prefix` switch in the `configure` command. To test that the `httpd` binary has been correctly built, type the following at the prompt:

```
# /usr/local/apache2/bin/httpd -v
```

You should see the following output (your version and build date will be different):

Server version: Apache/2.0.44

Server built: Jan 21 2003 07:37:05

You're now only a few steps away from starting up your new Apache server. To run a basic installation of Apache, the only changes you need to make are to the server name, which resides in the master configuration file called httpd.conf. This file lives in the conf directory, within the Apache installation directory. In this case, the configuration files will be in /usr/local/apache2/conf/.

In your text editor of choice, open the httpd.conf and make the following changes:

◆ Change the value of `ServerAdmin` to your e-mail address:

```
ServerAdmin you@yourdomain.com
```

◆ Change the value of `ServerName` to something accurate (or use the loop-back address of 127.0.0.1 for testing purposes, if you're connecting locally) and remove the preceding "#", so that the entry looks like this:

```
ServerName 127.0.0.7
```

You do not want it to look like this:

```
#ServerName somehost.somedomain.com
```

These two modifications are the only changes necessary for a basic installation of Apache on Linux/UNIX. Whenever you modify the configuration files you must restart Apache for the changes to take effect. Make sure you back up your original files before you modify them.

Now you can try to start Apache. There's a handy utility, called `apachectl`, in the bin directory within your Apache installation directory. It allows you to issue start, stop, and restart commands. Use this utility to start Apache for the first time by typing the following from within the bin subdirectory of the Apache installation directory:

```
# ./apachectl start
```

If you don't get an error, then Apache is happily chugging along and you can now connect to whatever value you put in ServerName. When you connect to this new installation of Apache, you should see the Apache default start page, as shown in Figure 1.1.

This page comes from the htdocs directory within your Apache installation directory. You can go into that directory and delete all the default files if you want to, or you can leave them there. They're not hurting anything, but you'll eventually be filling the htdocs directory with your own files and subdirectories, so you might want to delete them for the sake of good housekeeping.

If you do get an error when you try to start Apache, the output of apachectl will usually tell you why—most likely it'll be a typo in httpd.conf that you can easily fix.

Unless you've got some extra time on your hands and an extra machine, you can skip the next section regarding installation of Apache on Windows and jump ahead to "Installing and Configuring PHP."

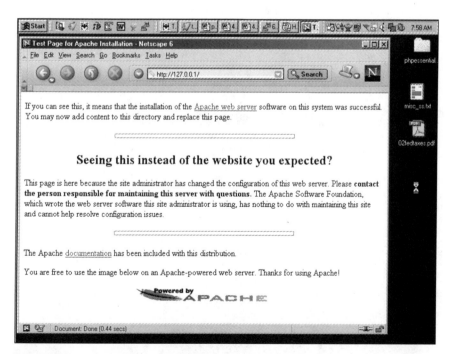

FIGURE 1.1 *Successful Apache installation*

Installing and Configuring Apache on Windows

Although Apache 2.0 is designed to run on Windows NT, Windows 2000, and Windows XP, you can also run it on Windows 95 and Windows 98 without difficulty. However, do so for testing purposes only, as these platforms are intended for personal use, not as a server platform. If you are installing on Windows 95 or Windows 98, be sure to read the notes found at http://httpd.apache.org/dist/binaries/win32/ and make sure your operating system is up-to-date. Also, before embarking on the Apache installation, make sure that you do not already have a Web server running on your machine (for instance, a previous version of Apache, Microsoft Internet Information Server, or Microsoft Personal Web Server). While you can run several Web servers on the same machine, they will need to run under different address and port combinations.

Installing Apache on Windows is easily performed via the pre-packaged installer program. Go to the official Apache download page at http://httpd.apache.org/download.cgi, and look for the link to the Windows installer, which is clearly marked as such. The naming convention is apache_*version*-win32-x86-no_ssl.msi, where *version* is the current version number. The installer file used for these instructions is called apache_2.0.44-win32-x86-no_ssl.msi.

After you download the installer, the process begins with the basic double-click on the installer file. This launches the program, complete with the welcome screen shown in Figure 1.2.

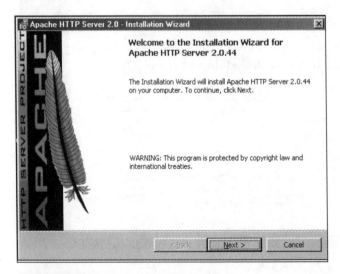

FIGURE 1.2 *Apache Installer Welcome screen*

Select Next to continue the installation process, and then read and accept the Apache license. After you accept the license, the installer presents you with a brief introduction to Apache. Following that, it asks you to provide basic information about your computer, as shown in Figure 1.3.

The information you'll need to provide includes the full network address for your server (for instance, yourmachine.yourdomain.com) and the administrator's e-mail address.

 NOTE

If your machine does not have a full network address, use localhost or 127.0.0.1 as the `ServerName`, as shown in Figure 1.3.

After continuing to the next step, select the type of installation. *Typical* installation means that Apache binaries and documentation will be installed, but headers and libraries will not. This is the best option to choose unless you plan to compile your own modules.

A *custom* installation enables you to choose whether to install header files or documentation. After selecting the target installation directory, which defaults to C:\Program Files\Apache Group, the program will proceed through the

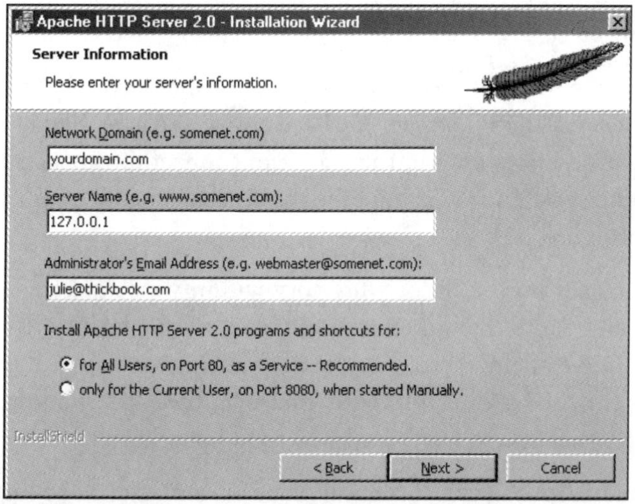

FIGURE 1.3 *Provide information about your server*

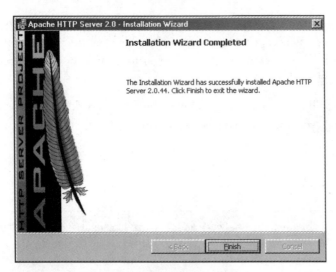

FIGURE 1.4 *Apache installer has finished*

installation process. If everything goes well, it will present you with the final screen, shown in Figure 1.4.

With Apache installed, you can now check its configuration file to ensure that the installer did its job. To check the configuration, go to Start>Programs>Apache HTTP Server 2.0.44>Configure Apache Server>Test Configuration. A window will appear, containing the result of the test. If the test is successful, the window will disappear on its own. If there is a problem, the correctable error message will appear in the window.

After your configuration file has been validated, start the server by going to Start>Programs>Apache HTTP Server 2.0.44>Control Apache Servers>Start Apache in Console. If no errors appear, then you can connect to this new installation of Apache. When you do, you should see the Apache default start page (as shown previously, in Figure 1.1).

The default page comes from the htdocs directory within your Apache installation directory. You can go into that directory and delete all the default files if you want to, or you can leave them there. They're not hurting anything, but you'll eventually be filling the htdocs directory with your own files and subdirectories, so you might want to delete them for the sake of good housekeeping.

With the installation of Apache out of the way, you can continue on to installing PHP.

Installing and Configuring PHP

PHP can be installed as a module, or even as a CGI processor if your Web server does not support SAPI (Server Application Programming Interface) or ISAPI module types. In the following sections, you'll install PHP as a dynamic shared object (DSO) for Apache on Linux/UNIX, and as a SAPI module for Apache on Windows. While the Linux/UNIX installation requires actual compilation and building of files, the Windows installation consists only of placing files in particular places. Neither method is terribly difficult—if you've made it through the Apache installation sections, then you have the skills to install PHP as well.

Installing PHP on Linux/UNIX

In this section, you'll learn how to install PHP with Apache on Linux/Unix as a dynamic shared object (DSO). While you might be able to find pre-built versions of PHP for your system, compiling PHP from the source gives you greater control over the features built into your binary.

To download the PHP distribution files, go to the home of PHP, http://www.php.net/, and follow the link to the Downloads section. Grab the latest version of the source code—this example uses version 4.3.0. Your distribution will be named something like php-*version*.tar.gz, where *version* is the most recent release number. Keep this file in the directory reserved for source files, such as /usr/src/ or /usr/local/src/.

Next, unzip and untar the software by typing the following command at the prompt (#):

```
# gunzip < php-4.3.0.tar.gz | tar xvf -
```

You should now have a structure of directories, with the top-level directory named php-*version*. Change your current directory to this top-level directory to prepare for configuring the software.

For example:

```
# cd php-4.3.0
```

Like the Apache build method, PHP compiling follows the configure/make/make install sequence of events. Within your distribution directory you will use the con-figure script, which accepts command-line arguments to control the features that PHP will support. In these installation instructions, you will include the basic options you need to use to install PHP with Apache, and support for using MySQL for your database applications. For now, type the following command at the prompt:

```
# ./configure --prefix=/usr/local/php --with-apxs2=/usr/local/apache2/bin/apxs
```

Once the configure script has run, and after you've received informational notes from the PHP Group, you will be returned to the prompt. Unless the `configure` script errors, simply take the PHP Group notes as sound advice, and then issue the `make` command, followed by the `make install` command. These commands should end the process of PHP compilation and installation and return you to your prompt.

```
...
Installing build environment:      /usr/local/php/lib/php/build/
Installing header files:           /usr/local/php/include/php/
Installing helper programs:        /usr/local/php/bin/
  program: phpize
  program: php-config
  program: phpextdist
#
```

Next, you will need to ensure that two very important files are copied to their correct locations. First, issue the following command to copy the distributed version of php.ini to its default location (the php.ini file is the configuration file for PHP, and you'll learn more about it later in this chapter):

```
# cp php.ini-dist /usr/local/php/lib/php.ini
```

Next, copy the PHP shared object file to its proper place in the Apache installation directory, if it has not already been placed there by the installation process:

```
# cp libs/libphp4.so /usr/local/apache2/modules/
```

To ensure that PHP and Apache get along with one another, you need to check for—and potentially add—a few items to the httpd.conf configuration file. First, look for a line like the following:

```
LoadModule php4_module        modules/libphp4.so
```

If this line is not present, or only appears with a # sign at the beginning of the line, you must add the line or remove the # sign. This line tells Apache to use the PHP shared object file (libphp4.so) that was created by the PHP build process.

Next, look for this section:

```
#
# AddType allows you to add to or override the MIME configuration
# file mime.types for specific file types.
#
```

and add the following line:

```
AddType application/x-httpd-php .php
```

This ensures that the PHP engine will parse files that end with the .php extension. Your selection of filenames may differ, and you may wish to add .html as an extension, which would parse every .html as PHP as well. When you're through adding your extensions, save the file and restart Apache. When you look in your error_log, found in the logs subdirectory of your Apache installation directory, you should see something like the following line:

```
[Tue Jan 21 09:48:44 2003] [notice] Apache/2.0.44 (Unix) PHP/4.3.0 configured
```

Congratulations are in order, as PHP is now part of the Apache Web server. If you want to learn how to install PHP on a Windows platform, keep reading. Otherwise, you can skip ahead to the "Testing Your Installation" section later in this chapter.

Installing PHP on Windows

Unlike building and installing PHP on Linux/UNIX, installing PHP on Windows requires nothing more than downloading the distribution and moving a few files around. To download the PHP distribution files, go to the home of PHP, http://www.php.net/, and follow the link to the Downloads section. Grab the latest version of the Windows binaries—this example uses version 4.3.0. Your distribution will be named something like php-*version*.zip, where *version* is the most recent release number.

Once the file is downloaded to your system, double-click on it to launch your unzipper. The distribution is packed up with pathnames already in place, so if you extract the files to the root of your drive, it will create a directory called php-*version-Win32* and place all the files and subdirectories under that new directory.

Now that you have all the basic PHP distribution files, you just need to move a few of them around:

1. In the PHP installation directory, find the php.ini-dist file and rename it php.ini.
2. Move the php.ini file to C:\WINDOWS\ or wherever you usually put your *.ini files.
3. Move the php4ts.dll file to C:\WINDOWS\SYSTEM\ or wherever you usually put your *.dll files.

To get a basic version of PHP working with Apache, you'll need to make a few minor modifications to the Apache configuration file. First, find a section that looks something like this:

```
# Example:
# LoadModule foo_module modules/mod_foo.so
#
LoadModule access_module modules/mod_access.so
LoadModule actions_module modules/mod_actions.so
LoadModule alias_module modules/mod_alias.so
LoadModule asis_module modules/mod_asis.so
LoadModule auth_module modules/mod_auth.so
#LoadModule auth_anon_module modules/mod_auth_anon.so
#LoadModule auth_dbm_module modules/mod_auth_dbm.so
#LoadModule auth_digest_module modules/mod_auth_digest.so
LoadModule autoindex_module modules/mod_autoindex.so
#LoadModule cern_meta_module modules/mod_cern_meta.so
LoadModule cgi_module modules/mod_cgi.so
#LoadModule dav_module modules/mod_dav.so
#LoadModule dav_fs_module modules/mod_dav_fs.so
LoadModule dir_module modules/mod_dir.so
LoadModule env_module modules/mod_env.so
#LoadModule expires_module modules/mod_expires.so
#LoadModule file_cache_module modules/mod_file_cache.so
#LoadModule headers_module modules/mod_headers.so
```

At the end of this section, add the following:

```
LoadModule php4_module c:/php-version/sapi/php4apache2.dll
```

Next, look for this section:

```
#
# AddType allows you to add to or override the MIME configuration
# file mime.types for specific file types.
#
```

Add the following line:

```
AddType application/x-httpd-php .php
```

This ensures that the PHP engine will parse files that end with the .php extension. Your selection of filenames may differ, and you may wish to add .html as an extension, which would parse every .html as PHP as well. When you're through adding your extensions, save the file and restart Apache. When you look in your error_log, found in the logs subdirectory of your Apache installation directory, you should see something like the following line:

```
[Tue Jan 21 10:24:44 2003] [notice] Apache/2.0.44 (Win32) PHP/4.3.0 configured
```

Now that PHP is happily cohabitating with Apache, you can breathe easy and move on to bigger and better things.

Modifications with php.ini

Even after installing PHP, you can still change its behavior through the php.ini file. Directives in the php.ini file come in two forms: values and flags. Value directives take the form of a directive name and a value separated by an equals sign (=). Possible values vary from directive to directive. Flag directives take the form of a directive name and a positive or negative term separated by an equals sign. Positive terms include 1, On, Yes, and True. Negative terms include 0, Off, No, and False.

You can change your php.ini settings at any time, but after you do, be sure to restart the server so that the changes can take effect. At some point, take time to read through the php.ini file on your own, to see the types of things that can be configured.

Adding Database Support to PHP

One of the selling points of PHP is its ability to interface with numerous databases. This ability makes PHP a logical choice for generating database-driven dynamic content, as well as developing e-commerce applications, project and document management applications, and virtually any other application you can imagine that might use a database.

The examples of database usage in this book, in the context of application development, use MySQL as the database. However, the basic PHP functions for database connectivity with other popular database systems are located in Chapter 3, "Working with Databases." The other databases covered in Chapter 3 are PostgreSQL, Oracle, and Microsoft SQL Server.

In order to use the functions for these particular databases, you must enable their functionality when compiling PHP (on Linux/UNIX) or through the php.ini file (on Windows). During the installation instructions for Linux/UNIX, earlier in this chapter, the configuration directive `--with-mysql` was used. This directive told the compiler to include the MySQL-related functions as part of PHP. In the Windows installation, nothing additional was needed to enable MySQL functions—they are enabled by default.

Enabling Other Database Support on Linux/UNIX

To enable support for other databases on Linux/UNIX, configuration flags similar to `--with-mysql` are used at configuration time. For example:

- `--with-pgsql=DIR`. Enables PostgreSQL support. `DIR` is the base director of PostgreSQL, which defaults to /usr/local/pgsql
- `--with-oci8=DIR`. Enables Oracle support. `DIR` defaults to the `ORACLE_HOME` environment variable.
- `--with-mssql=DIR`. Enables Microsoft SQL Server support. `DIR` is the base director of the FreeTDS library, which defaults to /usr/local/freetds

Each of these directives assumes the database is already installed on your system. For additional notes regarding installation and configuration of PHP with these database types, please see their respective pages in the PHP Manual.

- PostgreSQL information can be found at http://www.php.net/manual/en/ref.oci8.php.
- Oracle 8 information can be found at http://www.php.net/manual/en/ref.oci8.php.

◆ Microsoft SQL Server information can be found at
http://www.php.net/manual/en/ref.oci8.php.

Enabling Other Database Support on Windows

To enable support for other databases on Windows, you must activate extensions
through the php.ini file. Extensions ship with the PHP distribution, and are
found in the extensions directory within your PHP installation directory.

Activating an extension simply means that you must uncomment the line in
php.ini that refers to the extension you wish to use. There is a section in php.ini
that looks something like this:

```
;Windows Extensions
;Note that MySQL and ODBC support is now built in, so no dll is needed for it.
;
;extension=php_bz2.dll
;extension=php_cpdf.dll
;extension=php_crack.dll
;extension=php_curl.dll
;extension=php_db.dll
;extension=php_dba.dll
;extension=php_dbase.dll
...
```

To uncomment an extension, simply remove the semicolon from the front of the line.

For example:

◆ `extension=php_pgsql.dll` will activate PostgreSQL support.

◆ `extension=php_oci8.dll` will activate Oracle 8 support.

◆ `extension=php_mssql.dll` will activate Microsoft SQL Server support.

After you have activated the appropriate extensions, save the php.ini file and
restart your server.

For additional notes regarding installation and configuration of PHP with these
database types, please see their respective pages in the PHP Manual.

◆ PostgreSQL information can be found at
http://www.php.net/manual/en/ref.oci8.php.

♦ Oracle 8 information can be found at
   http://www.php.net/manual/en/ref.oci8.php.

♦ Microsoft SQL Server information can be found at
   http://www.php.net/manual/en/ref.oci8.php.

Testing Your Installation

The simplest way to test your PHP installation is to create a small test script using
the phpinfo() function. This function will produce a long list of configuration
information.

Open a text editor and type the following line:

```
<? phpinfo(); ?>
```

Save this file as phpinfo.php and place it in the document root of your Web
server—the htdocs subdirectory of your Apache installation. Access this file via
your Web browser; you should see something like what's shown in Figure 1.5.

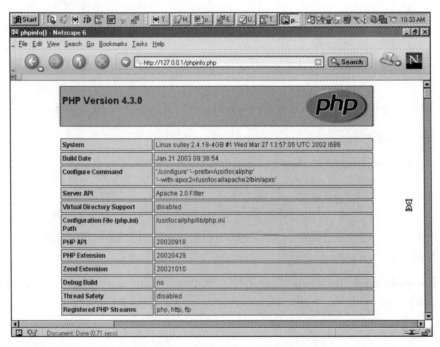

FIGURE 1.5 *The results of* phpinfo() *on a Linux/UNIX system.*

Getting Installation Help

Should you hit a brick wall during your installation attempt, your first recourse should be to the official PHP site, at http://www.php.net/ (particularly the annotated manual at http://www.php.net/manual/).

If you still can't find your answer, both the PHP site and the mailing list archives at http://www.php.net/search.php are searchable.

If you still can't figure out what's wrong, you may do the PHP community a service (and possibly get your solution) by explaining the problem you're having. You can join the PHP mailing lists at http://www.php.net/support.php. Although these lists often have high volume (and you may not want hundreds of extra e-mails in your inbox) you can learn a lot from them. If you are serious about PHP scripting, you should certainly subscribe to at least one digest list. Once you've subscribed to the list that matches your concerns, you might consider posting your problem.

Working with Other Web Servers

It's important to note that Apache is certainly not the only Web server that supports PHP. In fact, you'll be hard-pressed to find one that doesn't. In the next section you'll find some information on using Microsoft IIS and PHP; there is plenty more information for additional servers listed in the PHP Manual at http://www.php.net/manual/en/installation.php.

Installing on Microsoft IIS 4 (or Newer)

These instructions are the basics for installing PHP as an ISAPI module with IIS 4 (or newer). First, start the Microsoft Management Console (also known as the Internet Services Manager on some systems). Right-click on your Web server and select the Properties tab to get to the starting point. Then do the following:

1. Under ISAPI Filters, add the PHP filter (php4isapi.dll) as a new filter.

2. Under Home Directory, click the Configuration button.

3. Add a new entry in the Application Mappings area, using the path to php4isapi.dll as the value for Executable. Use .php as the extension for PHP pages.

   4. Check the Script Engine checkbox.

   5. Close the dialog box.

   6. Stop IIS completely, and then start it.

PHP and IIS should now be functioning together.

Chapter 2

Basic PHP
Techniques

Before delving directly into PHP scripting, it's important to get a handle on basic HTML techniques. As PHP is embedded within HTML, or perhaps because the script itself generates marked-up text, knowing the fundamental structure of HTML will help you avoid potential problems with your script output. For example, if your PHP script is generating a table layout and that table does not render onscreen, don't jump to the assumption that there's a problem with your PHP code. Most likely, the problem is a missing table end tag!

An HTML Refresher

Hypertext Markup Language, or HTML, isn't a programming language in the same vein as C++ or Java. Instead, it is, as its name implies, a markup language. You take a simple ASCII text file and "mark up" that text by putting text in brackets around other text. Now put that page on a Web server and then request it in your Web browser by typing its URL, such as http://www.yourserver.com/yourpage.html. Your Web browser makes a request to the Web server, and the Web server responds with the file. This transaction essentially says, "Please take the file called yourpage.html that exists on this machine and send it to my Web browser."

Your Web browser then "renders" the document by taking the file, looking at the text in funny brackets, and following the directions they contain. These directions tell the Web browser how the information displayed on the page should appear: bold, italicized, blue, with line breaks, and so on.

This very brief HTML refresher lesson may be unnecessary for you, and if so, feel free to skip it. However, if you've only ever created Web pages with a WYSIWYG editor or some other tool that eliminates the need to know HTML, please glance at this information. In many Web applications, you will be coding PHP that will generate HTML, and you'll want to be sure that the HTML you're generating is correct!

HTML Tags

HTML tags define elements of the document: titles, headings, paragraphs, lists, and so on. Without tags, the Web browser has no way to determine how to display the elements.

Tags begin with a left-angle bracket (<) and end with a right-angle bracket (>). Tags, which are case insensitive, are usually in pairs: the opening tag and the closing tag. Here's an example:

- ◆ `<HTML>`. The opening tag, which tells the browser that everything from that point forward is HTML.

- ◆ `</HTML>`. The closing tag, which tells the browser that the HTML document should end at that point. Note the / before the tag name, defining it as a closing tag.

Certain HTML tags can contain *attributes,* or additional information included in the tag, such as alignment directives.

```
<P align=center>This is a centered paragraph.</P>
```

The attribute `align=center` tells the browser to center the paragraph.

There are two main types of HTML tags: block-level and text-level. An HTML document contains one or more block-level elements, or text surrounded by block-level tags.

Block-Level Tags

Block-level tags, such as the logical division tag (`<DIV></DIV>`), contain block-level elements. Block-level elements can contain other block-level elements, as well as text-level elements. For example, a logical division can contain a paragraph, and the paragraph can contain emphasized text:

```
<DIV>
            <P>This paragraph introduces the next paragraph.</P>
            <P>This paragraph contains <em>very</em> useful information.</P>
            <P>Both paragraphs are within a logical division.</P>
</DIV>
```

Following are some examples of block-level tags:

- `<H1></H1>`, `<H2></H2>`, `<H3></H3>`, `<H4></H4>`, `<H5></H5>`, `<H6></H6>`. These are the level heading tags. The level 1 heading (`<H1></H1>`) appears more prominently than other level heading tags, followed by `<H2></H2>` and `<H3></H3>`, through `<H6></H6>`. Use level heading tags in a hierarchical order: level 2 after level 1, level 3 after level 2, and so on.

- `<BLOCKQUOTE></BLOCKQUOTE>`. Used when quoting large blocks of text from another document.

- `<UL></UL>`. The unordered list. Unordered list items, indicated with the `<LI>` tag, are preceded by a bullet symbol.

- `<OL></OL>`. The ordered list. Ordered list items, indicated with the `<LI>` tag, are preceded by a number.

- `<TABLE></TABLE>`. Create a table when surrounding the `<TH></TH>` and `<TD></TD>` text-level tags.

- `<TR></TR>`. These tags insert a table row within a `<TABLE>` element. Table rows contain `<TH></TH>` and `<TD></TD>` elements.

- `<TH></TH>`. These tags insert a table header cell within a `<TR>` element.

- `<TD></TD>`. These tags insert a table data cell within a `<TR>` element.

Text-Level Tags

Text-level tags are applied to specific text within block-level elements. For example, a paragraph can contain emphasized text and a hypertext link, both of which are examples of text-level elements.

```
<P>This paragraph contains a link to a <em>very</em> interesting <a
href="http://www.yourserver.com/story.html">story</a>.</P>
```

Following are some examples of text-level tags:

- `<STRONG></STRONG>`. Strongly emphasized text.

- `<IMG>`. Displays an image. No closing tag is necessary.

- `<BR>`. Inserts a line break. No closing tag is necessary.

Creating a Valid HTML Document

HTML documents have a specific structure that should be followed in order to avoid display problems. Understanding the structure of an HTML document is especially important when integrating it with PHP code, because in some instances PHP code must exist before certain HTML elements. For example, when starting a session or sending cookies, the PHP code used to create and send the cookie must exist before any text, line breaks, or other HTML is sent to the browser.

The following steps will create a structurally sound HTML document:

1. Using a document type declaration tag, define the document type according to the HTML standard it follows (3.0, 4.0, and so forth).

2. Open the <HTML> tag, stating that the information that follows is in HTML.

3. Open the <HEAD> tag. This area contains the title of your document, as well as other document information. With the exception of the document title, none of the information in the <HEAD> element is displayed by the browser.

4. Insert the title of the document within the <TITLE></TITLE> tag pair.

5. Insert any <META> information. Examples of <META> information include document descriptions and expiration dates.

6. Insert any <LINK> information. Examples of <LINK> information include the e-mail address of the document's author and the location of the associated style sheet.

7. Insert the closing <HEAD> tag: </HEAD>.

8. Open the <BODY> tag. This area contains all of the information displayed by the browser. Only one <BODY> element exists in each document.

9. Insert your content, in HTML format.

10. Insert the closing <BODY> tag: </BODY>.

11. Insert the closing <HTML> tag: </HTML>.

Following these steps produces a valid HTML document, something like this:

```
<!DOCTYPE HTML PUBLIC "-//W3C//DTD HTML 4.0 Transitional//EN">
<HTML>
<HEAD>
<TITLE>Your Title</TITLE>
<META NAME="description" CONTENT="My first document">
<LINK REV="made" HREF="mailto:you@yourserver.com">
</HEAD>
```

```
<BODY>
<P>All of your content goes here!</P>
</BODY>
</HTML>
```

Understanding valid HTML document structure is the first step in creating error-free PHP scripts.

The next two sections provide a quick overview of HTML tables and forms.

Understanding HTML Tables

HTML tables follow a structure as strict as the overall HTML document structure. One miscue, such as a missing closing tag, can cause great debugging headaches. Many programmers have examined their code for hours, calling in reinforcements to help them debug the mystery of the non-displaying pages, only to discover that they simply failed to insert the </TABLE> tag to close the table. This is known as "Smack the Forehead" syndrome. Repeat the mantra "Close all table tags," and you probably won't suffer from "Smack the Forehead" syndrome.

A simple table contains one row and two columns. The row starts with a <TR> tag and ends with a </TR> closing tag. Within the <TR> tags are the <TD> opening tag, followed by the data for that cells and the </TD> closing tag. Each <TD></TD> tag pair represents a column, so if you have two columns, you'll need two tag pairs. For example:

```
<TABLE>
<TR>
            <TD>Cell 1</TD>
            <TD>Cell 2</TD>
</TR>
</TABLE>
```

The browser will display this code as follows:

```
Cell 1      Cell 2
```

To place a column heading above each column, use the <TH></TH> tag pair. For example:

```
<TABLE>
<TR>
```

```
            <TH>Heading 1</TH>
            <TH>Heading 2</TH>
</TR>
<TR>

            <TD>Cell 1</TD>
            <TD>Cell 2</TD>
</TR>
</TABLE>
```

Table headings are usually displayed in bold text. The browser will display this code like this:

Heading 1   **Heading 2**

Cell 1   Cell 2

HTML tables can be as complex or as simple as you need them to be, and can even be nested within one another. The more complex the table code, the greater the chance for rendering errors. If you remember to close all open table tags, including row and data tags, the likelihood of errors will certainly decrease.

Understanding HTML Forms

This section explains the display and internal elements of an HTML form. Later in this chapter you'll learn how to make functional forms using PHP scripts; but first, the basics. Committing form basics to memory will alleviate script-debugging headaches, just like remembering to close all table tags!

Forms begin with an opening <FORM> tag and end with the closing </FORM> tag. The form's method and action are defined in the opening <FORM> tag, like this:

```
<FORM METHOD="POST" ACTION="go.php">
```

Two methods exist for sending forms.

♦ GET. The default method. Sends input to a script via a URL. The GET method has a limit to the amount of data that can be sent, so if you plan to send a large amount, use POST.

♦ POST. Sends input in the body of the submission, allowing for larger form submissions.

The action is the name of the script receiving the input.

After defining the method and action, you need a way to get data to your script: input elements.

There are three input element tags—<INPUT>, <TEXTAREA>, and <SELECT>—and there are several types within those elements. Following are the common types:

♦ **Text fields.** An input field with a size indicated in the SIZE attribute and a maximum length indicated in the MAXLENGTH attribute. Here's a 20-character text field named "Field1" with a character limit of 50 characters:

```
<input type="text" name="Field1" size=20 maxlength=50>
```

♦ **Password fields.** Similar to text fields, except each typed character is displayed as an asterisk (*). Here's an example of a 20-character password field named "Pass1" with a character limit of 50 characters:

```
<input type="password" name="Pass1" size=20 maxlength=50>
```

♦ **Radio buttons.** A radio button exists in a group. Each member of the group has the same name but a different value. Only one member of the group can be checked—for example, a button with the value "yes" or a button with the value "no." Additionally, you can specify that one of the values be checked by default. Here's an example of a radio button group named "like_coffee", with "yes" and "no" as available answers:

```
<input type="radio" name="like_coffee" value="yes" checked> yes
<input type="radio" name="like_coffee" value="no"> no
```

♦ **Checkboxes.** Like radio buttons, checkboxes exist in a group. Each member of the group has the same name but a different value. However, multiple checkboxes in each group can be selected. Additionally, you can specify that one or more of the values be checked by default. Here's an example of a checkbox group named "drink", with "coffee", "tea", "water", and "soda" as available answers:

```
<input type="checkbox" name="drink[]" value="coffee"> coffee
<input type="checkbox" name="drink[]" value="tea"> tea
<input type="checkbox" name="drink[]" value="water"> water
<input type="checkbox" name="drink[]" value="soda"> soda
```

The use of brackets ([]) after "drink" indicates that the responses are to be placed in an array. You'll learn more about retrieving information from forms later in this chapter.

◆ **Text areas.** These are displayed as a box with a width indicated by the number of COLS and a height indicated by the number of ROWS. Text areas must have a closing </TEXTAREA> tag. Here's an example of a text area named "message" with a width of 20 characters and a height of five characters:

```
<textarea name="message" cols=20 rows=5></textarea>
```

◆ **List boxes/drop-down list boxes.** These input types begin with the <SELECT> tag, contain one or more <OPTION> tags, and must end with the closing </SELECT> tag. The SIZE attribute indicates the number of <OPTION> elements displayed. If SIZE=1, a drop-down list will appear; otherwise, the user will see a scrollable list box. If the MULTIPLE attribute is present within a list box, then the user can select more than one <OPTION> from the list. <OPTION>tags have unique values. The default <OPTION> tag is set using the SELECTED attribute. Here's a drop-down list named "year", with "2003" as the default selection from the options 2003, 2004, and 2005:

```
<select name="year" size="1">
<option value="2003" selected>2003</option>
<option value="2004">2004</option>
<option value="2005">2005</option>
</select>
```

When you create forms, the NAME attributes of your input elements must all be unique. These element names become the variables interpreted by your scripts, which you'll learn about later in this chapter. So, if you have a field called "my_name" with a value of "Joe", and you have another field called "my_name" with a value of "coffee", then the script will overwrite the former value with the latter. From that point forward, according to the script, your name would be "coffee" and not "Joe".

The final element of a form is crucial—it's the button that submits the form to the script! Submit buttons can be the default gray 3D form buttons with text, or you can use images.

For a gray 3D button that displays SUBMIT, use

```
<INPUT TYPE="submit" NAME="submitme" VALUE="SUBMIT">
```

The VALUE attribute contains the text that appears on the face of the button. If you wanted this button to say "Send Form", the code would look like this:

```
<INPUT TYPE="submit" NAME="submitme" VALUE="Send Form">
```

To use an image as a submission button, use

```
<INPUT TYPE="image" NAME="submitme" SRC="button_image.gif" alt="Submit Me"
border=0>
```

When the user clicks the form submission button, the input field names and their associated values are sent to the script specified as the form's ACTION.

Understanding How PHP Is Parsed

Previously, you were reminded of how a Web server responds to a request for a static HTML file. The following steps describe the request-response sequence for a PHP file:

1. The Web browser requests a document with a .php extension (or any extension set to be treated as a PHP file).
2. The Web server sends the request on to the PHP parser, which is either built into the Web server binary or exists separately as a filter or CGI executable.
3. The PHP parser scans the requested file for PHP code.
4. When the PHP parser finds PHP code, it executes that code and places the resulting output (if any) into the place in the file formerly occupied by the code.
5. This new output file is sent back to the Web server.
6. The Web server sends the output file along to the Web browser.
7. The Web browser displays the output.

Because the PHP code is parsed by the server, this method of code execution is called *server-side*. When code is executed by the browser, such as with JavaScript, it is called *client-side*.

Code Cohabitation and PHP Tags

To combine PHP code with HTML, the PHP code must be *escaped*, or set apart, from the HTML. The following method is the default configuration of the PHP engine:

```
<?php
// PHP code goes here.
?>
```

The PHP engine will consider anything within the `<?php` opening tag and the `?>` closing tag as PHP code. You can also escape your PHP code by using the `<?` opening tag and the `?>` closing tag, or by using the `<SCRIPT Language=php>` opening tag and the `</SCRIPT>` closing tag.

Now it's time to write that first script. Your first PHP script will display "Hello World! I'm using PHP!" in the browser window.

First, open your favorite text editor and create a simple text file called first.php. In this text file, type the following code:

```
<!DOCTYPE HTML PUBLIC "-//W3C//DTD HTML 4.0 Transitional//EN">
<HTML>
<HEAD>
<TITLE>My First PHP Script</TITLE>
</HEAD>
<BODY>
            <?php
                echo "<P>Hello World! I'm using PHP!</P>\n";
?>
</BODY>
</HTML>
```

Save this file and place it in the document root of your Web server. Now access it with your browser at its URL, http://127.0.0.1/first.php. In your browser window, you should see this:

```
Hello World! I'm using PHP!
```

 NOTE

If your server has an actual machine and domain name, such as www.yourcompany.com, feel free to use it in place of 127.0.0.1 (which is the default localhost).

If you use your browser to view the source of the document, you should just see this:

```
<!DOCTYPE HTML PUBLIC "-//W3C//DTD HTML 4.0 Transitional//EN">
<HTML>
<HEAD>
<TITLE>My First PHP Script</TITLE>
</HEAD>
<BODY>
          <P>Hello World! I'm using PHP!</P>
</BODY>
</HTML>
```

As the PHP code was rendered by the PHP parser, all that remains visible is the HTML output.

Now, take a look at the PHP code used in the script. It contains three elements: the command (echo), the string (<P>Hello World...), and the instruction terminator (;).

Familiarize yourself now with echo, because it will likely be your most often-used command. The echo() function is used to output information—in this case, to print <P>Hello World! I'm using PHP!</P> in the HTML file. The instruction terminator is such an important concept that it warrants its own section.

The Importance of the Instruction Terminator

The instruction terminator, also known as the semicolon, is absolutely required. If you do not end your command with a semicolon, the PHP engine will not parse your PHP code properly, and ugly errors will occur. For example, this code:

```
<?php
          echo "<P>Hello World! I'm using PHP!</P>\n"
          echo "<P>This is another message.</P>";
?>
```

produces this nasty error:

```
Parse error: parse error, expecting "," or ";" in
/path/to/your/file/filename.php on line 9
```

Avoid this error at all costs—remember to terminate commands with a semicolon!

Escaping Your Code

Right up there with remembering to end your commands with semicolons is remembering to escape elements like quotation marks. When you use quotation marks inside other quotation marks, the inner pairs must be delineated from the outside pair using the escape (\) character (also known as a backslash). For example, the following code will produce another parse error, because the term "cool" is surrounded by double quotes, within a double-quoted string:

```php
<?php
echo "<P>I think this is really "cool"!</P>";
?>
```

This code should instead look like this:

```php
<?php
echo "<P>I think this is really \"cool\"!</P>";
?>
```

Now that the inner quotation marks are escaped, the PHP parser will skip right over them because it knows that these characters should just be printed and that they have no other meaning. The same concept holds true for single-quoted elements within other single-quoted strings—escape the inner element. Single-quoted strings within double-quoted strings, and vice versa, require no escaping of characters.

Commenting Your Code

Whether you're adding comments to static HTML documents or to PHP scripts, code-commenting is a good habit to cultivate. Comments will help you, and others who might have to edit your documents later, get a handle on what's going on in your documents.

HTML comments are ignored by the browser and are contained within <!-- and --> tags. For example, the following comment reminds you that the code following it contains your logo graphic:

```html
<!-- logo graphic goes here -->
```

Similarly, PHP comments are ignored by the parsing engine. PHP comments are usually preceded by double slashes, like this:

```php
// this is a comment in PHP code
```

Other types of commenting can be used in PHP files, as in the following:

```
# This is shell-style style comment
```

and

```
/* This begins a C-style comment that runs
onto two lines */
```

HTML and PHP comments are used extensively throughout this book to explain blocks of code. Get used to reading comments, and try to pick up the habit of using them. Writing clean, bug-free code, with plenty of comments and white space, will make you popular among your developer peers because they won't have to work extra hard to figure out what your code is trying to do!

Now that you have a handle on how PHP documents are created and used, the next section will introduce you to the PHP variables and operators that will become integral parts of your scripts.

PHP Variables and Operators

Very simply put, variables represent data. If you want your script to hold onto a specific piece of information, first create a variable and then assign a literal value to it using the equal sign (=).

For example, the variable username holds the literal value "joe" when appearing in your script as

```
$username = "joe";
```

Variable names begin with the dollar sign ($) and are followed by a concise, meaningful name. The variable name cannot begin with a numeric character, but it can contain numbers and the underscore character (_). Additionally, variable names are case sensitive, meaning that $YOURVAR and $yourvar are two different variables.

Creating meaningful variable names is another way to lessen headaches while coding. If your script deals with name and password values, don't create a variable called $n for the name and $p for the password—those are not meaningful names. If you pick up that script weeks later, you might think that $n is the variable for "number" rather than "name," and that $p stands for "page" rather than "password."

This section describes several kinds of variables. Some variables change values as your script runs, and others are assigned values outside of your PHP script—such as HTML forms.

Variables and Value Types

You will create two main types of variables in your PHP code: scalar varriables and arrays. Scalar variables contain only one value at a time, while arrays contain a list of values or another array (thus producing a multi-dimensional array). Within variables, their associated values can be of different types, such as the following:

- ◆ **Integers.** Whole numbers (numbers without decimals). Examples are 1, 345, and 9922786. You can also use octal and hexadecimal notation: the octal 0123 is decimal 83 and the hexadecimal 0x12 is decimal 18.

- ◆ **Floating-point numbers ("floats" or "doubles").** Numbers with decimals. Examples are 1.5, 87.3446, and 0.88889992.

- ◆ **Strings.** Text and/or numeric information, specified within double quotes (" ") or single quotes (' ').

As you begin your PHP script, plan your variables and variable names carefully, and use comments in your code to remind you of the assignments you've made.

Local and Global Variables

Variables can be *local* or *global*, the difference having to do with their definition and use by the programmer, as well as where they appear in the context of the scripts you're creating. The variables described in the previous section—and in the majority of this book—are local variables.

By default, PHP variables can be used only by the script they live within. Scripts cannot magically reach inside other scripts and use the variables created and defined within them—unless you purposely share them with other scripts. For example, when creating your own functions (blocks of reusable code that perform a particular task), you define the shared variables as *global*—that is, able to be accessed by other scripts and functions that need them.

You will learn more about creating your own functions, and about using global as well as local variables, later in this chapter. For now, just understand that there are two different variable scopes—local and global—that will come into play as you write more advanced scripts.

Pre-defined Variables

In all PHP scripts, a set of pre-defined variables is in use. You may have seen some of these variables in the output of the phpinfo() function if you scrolled down and read through the entire results page. Some of these pre-defined variable are also called *superglobals*, essentially meaning that they are always present and available in your scripts.

Study the following list of superglobals, as they will be used throughout this book. Each of these superglobals is actually an array of other variables. Don't worry about fully understanding this concept now, as it will be explained as you move along through the book.

- ◆ **$_GET**. Any variables provided to a script through the GET method.
- ◆ **$_POST**. Any variables provided to a script through the POST method.
- ◆ **$_COOKIE**. Any variables provided to a script through a cookie.
- ◆ **$_FILES**. Any variables provided to a script through file uploads.
- ◆ **$_ENV**. Any variables provided to a script as part of the server environment.
- ◆ **$_SESSION**. Any variables that are currently registered in a session.

 NOTE

If you are using a version of PHP earlier than 4.1.x and cannot upgrade to a newer version of PHP (as described in Chapter 1), you must adjust the names of these variables when following the scripts in this book. The old names are $HTTP_GET_VARS, $HTTP_POST_VARS, $HTTP_COOKIE_VARS, $HTTP_POST_FILES, $HTTP_ENV_VARS, and $HTTP_SESSION_VARS.

Using Constants

A *constant* is an identifier for a value that cannot change during the course of a script. Once a constant has a value, that value remains throughout its execution lifetime. Constants can be user-defined, or you can use some of the predefined constants that PHP always has available. Unlike simple variables, constants do not have a dollar sign before their name, and they are usually uppercase, in order to distinguish them from scalar variables.

The function used to define a constant is called define(), and it requires the name of the constant and the value you want to give it. In the following code snippet, you define a constant called MYCONSTANT with a value of "This is a test of defining constants." Then the echo command will echo the value of the constant to the screen.

```
<?
define("MYCONSTANT", "This is a test of defining constants.");
echo MYCONSTANT;
?>
```

The output of this script is just

> This is a test of defining constants.

There are some common pre-defined constants in PHP, including:

- **__FILE__**. The name of the script file being parsed.
- **__LINE__**. The number of the line in the script being parsed.
- **PHP_VERSION**. The version of PHP in use.
- **PHP_OS**. The operating system using PHP.

You can create a script to test them all out.

```
<?
echo "<br>This file is ".__FILE__;
echo "<br>This is line number ".__LINE__;
echo "<br>I am using ".PHP_VERSION;
echo "<br>This test is being run on ".PHP_OS;
?>
```

Save the file with the name constants.php and place it on your Web server. When you access this file, you should see the strings you typed, plus the values of the constants. For example:

```
This file is /usr/local/bin/apache/htdocs/constants.php
This is line number 4
I am using 4.3.0
This test is being run on Linux
```

Operator Types

Values are assigned to variables using different types of operators. A list of common operators and operator types follows. For a complete list, see the "Operators" section in Appendix A, "Essential PHP Language Reference."

Assignment Operators

You've already seen an assignment operator at work: the equal sign (=) in $username = "joe"; is the basic assignment operator.

 NOTE

The single equal sign does not mean "equal to." Instead, the single equal sign always means "is assigned to." The double equal sign ("==") means "equal to." Commit this to memory to alleviate debugging headaches.

Other assignment operators include +=, -=, and .=.

```
$ex += 1;    // Assigns the value of ($ex + 1) to $ex.
                 // If $ex = 2, then the value of ($ex += 1) is 3.
$ex -= 1;    // Assigns the value of ($ex - 1) to $ex.
                 // If $ex = 2, then the value of ($ex -= 1) is 1.
$ex .= "coffee";  // Concatenates (adds to) a string. If $ex = "I like "
// then the value of ($ex .= "coffee") is "I like coffee".
```

Arithmetic Operators

Even if you've never written a line of code in your life, you already know most of the arithmetic operators—they're basic math!

- \+   Addition
- \-   Subtraction
- *   Multiplication
- /   Division
- %   Modulus, or "remainder"

In the following examples, $a = 5 and $b = 4.

```
$c = $a + $b;      // $c = 9
$c = $a - $b;      // $c = 1
$c = $a * $b;      // $c = 20
$c = $a / $b;      // $c = 1.25
$c = $a % $b;      // $c = 1
```

You don't have to limit mathematical operations to variables—you can use hard-coded numbers as well. For example:

```
$c = 3 + 4;        // $c = 7
$c = 8 * 4;        // $c = 32
$c = $a * 10;      // $c = 50
```

Comparison Operators

It should come as no surprise that comparison operators compare two values. As with the arithmetic operators, you already know most of the comparison operators.

==	Equal to
!=	Not equal to
>	Greater than
<	Less than
>=	Greater than or equal to
<=	Less than or equal to

In the following examples, $a = 5 and $b = 4.

- Is $a == $b? No; 5 does not equal 4. The comparison is FALSE.
- Is $a != $b? Yes; 5 does not equal 4. The comparison is TRUE.
- Is $a > $b? Yes; 5 is greater than 4. The comparison is TRUE.
- Is $a < $b? No; 5 is not less than 4. The comparison is FALSE.
- Is $a >= $b? Yes; although 5 does not equal 4, 5 is greater than 4. The comparison is TRUE.
- Is $a <= $b? No; 5 does not equal 4, and 5 is not less than 4. The comparison is FALSE.

Comparison operators are often used in conjunction with control statements (if...else, while) to perform a specific task based on the validity of expressions. For example, if you are writing a number-guessing program and you want your script to print "That's the right number!" when a successful guess is made, you might include the following code:

```
// secret number 5
if ($guess == "5") {
          echo "That's the right number!";
} else {
          echo "Sorry. Bad guess.";
}
```

Logical Operators

Logical operators, like comparison operators, are often found within if...else and while control statements. These operators allow your script to determine the status of conditions and, in the context of your if...else or while statements, execute certain code based on which conditions are true and which are false.

A common logical operator is ||, meaning OR. The following example shows the evaluation of two variables and the result of the statement. In this example, I really want to drink coffee. I have two options, $drink1 and $drink2. If either of my options is "coffee", I will be happy. Otherwise, I'll still need caffeine.

```
$drink1 = "coffee";
$drink2 = "milk";
          if (($drink1 == "coffee") || ($drink2 == "coffee")) {
              echo "I'm happy!";
          } else {
              echo "I still need caffeine.";
          }
```

In this example, because the value of the $drink1 variable is "coffee", the logical OR comparison of $drink1 and $drink2 is TRUE, and the script returns "I'm happy!"

Other logical operators include AND (&&) and NOT (!).

Using Variables and Operators: A Calculation Script

You now have a fundamental knowledge of variables and operators—enough to create a PHP script that does some sort of variable calculation and displays results. To begin, open your favorite text editor, create a file called calc01.php, and set up the HTML "shell" around your script.

```
<!DOCTYPE HTML PUBLIC "-//W3C//DTD HTML 4.0 Transitional//EN">
<HTML>
<HEAD>
<TITLE>Calculate Values</TITLE>
</HEAD>
<BODY>
<?php
        // PHP code goes here.
?>
</BODY>
</HTML>
```

 NOTE

In the following examples, replace the `<?php ... ?>` block with the code provided.

This script will use hard-coded values. In later sections, you'll learn how to use values from outside your PHP script in order to make this a working calculation form.

The calc01.php script will calculate an order for coffee beans. We know only the following information:

- ◆ The price of one bag of beans is $10.00, including shipping.
- ◆ Sales tax is 8.25 percent.
- ◆ Joe wants four bags.

Begin the PHP portion of the script by creating variables for your known information and assigning values to those variables.

```
$price = 10.00;
$sales_tax = 8.25;
$quantity = 4;
```

You know that to find the subtotal of an order, you multiply the price of the item by the quantity ordered. You've just found another variable: $sub_total. Your list now looks like this:

```
$price = 10.00;
$sales_tax = 8.25;
$quantity = 4;
$sub_total = $price * $quantity;
```

You also know that the grand total of an order is the subtotal of the order plus the sales tax amount. The sales tax amount is determined by multiplying the sales tax by the subtotal of the order. You now know all of your remaining variables: $sales_tax_amount and $grand_total. The final list of PHP variables looks like this:

```
$price = 10.00;
$sales_tax = .0825;
$quantity = 4;
$sub_total = $price * $quantity;
$sales_tax_amount = $sub_total * $sales_tax;
$grand_total = $sub_total + $sales_tax_amount;
```

Now that you have all the numbers, you'll want to display the results in the browser. You display the value of a variable with the echo command, just as if you were displaying a normal text string. The following chunk of code should go between the PHP start and end tags in your original shell:

```
$price = 10.00;
$sales_tax = .0825;
$quantity = 4;
$sub_total = $price * $quantity;
$sales_tax_amount = $sub_total * $sales_tax;
$grand_total = $sub_total + $sales_tax_amount;
```

```
echo "<P>You ordered $quantity bags of coffee.</p>";
echo "<P>Bags of coffee are $price each.</p>";
echo "<P>Your subtotal is $sub_total.</p>";
echo "<P>Sales tax is $sales_tax in this location.</p>";
echo "<P>$sales_tax_amount has been added to your order.</p>";
echo "<P>You owe $grand_total for your coffee.</p>";
```

Save the whole file and place it on your Web server. Now access it with your browser at its URL, http://127.0.0.1/calc01.php.

In your browser window, you should see this:

> You ordered 4 bags of coffee.
>
> Bags of coffee are 10 each.
>
> Your subtotal is 40.
>
> Sales tax is 0.0825 in this location.
>
> $3.3 has been added to your order.
>
> You owe 43.3 for your coffee.

While these calculations are correct, the results could use a little formatting help—you could place a dollar sign before the amount, display the sales tax as a percentage, and show the amount with two decimal places.

To print a dollar sign, place a backslash (\) before it. Dollar signs must be *escaped*, or delineated, in this way because dollar signs are also used to indicate the presence of a variable. In your script, use

```
echo "<P>Bags of coffee are \$$price each.</p>";
```

to print a dollar sign before the value of $price. The result will look like this:

> Bags of coffee are $10 each.

Add the escaped dollar sign to other echo statements containing dollar amounts.

To get the percentage value of $sales_tax, first create a new variable called $sales_tax_pct. Then transform the value 0.0825 into 8.25 by multiplying 0.0825 by 100.

```
$sales_tax_pct = $sales_tax * 100;
```

The variable $sales_tax_pct now contains the value 8.25. Rewrite the echo statement to include the new variable and the percent sign.

```
echo "<P>Sales tax is $sales_tax_pct% in this location.</p>";
```

Here's the result:

Sales tax is 8.25% in this location.

The final bit of formatting, which ensures that the dollar amount prints to two decimal places, involves the use of the sprintf() function. This function takes two arguments: the formatting argument and the name of the value to be formatted. The following code takes the value of $price, formats it by creating a floating-point number with two decimal places, and puts the value (10.00) into a new variable called $fmt_price:

```
$fmt_price = sprintf("%0.2f",$price);
```

Repeat this process for the other monetary values in the script: $sub_total and $grand_total.

```
$fmt_price = sprintf("%0.2f",$price);
$fmt_sub_total = sprintf("%0.2f",$sub_total);
$fmt_sales_tax_amount = sprintf("%0.2f",$sales_tax_amount);
$fmt_grand_total = sprintf("%0.2f",$grand_total);
```

In your echo statements, replace the old variables with the newly formatted variables. The PHP portion of your script should now look something like this:

```
<?php
        $price = 10.00;
        $sales_tax = .0825;
        $quantity = 4;
        $sub_total = $price * $quantity;
        $sales_tax_amount = $sub_total * $sales_tax;
        $sales_tax_pct = $sales_tax * 100;
        $grand_total = $sub_total + $sales_tax_amount;
        $fmt_price = sprintf("%0.2f",$price);
        $fmt_sub_total = sprintf("%0.2f",$sub_total);
        $fmt_sales_tax_amount = sprintf("%0.2f",$sales_tax_amount);
        $fmt_grand_total = sprintf("%0.2f",$grand_total);
        echo "<P>You ordered $quantity bags of coffee.</p>";
        echo "<P>Bags of coffee are \$$fmt_price each.</p>";
        echo "<P>Your subtotal is \$$fmt_sub_total.</p>";
```

```
        echo "<P>Sales tax is $sales_tax_pct% in this location.</p>";
        echo "<P>\$$fmt_sales_tax_amount has been added to your order.</p>";
        echo "<P>You owe \$$fmt_grand_total for your coffee.</p>";
?>
```

Name this version of the script calc02.php, place it on your Web server, and access it with your browser at its URL, http://127.0.0.1/calc02.php. In your browser window, you should now see this:

> You ordered 4 bags of coffee.
>
> Bags of coffee are $10.00 each.
>
> Your subtotal is $40.00.
>
> Sales tax is 8.25% in this location.
>
> $3.30 has been added to your order.
>
> You owe $43.30 for your coffee.

You've just completed your first script using variables and operators. In the next section, you'll learn the basics of working with arrays.

Working with Arrays

In brief, an array in PHP is a structure that acts as a map of keys and values. Single-dimensional arrays, wherein you have a single set of keys that maps to a single set of values, are the most commonly used arrays. For example, suppose you wanted to store your favorite colors in an array, for use later in a script. If you have three favorite colors, say, blue, black, and red, then you know you're going to have a set of three keys and values.

In the following example, $fave_colors is an array that contains strings representing array elements. In this case, the array elements are names of colors. Array elements are counted with 0 as the first position in the numerical index.

```
$fave_colors[0] = "blue";
$fave_colors[1] = "black";
$fave_colors[2] = "red";
```

To create a single-dimensional array, you use the array() function.

For example, to create an array called $fave_colors, which holds the values "blue", "black", and "red" in positions 0, 1, and 2, use the following:

```
$fave_colors = array("blue", "black", "red");
```

If you wanted to explicitly define the keys used in your array—for example, if you wanted to use strings, then you would use:

```
$fave_colors = array("1st" => "blue", "2nd" => "black", "3rd" => "red");
```

The keys in this array would be "1st", "2nd" and "3rd", mapping to elements "blue", "black", and "red". Arrays are very useful for storing elements in lists and tables for later use.

Multidimensional Arrays

A multidimensional array is just what it sounds like—an array with more than one dimension, or a bunch of arrays within an array. Say, for example, you wanted to create an array just called $favorites, which would hold your favorite colors, numbers, and foods. You still use the array() function, just several times over.

```
$favorites = array("colors" => array("blue", "black", "red"),
                   "numbers" => array(3, 5, 21),
                   "foods" => array("pizza", "sushi", "prime rib")
            );
```

The keys in the $favorites array would be "colors", "numbers", and "foods", mapping to the second level of arrays. Those arrays each use their own index, starting with position 0. So, to get the value of "sushi", you would use $favorites["foods"][1].

In the next section, you'll learn how to easily get values out of arrays.

Traversing Arrays

Once you have elements in an array, you'll obviously want to retrieve them! The most efficient method for retrieving keys and values from a single-dimensional array is to use the foreach construct. Here's how it works—given an array, the foreach function will read the key name and value of the current element, and then advance its internal pointer by one step. Then it will keep going on to the next element.

Check out the following array:

```
$fave_colors = array("1st" => "blue", "2nd" => "black", "3rd" => "red");
```

Use this snippet to produce a list of elements in the array.

```php
<?php
$fave_colors = array("1st" => "blue", "2nd" => "black", "3rd" => "red");
foreach ($fave_colors as $key => $value) {

    echo "Key: $key ... Value: $value<br>";
}
?>
```

The resulting output is:

> Key: 1st ... Value: blue
>
> Key: 2nd ... Value: black
>
> Key: 3rd ... Value: red

There are plenty of PHP functions designed especially for working with arrays. See the "Array Functions" section of Appendix A, "Essential PHP Language Reference," or the Arrays section of the PHP Manual, at http://www.php.net/array.

User-Defined Functions

When you program in PHP, you will use predefined functions to achieve certain results. For example, the mail() function is a predefined function that sends mail. The mysql_connect() function is a predefined function that connects to a MySQL database. The code that makes up these functions is built into the PHP scripting engine, so you never see it. However, you can write your own functions and use them in your scripts, even storing your own functions in external files for use only when you need them.

Defining a Function

Functions have a very specific structure, wherein [function name] and [arguments] should be replaced with your own function name and any arguments you may want to use.

```php
function [function_name] ([arguments]) {
        // code
}
```

When you create a function, you precede the name of the function with the literal word `function`. After the name of your function comes the list of arguments inside a set of parentheses. The arguments—which are optional, as you don't have to pass any arguments to a function if you don't want to—are separated by commas and hold values that your function needs in order to complete its task or tasks.

After the arguments, you open a set of curly braces, type in all of your code, and finally close the set of braces. For example, the following function (called `multiplier`) takes an argument called `$num` and multiplies the value by 5:

```
function multiplier ($num) {
        $answer = $num * 5;
}
```

Say you have already determined that `$num` equals 8, and that's what you're passing to the `multiplier` function. Using your math skills, you know that `$answer` will equal 40. To get that number back to your script, outside of the function, you must return the value.

Returning Values from Functions

The basic method for returning values from your functions is to use the `return` statement. Usually, this statement comes at the end of the function, like so:

```
function multiplier ($num) {
        $answer = $num * 5;
        return $answer;
}
```

When you use a `return` statement, you can then call the function in your code, like so:

```
echo multiplier(5);
```

This usage would result in the following on your screen:

40

As you are passing 8 as the `$num` argument to the `multiplier()` function, `$answer` becomes 40. As `$answer` is being returned as the result of the function's actions, and you're using `echo` followed by the function call, you're telling PHP to print the result of the code within the function. In this case, that result is the number 40.

Using a return statement to pass results from your functions to your main script is simple and safe, and it's one of the most common methods for doing so. If you do not use a return statement, then you must declare as global any variables you wish to pass back to your main script. For example:

```
function multiplier($num) {
            global $answer;
            $answer = $num * 5;
}
```

In this case, you call the multiplier() function and then use the name of the variable in the echo statement, as it's not returned directly from your function. For example, using the modified function, the following code will print the number 40 to your screen:

```
multiplier(5);
echo $answer;
```

If you had not declared $answer as a global variable, the result would have been a blank screen.

Using Functions in Your Code

So far, you've learned the basic structure of a user-defined function, but not how it fits within your own scripts. In the case of the multiplier() function, it does seem awfully time-consuming to create a script like the following just to print a number on the screen:

```
<?
function multiplier($num) {
            $answer = $num * 5;
return $answer;
}
echo multiplier(5);
?>
```

Take a look at the function below, called db_connect(), which contains a database connection and selection code (don't worry about understanding this code right now; you'll learn more about database connections in the next chapter):

```
function db_connect();
$connection = @mysql_connect("localhost", "username", "password")
            or die(mysql_error());
```

```
$db = @mysql_select_db($db_name, $connection)
                  or die(mysql_error());
}
```

Instead of typing all that information over and over in each script just to connect to a database server and select a database to use, imagine simply typing

```
db_connect();
```

If your host name, username, password, or database name changes, you only have to change this information in one place—the db_connect() function code.

Retrieving Values from Forms

Now that you've learned a little bit about working with PHP, it's time to put together a static document and a PHP script and make them talk to each other. To be exact, you'll create an HTML form and a PHP script to retrieve values from that form.

As you'll recall, HTML forms always have three elements: a method, an action, and a submit button. When you click on a submit button in an HTML form, variables are sent to the script specified by the ACTION via the specified METHOD. The method can be either POST or GET. Variables passed from a form to a PHP script are placed in the global associative array (or *superglobal*) called $_POST or $_GET, depending on the form method. For example, the following HTML snippet calls a script called docalc.php using the POST method:

```
<FORM method="POST" action="docalc.php">
<!--some form elements go here -->
<INPUT type="submit" value="Calculate">
</FORM>
```

The following form has one input text field and therefore passes one variable to a script called goform.php:

```
<FORM method="POST" action="goform.php">
<P>Name: <INPUT type="text" name="your_name" size=10></P>
<INPUT type="submit" value="Submit">
</FORM>
```

Upon submission, the script goform.php receives a variable called $_POST[your_name], with a value of whatever the user typed in the form field. Variables are named according to the name attribute of the input field.

Putting a Form to Work

In this section, you'll use your knowledge of HTML forms and basic PHP scripting to develop an interactive version of the coffee bean calculator from earlier in this chapter. Before you create the form, recall some hard-coded variables from the calc01.php script earlier in this chapter: $price and $quantity. To make the script interactive, just create a form that allows the user to specify the values of these variables, and rewrite a little bit of the PHP to accommodate the usage of the $_POST superglobal.

To begin, open your favorite text editor, create a file called show_calculate.html, and set up an HTML shell:

```
<!DOCTYPE HTML PUBLIC "-//W3C//DTD HTML 4.0 Transitional//EN">
<HTML>
<HEAD>
<TITLE>Bean Counter Form</TITLE>
</HEAD>
<BODY>
            <!-- your HTML form will go here -->
</BODY>
</HTML>
```

To create the form code, assume that your PHP script will be called do_calculate.php and that your form will use the POST method.

```
<FORM method="POST" action="do_calculate.php">
```

Next, create two simple text fields to capture the values for price and quantity.

```
<P>Enter the price per bag of coffee beans: $ <INPUT type="text" name="price"
size=10 maxlength=10></P>
```

Use the MAXLENGTH attribute to set a maximum number of characters entered in the text field, including spaces.

```
<P>How many bags would you like? <INPUT type="text" name="quantity" size=10
maxlength=10></P>
```

Finally, add a submit button.

```
<INPUT type="submit" value="Submit">
```

Don't forget the closing </FORM> tag!

Your HTML source code should look something like this:

```
<!DOCTYPE HTML PUBLIC "-//W3C//DTD HTML 4.0 Transitional//EN">
<HTML>
<HEAD>
<TITLE>Bean Counter Form</TITLE>
</HEAD>
<BODY>
<FORM method="POST" action="do_calculate.php">
<P>Enter the price per bag of coffee beans: <INPUT type="text" name="price"
size=10 maxlength=10></P>
<P>How many bags would you like? <INPUT type="text" name="quantity" size=10
maxlength=10></P>
<INPUT type="submit" value="Submit">
</FORM>
</BODY>
</HTML>
```

Place this file on your Web server, and access it with your browser at its URL, http://127.0.0.1/show_calculate.html. In your browser window, you should see a form like that in Figure 2.1.

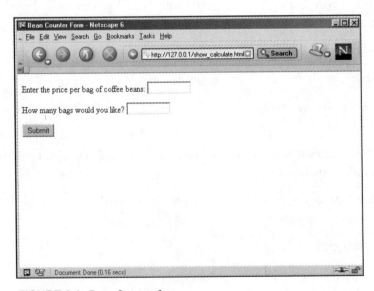

FIGURE 2.1 *Bean Counter form*

Now that you have a form all set to send two variables to a script, it's time to create the script. You'll be making a few modifications to the calc01.php script, so rename it do_calculate.php and open it in your favorite text editor.

Make the following modifications:

1. Change the title of the document to Bean Counter Results.

2. Delete the initial value assignment statements for $price and $quantity.

3. Replace all instances of $price and $quantity with $_POST[price] and $_POST[quantity], as these values will be coming from form input.

Your do_calculate.php script should look like this:

```
<!DOCTYPE HTML PUBLIC "-//W3C//DTD HTML 4.0 Transitional//EN">
<HTML>
<HEAD>
<TITLE>Bean Counter Results</TITLE>
</HEAD>
<BODY>
<?php
$sales_tax = .0825;
$sub_total = $_POST[price] * $_POST[quantity];
$sales_tax_amount = $sub_total * $sales_tax;
$sales_tax_pct = $sales_tax * 100;
$grand_total = $sub_total + $sales_tax_amount;
$fmt_price = sprintf("%0.2f",$_POST[price]);
$fmt_sub_total = sprintf("%0.2f",$sub_total);
$fmt_sales_tax_amount = sprintf("%0.2f",$sales_tax_amount);
$fmt_grand_total = sprintf("%0.2f",$grand_total);
echo "<P>You ordered $_POST[quantity] bags of coffee.</p>";
echo "<P>Bags of coffee are \$$fmt_price each.</p>";
echo "<P>Your subtotal is \$$fmt_sub_total.</p>";
echo "<P>Sales tax is $sales_tax_pct% in this location.</p>";
echo "<P>\$$fmt_sales_tax_amount has been added to your order.</p>";
echo "<P>You owe \$$fmt_grand_total for your coffee.</p>";
?>
</BODY>
</HTML>
```

Place this file on your Web server and open the Bean Counter form in your browser. Enter 10.00 in the first field and 4 in the second field, and then click the Submit button. You should see the same results as in the calc01.php script:

> You ordered 4 bags of coffee.
>
> Bags of coffee are $10.00 each.
>
> Your subtotal is $40.00.
>
> Sales tax is 8.25% in this location.
>
> $3.30 has been added to your order.
>
> You owe $43.30 for your coffee.

Try entering different values to see how the calculations turn out. Buying one bag of coffee at $14.25 should produce a grand total of $15.43, for example.

You can take the Bean Counter Form a step further by adding drop-down lists to your form and using conditional statements within your script to assign values to the variables sent from the form.

In your form, create a drop-down list of coffee types, replacing the question regarding the price of beans. Your form will pass the type of beans in a variable called $_POST[[beans].

```
<P>Select a bean type:</P>
<SELECT name="beans" size="1">
            <OPTION value="Ethiopian Harrar">Ethiopian Harrar - $14.25</OPTION>
            <OPTION value="Kona">Kona - $16.25</OPTION>
            <OPTION value="Sumatra">Sumatra - $13.00</OPTION>
</SELECT>
```

Next, create a drop-down list of quantities, replacing the question about bags of coffee:

```
<P>How many bags would you like?</P>
<SELECT name="quantity" size="1">
            <OPTION value="1">1</OPTION>
            <OPTION value="2">2</OPTION>
            <OPTION value="3">3</OPTION>
            <OPTION value="4">4</OPTION>
            <OPTION value="5">5</OPTION>
</SELECT>
```

Place this file on your Web server and access it with your browser at its URL, http://127.0.0.1/show_calculate.html. In your browser window, you should see the form shown in Figure 2.2.

Now you will make a few more modifications to the do_calculate.php script, including setting up the pricing assignments for the variable $_POST[beans]. Open the script in your favorite text editor and add the following at the beginning of your PHP block:

```
// set up the pricing assignments
if ($_POST[beans] == "Ethiopian Harrar") {
            $price = 14.25;
} else if ($_POST[beans] == "Kona") {
            $price = 16.25;
} else if ($_POST[beans] == "Sumatra") {
            $price = 13.00;
}
```

Previously, the user entered a number in a text field associated with the variable $_POST[price]. In the new version, the user selects a bean type and the script assigns a value to the variable $price, based on the value of $_POST[beans]. Replace all of the instances of $_POST[price] with $price, as that value is no longer coming from user input.

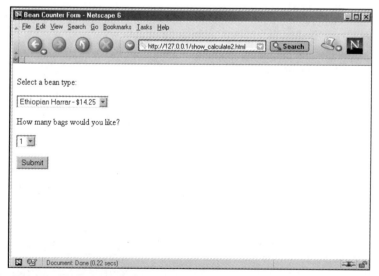

FIGURE 2.2 *Modified Bean Counter Form*

Using comparison operators, the script first checks to see if the value of $_POST[beans] is equal to the string "Ethiopian Harrar". If it is not, the script jumps to the next statement, to see if the value of $_POST[beans] is "Kona". If it still hasn't found a match, the script tries the last statement, to see if the value of $_POST[beans] is "Sumatra". As you are offering only three choices to the user, and the default value of the drop-down list is "Ethiopian Harrar", if you use the form interface you're assured of a match somewhere along the line.

Make two more modifications to the PHP script in order to return the selected bean type to the user instead of the generic term "coffee".

```
echo "<P>You ordered $_POST[quantity] bags of $_POST[beans].</P>";
```

and

```
echo "<P>Bags of $_POST[beans] are \$$fmt_price each.</P>";
```

The revised code for do_calculate.php should look something like this:

```
<!DOCTYPE HTML PUBLIC "-//W3C//DTD HTML 4.0 Transitional//EN">
<HTML>
<HEAD>
<TITLE>Bean Counter Results</TITLE>
</HEAD>
<BODY>
<?php
// set up the pricing assignments
if ($_POST[beans] == "Ethiopian Harrar") {
        $price = 14.25;
} else if ($_POST[beans] == "Kona") {
        $price = 16.25;
} else if ($_POST[beans] == "Sumatra") {
        $price = 13.00;
}
$sales_tax = .0825;
$sub_total = $price * $_POST[quantity];
$sales_tax_amount = $sub_total * $sales_tax;
$sales_tax_pct = $sales_tax * 100;
$grand_total = $sub_total + $sales_tax_amount;
$fmt_price = sprintf("%0.2f",$price);
$fmt_sub_total = sprintf("%0.2f",$sub_total);
```

```
$fmt_sales_tax_amount = sprintf("%0.2f",$sales_tax_amount);
$fmt_grand_total = sprintf("%0.2f",$grand_total);
echo "<P>You ordered $_POST[quantity] bags of $_POST[beans].</p>";
echo "<P>Bags of $_POST[beans] are \$$fmt_price each.</p>";
echo "<P>Your subtotal is \$$fmt_sub_total.</p>";
echo "<P>Sales tax is $sales_tax_pct% in this location.</p>";
echo "<P>\$$fmt_sales_tax_amount has been added to your order.</p>";
echo "<P>You owe \$$fmt_grand_total for your coffee.</p>";
?>
</BODY>
</HTML>
```

Save the file and place it on your Web server, and then open the Bean Counter form in your browser. Select Kona from the Bean Type drop-down list and 2 from the quantity drop-down list, and then click the Submit button. You should see the following results:

> You ordered 2 bags of Kona.
>
> Bags of Kona are $16.25 each.
>
> Your subtotal is $32.50.
>
> Sales tax is 8.25% in this location.
>
> $2.68 has been added to your order.
>
> You owe $35.18 for your coffee.

Try entering different values to see how the calculations turn out. Try buying five bags of Ethiopian Harrar, and see how expensive it is ($77.13)!

Displaying Dynamic Content

The Web is a dynamic environment, always changing and growing by leaps and bounds, so why not use your programming skills to display dynamic content? You can create a customized user environment by displaying specific content based on values sent through an HTML form, the type of browser being used, or (as you'll learn in later chapters) variables stored in cookies.

Redirecting to a New Location

Automatically redirecting a user to a new URL means that your script must send to the browser an HTTP header indicating a new location before it sends any other information. Many types of HTTP headers exist, from headers that indicate the character encoding and expiration date of the document to those that send the 404 - File Not Found error message. If you would like to learn more than anyone should ever know about headers, feel free to read the current HTTP 1.1 specification at http://www.w3.org/Protocols/rfc2068/rfc2068.

The format for sending an HTTP header from a PHP script is

```
header(string)
```

where string is the header text, in quotations.

NOTE

This information bears repeating over and over again: Do not attempt to send information of any sort to the browser before sending a header(). You can perform any sort of database manipulations or other calculations before the header(), but you cannot print anything to the screen—not even a new line character.

The following code will print a redirection header to send the browser to the PHP site:

```
<?php
header("Location: http://www.php.net/");
exit;
?>
```

Use the exit statement to ensure that the script does not continue to run.

Take the redirection script one step further, and add an HTML form with a drop-down list box as a front end to the redirection routine. Depending on the values sent by the form, the script redirects the browser to any of a number of URLs.

To begin, open your favorite text editor, create a file called show_menu.html, and set up an HTML shell. Next, create the form code with the assumption that your PHP script will be called do_redirect.php and your form will use the POST method.

```
<FORM method="POST" action="do_redirect.php">
```

Now create a drop-down list box containing some menu options.

```
<P>I want to go to:
<SELECT name="location" size="1">
        <OPTION value="http://www.premierpressbooks.com/">Premier Press</OPTION>
        <OPTION value="http://www.php.net/">PHP.net</OPTION>
        <OPTION value="http://www.thickbook.com/">thickbook.com</OPTION>
</SELECT>
```

Finally, add a submit button:

```
<INPUT type="submit" value="Go!">
```

Don't forget the closing `</FORM>` tag!

Your HTML source code should look something like this:

```
<!DOCTYPE HTML PUBLIC "-//W3C//DTD HTML 4.0 Transitional//EN">
<HTML>
<HEAD>
<TITLE>Redirection Menu</TITLE>
</HEAD>
<BODY>
<FORM method="POST" action="do_redirect.php">
<P>I want to go to:
<SELECT name="location" size="1">
        <OPTION value="http://www.premierpressbooks.com/">Premier Press</OPTION>
        <OPTION value="http://www.php.net/">PHP.net</OPTION>
        <OPTION value="http://www.thickbook.com/">thickbook.com</OPTION>
</SELECT>
<INPUT type="submit" value="Go!">
</FORM>
</BODY>
</HTML>
```

Place this file on your Web server, and access it with your browser at its URL, http://127.0.0.1/show_menu.html. In your browser window, you should see the menu shown in Figure 2.3.

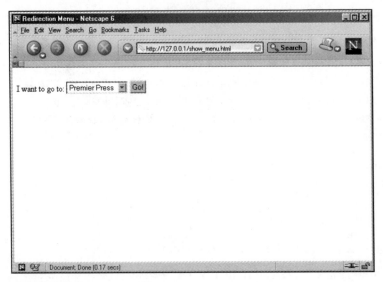

FIGURE 2.3 *Redirection Menu*

Now, create the do_redirect.php script, which simply captures the value in $_POST[location] and sends the redirection header.

```php
<?php
header("Location: $_POST[location]");
exit;
?>
```

Save this file and place it on your server, and then access the menu at its URL, http://127.0.0.1/show_menu.html. Then, select a destination, click the Go! button, and away you (should) go!

Basic Environment Variable Usage

When a Web browser makes a request of a Web server, it sends along with the request a list of extra variables. These are called *environment variables*, and they can be very useful for displaying dynamic content or authorizing users.

The phpinfo() function also displays a wealth of information about the version of PHP that you are running and your Web server software, in addition to the basic HTTP environment. Create a file called phpinfo.php, containing only the following line:

```php
<?php phpinfo(); ?>
```

To view a list of your environment variables and their values, place this file on your server and access it with your browser at its URL, http://127.0.0.1/phpinfo.php. For a list of general HTTP environment variables and their descriptions, visit http://hoohoo.ncsa.uiuc.edu/cgi/env.html.

Environment variables are part of the `$_SERVER` superglobal, and are referenced as `$_SERVER[VAR_NAME]`. For example, the `REMOTE_ADDR` environment variable is referenced as `$_SERVER[REMOTE_ADDR]`.

The `REMOTE_ADDR` environment variable contains the IP address of the machine making the request. Create a script called remote_address.php that contains the following code:

```php
<?php
echo "Your IP address is $_SERVER[REMOTE_ADDR].";
?>
```

Save this file and place it on your server, and then access it with your browser at its URL, http://127.0.0.1/remote_address.php.

You should see

> Your IP address is [some number]

on your screen. For example, I see

> Your IP address is 209.244.209.209.

This IP address is the address currently assigned to my computer by my Internet Service Provider.

In Chapter 4, "User Authentication," you'll learn how to use the `REMOTE_ADDR` environment variable as a form of user authentication by limiting the display of your Web site content to users accessing it from a specific domain or range of IP addresses.

Displaying Browser-Specific Code

The Browser War will never be won—no single Web browser will ever have 100 percent of the market share, nor will the browser makers ever fully comply with approved standards. So, using the `HTTP_USER_AGENT` environment variable, you can discern the specific attributes of the browser accessing your page and display code specifically designed for that browser type and platform. However, as you can imagine, there are hundreds of slightly different values. It's time to learn basic pattern matching!

Using the preg_match() PHP function, you'll create a script that finds a specific block of text within the value of $_SERVER[HTTP_USER_AGENT]. The syntax of preg_match() is

```
preg_match("/[what you want to find]/", "[where you're looking]");
```

So, to find "MSIE" somewhere in the $_SERVER[HTTP_USER_AGENT] value, use

```
(preg_match("/MSIE/i", "$_SERVER[HTTP_USER_AGENT]");
```

The i following /MSIE/ tells the script to match any instances, in uppercase or lowercase. Now, to find "Mozilla" in the $_SERVER[HTTP_USER_AGENT] value, use

```
(preg_match("/Mozilla/i", "$_SERVER[HTTP_USER_AGENT]");
```

Put all the pieces together within an if[...]else statement so that if the browser is MSIE, "Using MSIE" will be printed on the screen. Or, if the browser is Netscape, "Using Netscape" will be printed on the screen. Or, if the browser is neither of those types, the $_SERVER[HTTP_USER_AGENT] value for that browser will be printed. Your code should look something like this:

```php
<?php
if (preg_match("/MSIE/i", "$_SERVER[HTTP_USER_AGENT]")) {
        echo "Using MSIE.";
} else if (preg_match("/Mozilla/i", "$_SERVER[HTTP_USER_AGENT]")) {
        echo "Using Netscape.";
} else {
        echo "$_SERVER[HTTP_USER_AGENT]";
}
?>
```

Save this file as browser_match.php and place it on your Web server, then access it at its URL, http://127.0.0.1/browser_match.php.

In your browser window, you should see

> Using MSIE

or

> Using Netscape

or the value of $_SERVER[HTTP_USER_AGENT] for the browser you're using.

This sort of script is handy when you're developing a Web site using style sheets and you have one set of styles for MSIE and another set of styles for Netscape. You can use this same construct to print the style sheet link within the context of your code.

For example, a link to the style sheet,

```
<LINK REV="stylesheet" HREF="msie_style.css">
```

would appear in the area indicated by

```
<!-- stylesheet code goes here -->
```

in the following HTML example:

```
<!DOCTYPE HTML PUBLIC "-//W3C//DTD HTML 4.0 Transitional//EN">
<HTML>
<HEAD>
<TITLE>Your Page</TITLE>
<!-- stylesheet code goes here -->
</HEAD>
<BODY>
</BODY>
</HTML>
```

If you have three style sheets, msie_style.css for MSIE-specific styles, ns_style.css for Netscape-specific styles, and other_style.css for all other browsers, replace the style sheet comment with the following block of PHP:

```
<?php
if (preg_match("/MSIE/i", "$_SERVER[HTTP_USER_AGENT]")) {
        echo "<LINK REV=\"stylesheet\" HREF=\"msie_style.css\">.";
} else if (preg_match("/Mozilla/i", "$_SERVER[HTTP_USER_AGENT]")) {
        echo "<LINK REV=\"stylesheet\" HREF=\"ns_style.css\">.";
} else {
        echo "<LINK REV=\"stylesheet\" HREF=\"other_style.css\">.";
}
?>
```

This section of PHP code will seamlessly print the correct style sheet link in your HTML document, thus allowing you to safely use all the browser-specific styles you can think up.

Sending E-Mail

I can't think of any successful Web site that doesn't have some sort of feedback form or other mechanism for contact with users. When you see how incredibly easy it is to send e-mail with PHP, you might scratch your head in amazement and wonder why the rest of the world doesn't do this. That's a perfectly normal reaction (I still feel that way).

The mail() function takes four arguments: the recipient, the subject, the message, and the mail headers. So, if you want to send an e-mail to joe@yourcompany.com, with a subject of "Check this out!" and a message of "PHP is the best!", your entire PHP mail script could look like this:

```php
<?php
mail("joe@yourcompany.com", "Check this out!", "PHP is the best!", "From:
\"You\" <\"you@yourcompany.com\">\n");
?>
```

The e-mail will arrive in Joe's mailbox like any other mail message.

> Subject: Check this out!
> Date: [date sent]
> From: You <you@yourcompany.com>
> To: joe@yourcompany.com
> PHP is the best!

Now that you know how to send a simple e-mail, you can create a feedback form in HTML. A basic feedback form can contain text fields for the sender's name and e-mail address, a set of radio buttons asking if the user liked the site, and a text area for any additional message.

To begin, open your favorite text editor, create a file called show_feedback.html, and set up an HTML shell:

```html
<!DOCTYPE HTML PUBLIC "-//W3C//DTD HTML 4.0 Transitional//EN">
<HTML>
<HEAD>
<TITLE>Feedback Form</TITLE>
</HEAD>
<BODY>
            <!-- your HTML form will go here -->
```

```
</BODY>
</HTML>
```

To create the form code, assume that your PHP script will be called do_send-feedback.php and your form will use the POST method.

```
<FORM method="POST" action="do_sendfeedback.php">
```

Next, create two text fields to capture the values for $_POST[sender_name] and $_POST[sender_email]:

```
<P>Your Name: <br><INPUT type="text" name="sender_name" size=30></P>
<P>Your E-Mail Address: <br><INPUT type="text" name="sender_email" size=30></P>
```

Add the radio button group to gather the value of $_POST[like_site].

```
<P>Did you like this site?
<INPUT type="radio" name="like_site" value="Yes" checked> yes
<INPUT type="radio" name="like_site" value="No"> no
</p>
```

Add a text area so that the user can enter any additional message (captured in the variable $_POST[message]).

```
<P>Additional Message: <br>
<textarea name="message" cols=30 rows=5></textarea>
</P>
```

Finally, add the Send This Form button.

```
<INPUT type="submit" value="Send This Form">
```

Don't forget the closing </FORM> tag!

Your HTML source code should look something like this:

```
<!DOCTYPE HTML PUBLIC "-//W3C//DTD HTML 4.0 Transitional//EN">
<HTML>
<HEAD>
<TITLE>Feedback</TITLE>
</HEAD>
<BODY>
<FORM method="POST" action="do_sendfeedback.php">
<P>Your Name: <INPUT type="text" name="sender_name" size=30></P>
```

```
<P>Your E-Mail Address: <INPUT type="text" name="sender_email" size=30></P>
<P>Did you like this site?
<INPUT type="radio" name="like_site" value="Yes" checked> yes
<INPUT type="radio" name="like_site" value="No"> no
</P>
<P>Additional Message: <br>
<textarea name="message" cols=30 rows=5></textarea>
</P>
<INPUT type="submit" value="Send This Form">
</FORM>
</BODY>
</HTML>
```

Place this file on your Web server, and access it with your browser at its URL, http://127.0.0.1/show_feedback.html. In your browser window, you should see the form shown in Figure 2.4.

Next, create the do_sendfeedback.php script. This script will capture the form values $_POST[sender_name], $_POST[sender_email], $_POST[like_site], and $_POST[message].

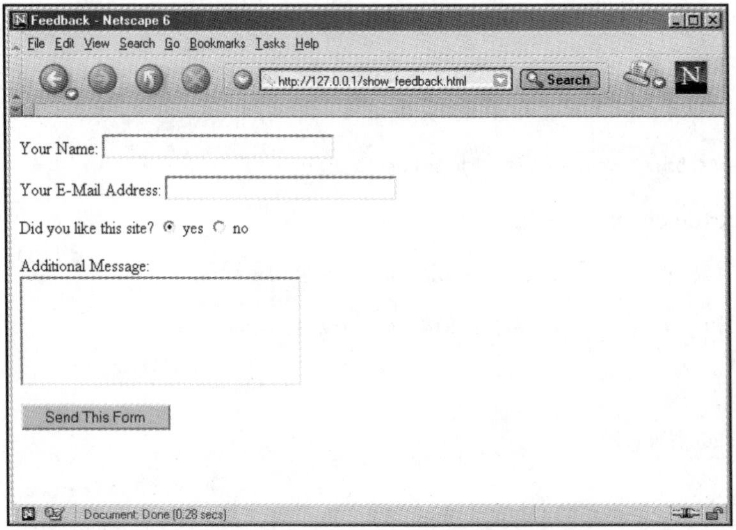

FIGURE 2.4 *Feedback form*

You must build the e-mail by concatenating strings to form one big message string (*concatenating* is a fancy word for "smashing strings together"). Use the newline (\n) and tab (\t) characters to add spacing where appropriate. Start building the message string in a variable called $msg.

```
$msg = "Sender's Full Name:\t$_POST[sender_name]\n";
```

In this line, you want the e-mail to display a field label before the variable $_POST[sender_name] so that you know what $_POST[sender_name] is. For all you know, $_POST[sender_name] could be "Dog's Name".

Repeat the process, setting up field labels and results for $_POST[sender_email], $_POST[like_site], and $_POST[message]. In these lines, however, use the concatenation operator (.=) instead of the assignment operator (=).

```
$msg .= "Sender's E-Mail:\t$_POST[sender_email]\n";
$msg .= "Did You Like the Site?\t$_POST[like_site]\n";
$msg .= "Additional Message:\t$_POST[message]\n\n";
```

Your message string ($msg) now will look like the following to the mail() function:

```
"Sender's Full Name:\t$_POST[sender_name]\nSender's E-
Mail:\t$_POST[sender_email]\nDid You Like the
Site?\t$_POST[like_site]\nAdditional Message:\t$_POST[message]\n\n";
```

The e-mail client will format this into a nice e-mail with line breaks and tabs between elements. Now, create a variable called $mailheaders to force particular values in the From and Reply-To headers of your e-mail.

```
$mailheaders = "From: My Web Site <myemail@domain.com>\n";
$mailheaders .= "Reply-To: $sender_email\n\n";
```

Create the mail function, replacing the fake e-mail address with your own:

```
mail("fakeemail@domain.com", "Feedback Form", $msg, $mailheaders);
```

After your mail is sent, you should return some sort of text message to the browser so that the person doesn't sit there wondering if the message was sent or not. If a user doesn't know if a message has been sent, chances are good that he or she will continue to click the Submit This Form button, thereby flooding your mailbox with the same feedback form.

Add a few echo statements. You can even include the user's name in your response, as you have access to the variable $_POST[sender_name]:

```
echo "<H1 align=center>Thank You, $_POST[sender_name]</H1>";
echo "<P align=center>We appreciate your feedback.</P>";
```

Your entire PHP script should look something like this:

```
<?php
$msg = "Sender's Full Name:\t$_POST[sender_name]\n";
$msg .= "Sender's E-Mail:\t$_POST[sender_email]\n";
$msg .= "Did You Like the Site?\t$_POST[like_site]\n";
$msg .= "Additional Message:\t$_POST[message]\n\n";

$mailheaders = "From: My Web Site <myemail@domain.com>\n";
$mailheaders .= "Reply-To: $sender_email\n\n";

mail("fakeemail@domain.com", "Feedback Form", $msg, $mailheaders);

echo "<H1 align=center>Thank You, $_POST[sender_name]</H1>";
echo "<P align=center>We appreciate your feedback.</P>";
?>
```

Return to your Web browser, open the feedback form at its URL, http://127.0.0.1/show_feedback.html, and enter your name, e-mail address, and a message. After I submitted the form, the resulting page properly displayed my name and provided a thank-you message, as shown in Figure 2.5.

I checked my e-mail, and I had indeed received a properly formatted message, including the $_POST[sender_name], $_POST[sender_email], $_POST[like_site], and $_POST[message] values.

So what about form validation? While ensuring that all fields are completed is not terribly crucial in this simple e-mail example, it will be important down the road when you start creating order forms. A very easy way to deal with required fields using PHP is to check for the required value and simply redirect the user back to the form if one of those values doesn't exist.

In the do_sendfeedback.php script, add the following code before building the message string, in order to check for an e-mail address and a message:

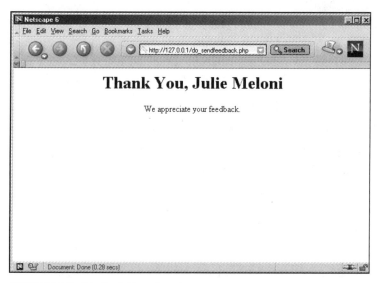

FIGURE 2.5 *Feedback Form Results page*

```
if (($_POST[sender_email] == "") || ($_POST[message] == "")) {
header("Location: http://127.0.0.1/show_feedback.html");
exit;
}
```

This code simply states, "If the value of $_POST[sender_email] is blank or if the value of $_POST[message] is blank, redirect the user back to a blank form so they can start again."

That's all there is to sending e-mail. In fact, you've made it through several simple areas of PHP functionality in this chapter, all of which you'll be able to put to good use in later chapters. In the remaining section of this chapter you'll learn the basics of reading and writing data files from the file system, including how to place the contents of a file into an e-mail and send it to a particular e-mail address.

Working with Your Filesystem

In addition to sending an e-mail full of data, you can create simple PHP scripts to create, open, and write to files on your Web server using the fopen() function, among others.

Writing Data Files

The fopen() function takes two arguments, file name and mode, and returns a file pointer. A file pointer provides information about the file and is used as a reference. The file name is the full path to the file you want to create or open, and mode can be any of the following:

- **r**. Opens the existing file in order to read data from it. The file pointer is placed at the beginning of the file, before any data.
- **r+**. Opens the existing file for reading or writing. The file pointer is placed at the beginning of the file, before any data.
- **w**. Opens a file only for writing. If a file with that name does not exist, *w attempts to create a new file. If the file does exist, it deletes all existing contents and places the file pointer at the beginning of the file.
- **w+**. Opens a file for reading and writing. If a file with that name does not exist, *w+ attempts to create a new file. If the file does exist, it deletes all existing contents and places the file pointer at the beginning of the file.
- **a**. Opens a file only for writing. If a file with that name does not exist, *a attempts to create a new file. If the file does exist, it places the file pointer at the end of the file, after all other data.
- **a+**. Opens a file for reading and writing. If a file with that name does not exist, *a+ attempts to create a new file. If the file does exist, it places the file pointer at the end of the file, after all other data.

So, to create a new file in your Web server document root (for example, /usr/local/apache/htdocs/) called mydata.txt, to be used to read and write data, use the following code:

```php
<?php
$newfile = fopen("/usr/local/apache/htdocs/mydata.txt", "a+");
?>
```

In this example, $newfile is the file pointer. You can refer to this file pointer when reading, closing, or performing other functions with the file.

 NOTE

Remember to read to and write from files that are in an area accessible by your server process.

After you open a file, be sure to close it using the `fclose()` function:

```
fclose($newfile);
```

Opening a file just to close it again can get boring, so use the `fwrite()` or `fputs()` function to place data in the open file:

```
fwrite([file], [data]);
```

 NOTE

For all intents and purposes, `fwrite()` and `fputs()` are exactly the same.

Create a script called write_data.php, containing the following code:

```
<?php
$newfile = fopen("/usr/local/apache/htdocs/mydata.txt", "a+");
fwrite($newfile, "This is a new file.");
fclose($newfile);
echo "All done!";
?>
```

Be sure to modify the path to the file to match your own environment. Adding the `echo` statement after the file has been opened, written to, and closed will cause the message to be displayed after the actions have occurred. If any errors arise, such as problems with file permissions, you'll see those on the screen as well.

 NOTE

If your Web server runs on the Windows platform, escape the backslashes in your file path, like this:

```
$newfile = fopen("c:\\Apache\\htdocs\\mydata.txt", "a+");
```

Place the PHP script on your Web server and access it with your browser at its URL, http://127.0.0.1/write_data.php. In your browser window, you should see the "All done!" message.

To verify that the message "This is a new file." has been written to mydata.txt, you can access it via URL if it has been placed above the document root, http://127.0.0.1/mydata.txt. If you placed the file in your home directory, such as /home/username/, navigate through your filesystem and open the file.

Reading Data Files

You can also use PHP to verify that a file has been written to by using the `fread()` function to gather the data into a variable. The `fread()` function takes two arguments:

```
fread([filename], [length]);
```

To read the complete file, `length` can be found using the `filesize()` function:

```
fread([filename], filesize([filename]));
```

To verify that the file mydata.txt, created in the preceding section, contains the string "This is a new file.", first create a script called read_data.php containing the following code:

```php
<?php
// this variable contains the full path to the filename
$file_loc = "/usr/local/apache/htdocs/mydata.txt";
// opens the file for reading only
$whattoread = fopen($file_loc, "r");
// puts the contents of the entire file into a variable
$file_contents = fread($whattoread, filesize($file_loc));
// close the file
fclose($whattoread);
echo "The file contains:<br>$file_contents";
?>
```

Be sure to modify the path to the file to match your own environment, then place the PHP script on your Web server and access it with your browser at its URL, http://127.0.0.1/read_data.php. In your browser window, you should now see the following:

> The file contains:
>
> This is a new file.

As well as reading the results on the screen, you can also send the contents in an e-mail. Add the following lines before the `echo` statement:

```
$mailheaders = "From: My Web Site <myemail@domain.com> \n";
mail("youremail@domain.com", "File Contents", $file_contents, $mailheaders);
```

And change the echo statement to:

```
echo "Check your mail!";
```

The complete script should now look something like this:

```php
<?php
// this variable contains the full path to the filename
$file_loc = "/usr/local/apache/htdocs/mydata.txt";
// opens the file for reading only
$whattoread = fopen($file_loc, "r");
// puts the contents of the entire file into a variable
$file_contents = fread($whattoread, filesize($file_loc));
// close the file
fclose($whattoread);
//send the mail
$mailheaders = "From: My Web Site <myemail@domain.com> \n";
mail("youremail@domain.com", "File Contents", $file_contents, $mailheaders);
echo "Check your mail!";
?>
```

Place the PHP script on your Web server and access it with your browser at its URL, http://127.0.0.1/read_data.php. In your browser window, you should now see the message telling you to check your mail. When you do, a message should be waiting for you, containing file contents.

Later, you'll learn how to save form data on the filesystem and e-mail it to yourself on demand. But for now, pat yourself on the back for making it through all of these small examples of basic PHP functionality. You'll see, in later chapters, how actual applications are really based upon these basic types of functionality.

Chapter 3

Working with
Databases

I can't think of a time when I wouldn't want to use some sort of database—be it a simple flat-file operational database or a complex relational database—in a Web application. Whether you're saving form data, tracking inventory, or creating dynamic content, if you can grasp basic database concepts, you can begin to create database-driven Web applications. With the advent of open source, fully functional relational databases, dynamic Web applications are no longer only for those with enough money to play the game.

In this chapter, you'll learn some rudimentary database theory, a few basic SQL statements, and how to use PHP to connect and retrieve information stored in MySQL, PostgreSQL, Oracle, and Microsoft SQL Server database tables. These database types are only a few from the long list supported by PHP.

After this chapter, the remaining examples used in the book will be based on MySQL. However, the introductory examples for the other databases in this chapter will provide all you'll need to know to re-create the examples in this book for these other database types. If you need additional help, refer to the specific database section of the PHP Manual, online at http://www.php.net/, to find the functions for your particular database type.

Basic Database Information

Before I lead you down the path of database development, you should become familiar with the basic structure of a database. For some this may be an unnecessary review. However, as one of the strengths of PHP is its ability to interact with a database to create a truly dynamic environment, having a basic idea of database structure and theory will help you create even better overall applications. After learning about structure, you'll also learn a little bit about database normalization.

But back to the basics of a database:

- ◆ A database is a collection of tables.
- ◆ A table contains a set of records.
- ◆ All records have the same number of fields.
- ◆ Each field categorizes a piece of data.

Starting with the smallest element, suppose you have a few uncategorized, seemingly random pieces of data: Joe Smith, 1970-10-03, and blue. These pieces of data can be placed into categories such as Full Name, Birthday, and Favorite Color. Give these fields some database-friendly names, such as FULL_NAME, BIRTH_DATE and FAVE_COLOR.

Now visualize these fields horizontally as they become the labels for columns in a table:

```
+-------------+---------------+--------------+
|  FULL_NAME  |  BIRTH_DATE   |  FAVE_COLOR  |
+-------------+---------------+--------------+
```

To create the first record (row) in this table, enter Joe Smith's information. Your table then looks like this:

```
+-------------+---------------+--------------+
|  FULL_NAME  |  BIRTH_DATE   |  FAVE_COLOR  |
+-------------+---------------+--------------+
|  Joe Smith  |  1970-10-03   |  blue        |
+-------------+---------------+--------------+
```

Add additional records to your table by adding more friends:

```
+-------------+---------------+--------------+
|  FULL_NAME  |  BIRTH_DATE   |  FAVE_COLOR  |
+-------------+---------------+--------------+
|  Joe Smith  |  1970-10-03   |  blue        |
|  Mary Smith |  1962-07-25   |  red         |
|  Jane Smith |  1968-04-28   |  black       |
+-------------+---------------+--------------+
```

Your table gets its name when you initially create its structure, and you populate your table after it's created. You'll learn all about table creation a bit later, but for now just recognize that tables, records, and fields are the basic elements of a database.

The Importance of Unique Identifiers

The FRIEND_INFO table from the preceding section is missing something: a unique identifier. You might think that the FULL_NAME field is the unique identifier. If so, you better not have any additional friends named Joe Smith, Mary Smith, or Jane

Smith. If `FULL_NAME` is the unique identifier, then no one else with those exact names can be included in your `FRIEND_INFO` table.

Instead, how about a simple `FRIEND_ID` field? If you have two friends named Joe Smith, this ensures that you'll know their favorite color when it's time to get them a birthday present.

Add the `FRIEND_ID` field to your `FRIEND_INFO` table:

```
+-------------+--------------+--------------+-------------+
+  FRIEND_ID  |  FULL_NAME   |  BIRTH_DATE  |  FAVE_COLOR |
+-------------+--------------+--------------+-------------+
+  1          |  Joe Smith   |  1970-10-03  |  blue       |
+  2          |  Mary Smith  |  1962-07-25  |  red        |
+  3          |  Jane Smith  |  1968-04-28  |  black      |
+-------------+--------------+--------------+-------------+
```

You can now add your other friend named Joe Smith. The `FRIEND_INFO` table will now look like this:

```
+-------------+--------------+--------------+-------------+
+  FRIEND_ID  |  FULL_NAME   |  BIRTH_DATE  |  FAVE_COLOR |
+-------------+--------------+--------------+-------------+
+  1          |  Joe Smith   |  1970-10-03  |  blue       |
+  2          |  Mary Smith  |  1962-07-25  |  red        |
+  3          |  Jane Smith  |  1968-04-28  |  black      |
+  4|            Joe Smith   |  1975-11-07  |  green      |
+-------------+--------------+--------------+-------------+
```

What About Relationships?

Relational databases get their name from the relationships that exist between the multiple tables contained in them. You could have a series of disconnected tables in a relational database, but where's the fun in that? As you'll learn in the next section, not only is it not fun, it's also inefficient. That's where database normalization comes into play. But for now, just understand a bit about relationships.

Relationships between tables occur because they have fields in common. Usually these common fields are the unique fields, or *keys*. The simplest example of a relational database is a product catalog and ordering mechanism. One table has product information, and the other contains customer information. A third table has order information. Instead of creating one large table for orders, containing all product and customer information, simply use unique identifiers in the orders table to reference products in the product table and customers in the customer table.

For example, records in the MY_PRODUCTS table will have a unique PRODUCT_ID, a TITLE, a DESCRIPTION, and a PRICE:

```
+---------------+-----------+----------------------+---------------+
+ PRODUCT_ID    | TITLE     | DESCRIPTION          | PRICE         |
+---------------+-----------+----------------------+---------------+
+ 12557         | Hat       | Warm and fuzzy       | 7.50          |
+ 12558         | Jacket    | Waterproof           | 32.50         |
+ 12559         | Shirt     | Shiny and stylish    | 48.00         |
+ 12560         | Pants     | Pleated chinos       | 52.00         |
+ 12561         | Socks     | Wool!                | 14.99         |
+---------------+-----------+----------------------+---------------+
```

Next, records in the MY_CUSTOMERS table will have a unique CUSTOMER_ID, a NAME, and an ADDRESS:

```
+---------------+---------------+-----------------------------------+
+ CUSTOMER_ID   | NAME          | ADDRESS                           |
+---------------+---------------+-----------------------------------+
+ 125           | Mike Jones    | 112 Main St, Anywhere CA 95228    |
+ 268           | Jim Smith     | 458 Bee Ave, Blankville IN 55248  |
+ 275           | Nancy Jones   | 751 14th St NW, Notown MI 44322   |
+---------------+---------------+-----------------------------------+
```

Records in the MY_ORDERS table will have a unique ORDER_ID. You can use the CUSTOMER_ID and PRODUCT_ID identifiers to fill in the CUSTOMER and PRODUCT_ORDERED fields. Finally, if you're ordering something, you have to have a QUANTITY:

```
+-------------+------------+--------------------+------------+
+ ORDER_ID    | CUSTOMER   | PRODUCT_ORDERED    | QUANTITY   |
+-------------+------------+--------------------+------------+
+ 1           | 125        | 12558              | 1          |
+ 2           | 268        | 12560              | 1          |
+ 3           | 275        | 12557              | 1          |
+-------------+------------+--------------------+------------+
```

To create an invoice for these orders, use the values in the CUSTOMER and PROD-UCT_ORDERED fields to find the extended information about these people and items in their respective tables: MY_CUSTOMERS and MY_PRODUCTS.

Using the relationships between your tables, you could create an invoice like this:

```
ORDER NUMBER:     001
SHIP TO:          Mike Jones, 112 Main St, Anywhere CA 95228
ITEMS ORDERED:    1 Hat (Warm and Fuzzy)
TOTAL COST:       $ 7.50
```

With this basic understanding of unique fields and the relationships between tables in a database, it's time to delve further into what is called *database normalization*.

Understanding Database Normalization

Database normalization is essentially a set of rules that allows you to organize your database in such a way that your tables are related, where appropriate, and flexible for future growth and relationships. The sets of rules used in normalization are called *normal forms*. If your database design follows the first set of rules, it's considered to be in the *first normal form*. If the first three sets of rules of normalization are followed, your database is said to be in the *third normal form*. We'll go through the normal forms using the concept of students and courses within a school.

Looking at a Flat Table

Before looking at the first normal form, let's start with something that needs to be normalized. In the case of a database, it's the *flat table*. A flat table is like a spreadsheet with many columns for data. There are no relationships between multiple tables, as all of the data you could possibly want is right there in that single flat table. The flat table is not the most efficient design and will consume more physical space on your hard drive than a set of normalized database tables.

Suppose you have a table that holds student and course information for a school. You might have the fields shown in Table 3.1 in your flat table.

Table 3.1   Students and Courses Table

Field Name	Description
StudentName	Name of the student
CourseID1	ID of the first course taken by the student
CourseDescription1	Description of the first course taken by the student
CourseIntructor1	Instructor of the first course taken by the student
CourseID2	ID of the second course taken by the student
CourseDescription2	Description of the second course taken by the student
CourseIntructor2	Instructor of the second course taken by the student

You might then repeat the CourseID, CourseDescription, and CourseInstructor columns many more times to account for all the classes a student can take during his or her academic career. While redundant, this is the method used when creating a single flat table to store information. Eliminating this redundancy is the first step in normalization, so next you'll take this flat table to the first normal form. If your table remained in its flat format, you could have a lot of unclaimed space and a lot of space being used unnecessarily—not an efficient table design!

The First Normal Form

The main rules for the first normal form are

♦ Eliminate repeating information
♦ Create separate tables for related data

If you look at the flat table design, with its many repeated sets of fields for students and courses, you can identify students and courses as its two distinct topics. Taking your student and courses flat table to the first normal form would mean that you create two tables: one for students (call it students) and one for students plus courses (call it students_courses). You can see the new table designs in Tables 3.2 and 3.3.

Table 3.2   The *students* Table

Field Name	Description
StudentID	A unique ID for the student. This new field is now a primary key.
StudentName	Name of the student

Table 3.3 The _students_courses_ Table

Field Name	Description
StudentID	Unique ID of the student, matching an entry in the students table.
CourseID	ID of the course being taken by the student
CourseDescription	Description of the course taken by the student
CourseIntructor	Instructor of the course taken by the student

Your two tables now represent a one-to-many relationship of one student to many courses. Students can take as many courses as they wish and are not limited to the number of CourseID/CourseDescription/CourseInstructor groupings that existed in the flat table.

You still have some work to do; the next step is to put the tables into second normal form.

The Second Normal Form

The basic rule for the second normal form is

◆ No non-key attributes depend on a portion of the primary key

In plain English, this means that if fields in your table are not entirely related to a primary key, then you have more work to do. In the students and courses example we're using, this means breaking out the courses into their own table so that the original flat table is now just a table full of students.

CourseID, CourseDesc, and CourseInstructor can become a table called courses with a primary key of CourseID. The students_courses table should then just contain two fields: StudentID and CourseID. You can see the new table designs in Tables 3.4 and 3.5.

Table 3.4 The _courses_ Table

Field Name	Description
CourseID	Unique ID of a course
CourseDescription	Description of the course
CourseIntructor	Instructor of the course

Table 3.5   The New *students_courses* Table

Field Name	Description
StudentID	Unique ID of the student, matching an entry in the students table.
CourseID	Unique ID of the course being taken, matching an entry in the courses table.

Believe it or not, you can go even further with this example, to the third normal form.

The Third Normal Form

The rule for the third normal form is

◆ No attributes depend on other non-key attributes

This rule simply means that you need to look at your tables and see if more fields exist that can be broken down further and that aren't dependent on a key. Think about removing repeated data and you'll find your answer—instructors. Inevitably, an instructor will teach more than one class. However, the CourseInstructor field in the courses table is not a key of any sort. So if you break out this information and create a separate table purely for the sake of efficiency and maintenance, that's the third normal form. Take a look at the new courses table and the instructors table in Tables 3.6 and 3.7.

Table 3.6   The *courses* Table

Field Name	Description
CourseID	Unique ID of a course
CourseDescription	Description of the course
CourseIntructorID	ID of the instructor, matching an entry in the instructors table

Table 3.7   The *instructors* Table

Field Name	Description
InstructorID	Unique ID of an instructor
InstructorName	Name of the instructor
InstructorNotes	Any notes regarding the instructor

The third normal form is usually adequate for removing redundancy and allowing for flexibility and growth while remaining efficient. That, after all, is the goal of database normalization!

With all that theory behind you, it's time to learn some of the language of relational databases: SQL, or Structured Query Language.

Basic SQL Commands

Although the Structured Query Language (SQL) was developed by IBM, SQL is currently under the watchful eye of the American National Standards Institute (ANSI). As with all "standards," there are variations of SQL—"proprietary enhancements," if you will—for use with MySQL, Microsoft SQL Server, Oracle, and so on. However, learning the standard set of SQL commands will provide you with a fundamental knowledge of SQL that you can use with multiple database systems. Here are the standard commands:

- CREATE. Creates a new table.
- ALTER. Modifies the definition (structure, data types, and so on) of an existing table.
- DROP. Permanently removes elements such as tables and fields.
- INSERT. Adds a record to a table.
- UPDATE. Modifies data in an existing record.
- SELECT. Performs a query on a table, including mathematical functions, field comparison, pattern matching, and so on.
- DELETE. Permanently removes elements from a table.

The next several sections contain further descriptions and examples of these basic SQL commands. Be sure to read your database documentation thoroughly for the exact usage of these commands in your own environment, because they might differ slightly from these examples, which are geared toward the MySQL user. Additionally, you may enter SQL commands directly through a graphical user interface (GUI) or via the command line, depending on your database type. The next sections only provide examples of the SQL commands themselves; at the end of this chapter, you'll learn to send SQL commands to your database via PHP scripts.

CREATE

The CREATE command creates a table in the selected database. The basic syntax is as follows:

```
CREATE TABLE [table name] [(field_name field_data_type,....)] [options]
```

 NOTE

Some common data types are int, double, char, varchar, date, time, datetime, text, and blob. Refer to your database documentation for a list of supported data types and any size and data restrictions.

To create the FRIEND_INFO table used at the beginning of this chapter, the SQL statement would be something like this:

```
CREATE TABLE FRIEND_INFO (
FRIEND_ID int not null primary key,
FULL_NAME varchar (100),
BIRTH_DATE date,
FAVE_COLOR varchar (25)
);
```

This sample code uses a lot of white space. White space is irrelevant in SQL statements, but it certainly makes your code easier to read (and easier to edit later!). The preceding statement could just as easily have been written like this:

```
CREATE TABLE FRIEND_INFO (FRIEND_ID int not null primary key, FULL_NAME varchar
(100), BIRTH_DATE date, FAVE_COLOR varchar (25));
```

The CREATE command defines the attributes of the fields in your table; it gives each attribute a type and a length. In this example, the FRIEND_ID field is defined as "not null," meaning that when a record is added, if the field is empty, it is simply empty, or it has a default value such as "0" for numeric fields. A value of NULL means something entirely different from "empty", and this is an important distinction to remember. FRIEND_ID is also identified as the *primary key*, meaning that FRIEND_ID always holds unique data; although there may be multiple entries for a friend named Joe Smith, there will be only one FRIEND_ID of 1, 2, and so on.

ALTER

The ALTER command gives you the opportunity to modify elements of a particular table. For example, you can use ALTER to add fields or change field types. For instance, if you want to change the size of the FULL_NAME field of the FRIEND_INFO table from 100 to 150, you could issue this statement:

```
ALTER TABLE FRIEND_INFO CHANGE FULL_NAME FULL_NAME VARCHAR (150);
```

To add a column to the table, you could use the following statement, which adds a field called HAT_SIZE:

```
ALTER TABLE FRIEND_INFO ADD HAT_SIZE varchar(5);
```

Using the ALTER command alleviates the need to delete an entire table and re-create it just because you spelled a field name incorrectly or made other minor mistakes.

DROP

The DROP command is quite dangerous if you're not paying attention to what you're doing, because it will delete your entire table in the blink of an eye. The syntax is very simple:

```
DROP TABLE [table name];
```

If you wanted to delete the FRIEND_INFO table and rely on your brain to remember your friends' birthdays, the command would be

```
DROP TABLE FRIEND_INFO;
```

You can use the DROP command in conjunction with the ALTER command to delete specific fields (and all the data contained in them). To delete the HAT_SIZE field from the FRIEND_INFO table, issue this statement:

```
ALTER TABLE FRIEND_INFO DROP HAT_SIZE;
```

The HAT_SIZE field will no longer exist, but all other fields in your table will still be intact.

INSERT

You use the INSERT command to populate your tables one record at a time. The basic syntax of the INSERT command is

```
INSERT INTO [table name] ([name of field1] , [name of field2], ...)
VALUES ('[value of field 1]', '[value of field 2]'...);
```

To add a record to the FRIEND_INFO table, where the fields are FRIEND_ID, FULL_NAME, BIRTH_DATE, and FAVE_COLOR, the command would be:

```
INSERT INTO FRIEND_INFO (FRIEND_ID, FULL_NAME, BIRTH_DATE, FAVE_COLOR)
VALUES ('1', 'Joe Smith', '1970-10-03', 'blue');
```

To add the rest of your friends, simply issue additional INSERT statements:

```
INSERT INTO FRIEND_INFO (FRIEND_ID, FULL_NAME, BIRTH_DATE, FAVE_COLOR)
VALUES ('2', 'Mary Smith', '1962-07-25', 'red');
INSERT INTO FRIEND_INFO (FRIEND_ID, FULL_NAME, BIRTH_DATE, FAVE_COLOR)
VALUES ('3', 'Jane Smith', '1968-04-28', 'black');
INSERT INTO FRIEND_INFO (FRIEND_ID, FULL_NAME, BIRTH_DATE, FAVE_COLOR)
VALUES ('4', 'Joe Smith', '1975-11-07', 'green');
```

When inserting records, be sure to separate your strings with single quotes or double quotes. If you use single quotes around your strings, and the data you are adding contains apostrophes, avoid errors by escaping the apostrophe (\') within the INSERT statement. Similarly, if you use double quotes around your strings and you want to include double quotes as part of the data, escape them (\") within your INSERT statement.

For example, if you use single quotes around your strings and you want to insert a record for a friend named Mark O'Hara, you can use this statement:

```
INSERT INTO FRIEND_INFO (FRIEND_ID, FULL_NAME, BIRTH_DATE, FAVE_COLOR)
VALUES ('5', 'Mark O\'Hara', '1968-12-12', 'orange');
```

Or, you can surround your strings with double quotes and avoid escaping single quotes:

```
INSERT INTO FRIEND_INFO (FRIEND_ID, FULL_NAME, BIRTH_DATE, FAVE_COLOR)
VALUES ("5", "Mark O'Hara", "1968-12-12", "orange");
```

However, be aware that using single quotes around strings is the convention in SQL, and try to use this convention whenever possible.

UPDATE

The UPDATE command modifies parts of a record without replacing the entire record. Here is the basic syntax of the UPDATE command:

```
UPDATE [table name] SET [field name] = '[new value]' WHERE [expression];
```

For instance, suppose you have an incorrect birth date in the FRIEND_INFO table. Joe Smith, with a FRIEND_ID of 1, was born on November 3 instead of October 3. Instead of deleting the record and inserting a new one, just use the UPDATE command to change the data in the BIRTH_DATE field:

```
UPDATE FRIEND_INFO SET BIRTH_DATE = '1970-11-03' WHERE FRIEND_ID = '1';
```

If you issue an UPDATE statement without specifying a WHERE expression, you will update all the records. For example, to change everyone's favorite color to red, use this UPDATE statement:

```
UPDATE FRIEND_INFO SET FAVE_COLOR = 'red';
```

UPDATE can be a very powerful SQL command. For example, you can perform string functions and mathematical functions on existing records and use the UPDATE to command to modify their values.

SELECT

When you're creating database-driven Web sites, the SELECT command will likely be the most often-used command in your arsenal. The SELECT command causes certain records in your table to be chosen, based on criteria that you define. Here is the basic syntax of the SELECT command:

```
SELECT [field names] FROM [table] WHERE [expression] ORDER BY [fields];
```

To select all the records in a table, such as the FRIEND_INFO table, use this statement:

```
SELECT * FROM FRIEND_INFO;
```

To select just the entries in the FULL_NAME field of the FRIEND_INFO table, use this:

```
SELECT FULL_NAME FROM FRIEND_INFO;
```

To select all the records in a table and have them returned in a particular order, use an expression for ORDER BY. For example, to view the FRIEND_ID, FULL_NAME, and `BIRTH_DATE` in each record in the `FRIEND_INFO` table, ordered by youngest friend to oldest friend, use the following:

`SELECT FRIEND_ID, FULL_NAME, BIRTH_DATE FROM FRIEND_INFO ORDER BY BIRTH_DATE DESC;`

`DESC` stands for "descending." To view from oldest to youngest, use `ASC` for "ascending":

`SELECT FRIEND_ID, FULL_NAME, BIRTH_DATE FROM FRIEND_INFO ORDER BY BIRTH_DATE ASC;`

Using sample data, the preceding statement produces results like this:

```
+-------------+--------------+--------------+
+  FRIEND_ID  |  FULL_NAME   |  BIRTH_DATE  |
+-------------+--------------+--------------+
+  2          |  Mary Smith  |  1962-07-25  |
+  3          |  Jane Smith  |  1968-04-28  |
+  1          |  Joe Smith   |  1970-11-03  |
+  4          |  Joe Smith   |  1975-11-07  |
+-------------+--------------+--------------+
```

When preparing `ORDER BY` clauses, the default order is `ASC` (ascending).

You can also perform mathematical and string functions within SQL statements, thereby using `SELECT` to do more than just echo existing data. For example, to quickly find the number of friends in your `FRIEND_INFO` table, use

`SELECT COUNT(FRIEND_ID) FROM FRIEND_INFO;`

The result of this statement is 4. You could also use the `COUNT( )` function on any other field to count the number of those entries in the table.

I could write volumes on the many variations of `SELECT` commands, but luckily, others already have. Additionally, if you are using the MySQL database, the MySQL manual contains a wonderful SQL reference. Later in this chapter, and in fact throughout the book, you'll learn more uses of the `SELECT` command within the context of creating various applications.

DELETE

The `DELETE` command is not nearly as fun as `SELECT`, but it's useful nonetheless. Like the `DROP` command, using `DELETE` without paying attention to what you're doing can have horrible consequences in a production environment. Once you

DROP a table or DELETE a record, it's gone forever. The basic syntax of the DELETE command is as follows:

```
DELETE FROM [table name] WHERE [expression];
```

For example, to delete entries for Joe Smith from your FRIEND_INFO table, you could use:

```
DELETE FROM FRIEND_INFO WHERE FULL_NAME = 'Joe Smith';
```

But wait a minute! If you execute this statement, you'll delete *both* Joe Smith entries. So, use another identifier in addition to the name:

```
DELETE FROM FRIEND_INFO   WHERE FULL_NAME = 'Joe Smith' AND
BIRTH_DATE = '1970-11-03';
```

Or, since you now know the importance of unique identifiers, you could use this:

```
DELETE FROM FRIEND_INFO   WHERE FRIEND_ID = '1';
```

If you issue a DELETE command without specifying a WHERE expression, you will delete all the records. For example, this bit of SQL deletes all the records in the FRIEND_INFO table:

```
DELETE FROM FRIEND_INFO;
```

Also remember, if you don't want to delete an entire record, just a certain field from a table, you can use this:

```
ALTER TABLE [table name] DROP [field name];
```

Always back up your data if you're going to be using the DELETE and DROP commands, just in case something goes wrong.

Establishing a Database Connection with PHP

Using the built-in database connectivity functions in PHP, you can connect to virtually any database type and access its data (if you have the proper permissions, of course!). If PHP does not contain specific functions for your particular database type, you can make generic ODBC connections using PHP's ODBC functions. Before trying to use any of the database connectivity functions, be sure that you have a database installed and the proper extensions were compiled into PHP or loaded through your `php.ini` file.

In the next several pages, you'll find function definitions and code samples for the more popular database types. The PHP Manual at http://www.php.net/manual/ is the first place you should look to find a complete list of all the functions for supported databases, not just those listed in this chapter. After searching the manual and the FAQ, search the PHP Mailing List Archives. Chances are good that if you have a database connectivity question, someone else has asked it and a developer has answered it. If not, asking a well-phrased question will undoubtedly elicit numerous responses.

The following sections are by no means all there is to know about connecting to databases with PHP. Instead, these sections detail the basic elements of database connectivity:

1. Connect to a server
2. Select a database
3. Query
4. View results

Additionally, the code samples provided in the next sections are not the only ways to make a simple connection and print results. Some of the examples are more verbose than they really need to be, but they give you a solid foundation for understanding the steps that follow. When you become an expert with your database type, you can find your own ways to optimize your code, eliminating extra steps and some processing time and resource overhead.

Connecting to a MySQL Database

The MySQL database is one of the most popular among PHP developers. It's my database of choice, as well as the database used in the examples found in this book. Understandably, there are numerous well-documented PHP functions you can use in conjunction with your MySQL databases; see the PHP Manual for a complete list. However, you need only a few of these functions in order to make a simple connection and select some data:

♦ `mysql_connect()`. Opens a connection to the MySQL server. Requires a hostname, username, and password.

- `mysql_select_db()`. Selects a database on the MySQL server.
- `mysql_query()`. Issues the SQL statement.
- `mysql_fetch_array()`. Puts an SQL statement result row in an array.
- `mysql_result()`. Gets single element result data from a successful query.
- `mysql_error()`. Returns a meaningful error message from MySQL.

First, you must know the name of the server on which the database resides, as well as the valid username and password for that server. In this example, the database name is MyDB on localhost, your username is joeuser, and your password is 34Nhjp. Start your PHP code by creating a connection variable:

```
$conn = mysql_connect("localhost","joeuser","34Nhjp") or die(mysql_error());
```

The `die()` function is used in conjunction with the `mysql_error()` function, to print an error message and exit a script when the function cannot perform as required. In this case, `die()` would execute if the connection failed. The error message would be printed so that you'll know where the error occurred, and no further actions would take place. Using `die()` properly will alleviate many headaches as you attempt to debug your code.

If you make it through the connection step, the next step is to select the database and issue the SQL statement. Suppose that the `FRIEND_INFO` table, used in previous examples, exists in a MySQL database called MyDB. Create a database variable like this one:

```
$db = mysql_select_db("MyDB", $conn) or die(mysql_error());
```

Up to this point, you've told PHP to connect to a server and select a database. If you've made it this far, you can issue a SQL statement and hopefully see some results!

Suppose you want use the `FRIEND_INFO` table to view your friends' names, birthdays, and favorite colors, ordered from oldest to youngest friend. Create a variable that holds your SQL statement:

```
$sql = "SELECT FULL_NAME, BIRTH_DATE, FAVE_COLOR FROM FRIEND_INFO ORDER BY
BIRTH_DATE ASC";
```

Next, create a variable to hold the result of the query, carried out by the `mysql_query()` function. The `mysql_query()` function takes two arguments: the connection and the SQL statement variables you just created.

```
$sql_result = mysql_query($sql,$conn) or die(mysql_error());
```

To format the results currently held in $sql_result, first separate the results by row, using the mysql_fetch_array() function:

```
while ($row = mysql_fetch_array($sql_result)) {
            // more code here...
}
```

The while loop creates an array called $row for each record in the result set. To get the individual elements of the record (FULL_NAME, BIRTH_DATE, FAVE_COLOR), create specific variables:

```
$full_name = $row["FULL_NAME"];
$birth_date = $row["BIRTH_DATE"];
$fave_color = $row["FAVE_COLOR"];
```

Suppose you want to print the results in a simple HTML table. Step back and place this statement before the while loop begins, in order to open the table tag and create the row headings:

```
echo "<TABLE BORDER=1>
<TR>
<TH>Full Name</TH>
<TH>Birthday</TH>
<TH>Favorite Color</TH>
</TR>";
```

After defining the variables within the while loop, print them in table format:

```
echo "<TR>
<TD>$full_name</TD>
<TD>$birth_date</TD>
<TD>$fave_color</TD>
</TR>";
```

The new while loop looks like this:

```
while ($row = mysql_fetch_array($sql_result)) {
$full_name = $row["FULL_NAME"];
$birth_date = $row["BIRTH_DATE"];
$fave_color = $row["FAVE_COLOR"];
echo "<TR>
<TD>$full_name</TD>
<TD>$birth_date</TD>
```

```
<TD>$fave_color</TD>
</TR>";
}
```

After the while loop, close the HTML table:

```
echo "</TABLE>";
```

The full script to perform a simple connection and data selection from a MySQL database could look something like this:

```php
<?php
// create connection; substitute your own information!
$conn = mysql_connect("localhost","joeuser","34Nhjp")
or die(mysql_error());

// select database; substitute your own database name
$db = mysql_select_db("MyDB", $conn) or die(mysql_error());

            // create SQL statement
$sql = "SELECT FULL_NAME, BIRTH_DATE, FAVE_COLOR FROM
FRIEND_INFO ORDER BY BIRTH_DATE ASC";

// execute SQL query and get result
$sql_result = mysql_query($sql,$conn) or die(mysql_error());

// start results formatting
echo "<TABLE BORDER=1>
<TR>
<TH>Full Name</TH>
<TH>Birthday</TH>
<TH>Favorite Color</TH>
</TR>";

// format results by row
while ($row = mysql_fetch_array($sql_result)) {
$full_name = $row["FULL_NAME"];
$birth_date = $row["BIRTH_DATE"];
$fave_color = $row["FAVE_COLOR"];
echo "<TR
```

```
<TD>$full_name</TD>
<TD>$birth_date</TD>
<TD>$fave_color</TD>
</TR>";
}
echo "</TABLE>";
?>
```

This example didn't use the `mysql_result()` function because `mysql_fetch_array()` is more useful for retrieving multiple records. If your SQL query was meant to select only one record, you could have used `mysql_result()`.

For example, say your SQL statement was

```
SELECT BIRTH_DATE FROM FRIEND_INFO WHERE ID = 1;
```

After issuing the query

```
$sql_result = mysql_query($sql,$conn) or die(mysql_error());
```

simply use `mysql_result()` like so:

```
$birthday = mysql_result($sql_result, 0, "BIRTH_DATE") or die(mysql_error());
```

The first argument used in the function is the resource result of the SQL statement. Next in the list comes the row (starting with number 0), and finally, there's the name of the field you selected.

See the PHP Manual, at http://www.php.net/mysql, for the forty or so additional MySQL functions, and try using your own tables and SQL statements in place of the examples shown here. The basic idea of connecting, querying, and retrieving a result is fundamental to all other actions.

Connecting to a PostgreSQL Database

Like MySQL, the PostgreSQL database is quite popular among PHP developers. Understandably, there are numerous well-documented PHP functions you can use in conjunction with PostgreSQL; see the PHP Manual at http://www.php.net/pgsql for a complete list. However, you need only a few of these functions in order to make a simple connection and select some data:

- ◆ **pg_connect()**. Opens a connection to PostgreSQL. Requires a hostname, database name, username, and password.

- ◆ pg_query(). Executes the SQL statement.
- ◆ pg_fetch_array(). Puts a SQL statement result row in an array.
- ◆ pg_fetch_result(). Gets single element result data from a successful query.
- ◆ pg_result_error(). Returns a meaningful error message from PostgreSQL.

First, you must know the name of the server on which the database resides, as well as a valid username and password for that server. In this example, the database name is MyDB on localhost, your username is joeuser, and your password is 34Nhjp. Start your PHP code by creating a connection variable:

```
$conn = pg_connect("host=localhost dbname=MyDB user=joseuser password=34Nhjp")
or die("Couldn't make a connection.");
```

The die() function in this case is used to print an error message and exit a script when the function cannot perform as required. In this case, die() would execute if the connection failed. The error message would be printed so you know where the error occurred ("Couldn't make a connection."), and no further actions would take place. Using die() properly will alleviate many headaches as you attempt to debug your code.

If you make it through the connection test, the next step is to create the SQL statement. Using the FRIEND_INFO table, suppose you want to view your friends' names, birthdays, and favorite colors, ordered from oldest to youngest friend. Create a variable that holds your SQL statement:

```
$sql = "SELECT FULL_NAME, BIRTH_DATE, FAVE_COLOR FROM FRIEND_INFO ORDER BY
BIRTH_DATE ASC";
```

Next, create a variable to hold the result of the query, carried out by the pg_query() function. This function takes two arguments: the connection and the SQL statement variables you just created.

```
$sql_result = pg_query($conn,$sql) or die(pg_result_error());
```

In this instance, the die() function works in conjunction with the pg_result_error() function, to produce an actual error from PostgreSQL instead of one you just made up.

Now that you have queried the database, you'll want to format the results currently held in $sql_result. Since you have more than one record to loop through, first separate the results by row, using the pg_fetch_array() function:

```
while ($row = pg_fetch_array($sql_result)) {
            // more code here...
}
```

The while loop creates an array called $row for each record in the result set. To get the individual elements of the record (FULL_NAME, BIRTH_DATE, FAVE_COLOR), create specific variables:

```
$full_name = $row["FULL_NAME"];
$birth_date = $row["BIRTH_DATE"];
$fave_color = $row["FAVE_COLOR"];
```

Suppose you want to print the results in a simple HTML table. Step back and place the following statement before the while loop begins, in order to open the table tag and create the row headings:

```
echo "<TABLE BORDER=1>
<TR>
<TH>Full Name</TH>
<TH>Birthday</TH>
<TH>Favorite Color</TH>
</TR>";
```

After defining the variables within the while loop, print them in table format:

```
echo "<TR>
<TD>$full_name</TD>
<TD>$birth_date</TD>
<TD>$fave_color</TD>
</TR>";
```

The new while loop looks like this:

```
while ($row = pg_fetch_array($sql_result)) {
$full_name = $row["FULL_NAME"];
$birth_date = $row["BIRTH_DATE"];
```

```
$fave_color = $row["FAVE_COLOR"];
echo "<TR>
<TD>$full_name</TD>
<TD>$birth_date</TD>
<TD>$fave_color</TD>
</TR>";
}
```

After the while loop, close the HTML table:

```
echo "</TABLE>";
```

The full script to perform a simple connection and data selection from a PostgreSQL database could look something like this:

```
<?php
// create connection; substitute your own info
$conn = pg_connect("host=localhost dbname=MyDB user=joeuser
password=34Nhjp") or die("Couldn't make a connection.");

// create SQL statement
$sql = "SELECT FULL_NAME, BIRTH_DATE, FAVE_COLOR FROM FRIEND_INFO
ORDER BY BIRTH_DATE ASC";

// execute SQL query and get result
$sql_result = pg_query($conn,$sql) or die(pg_result_error());

// start results formatting
echo "<TABLE BORDER=1>
<TR>
<TH>Full Name</TH>
<TH>Birthday</TH>
<TH>Favorite Color</TH>
</TR>";

// format results by row
while ($row = pg_fetch_array($sql_result)) {
$full_name = $row["FULL_NAME"];
$birth_date = $row["BIRTH_DATE"];
```

```
$fave_color = $row["FAVE_COLOR"];
echo "<TR>
<TD>$full_name</TD>
<TD>$birth_date</TD>
<TD>$fave_color</TD>
</TR>";
}
echo "</TABLE>";
?>
```

This example didn't use the `pg_fetch_result()` function, because `pg_fetch_array()` is more useful for retrieving multiple records. If your SQL query was meant to select only one record, you could have used `pg_fetch_result()`.

For example, say your SQL statement was

```
SELECT BIRTH_DATE FROM FRIEND_INFO WHERE ID = 1;
```

After issuing the query

```
$sql_result = pg_query($sql,$conn) or die(pg_result_error());
```

simply use `pg_fetch_result()` like so:

```
$birthday = pg_fetch_result($sql_result, 0, "BIRTH_DATE") or
die(pg_result_error());
```

The first argument used in the function is the resource result of the SQL statement. Next in the list comes the row (starting with number 0) and, finally, there's the name of the field you selected.

See the PHP Manual, at http://www.php.net/pgsql, for the numerous other PostgreSQL functions, and try using your own tables and SQL statements in place of the examples shown here. The basic idea of connecting, querying, and retrieving a result is fundamental to all other actions.

Connecting to an Oracle Database

PHP has numerous functions for connecting to Oracle databases. This is good because if you've spent the money to purchase an Oracle database, you'll want to be able to connect to it using PHP. The PHP Manual has the definitive list of

PHP-to-Oracle connectivity functions; however, you need only a few in order to make a simple connection and select some data:

- ◆ OCILogon(). Opens a connection to Oracle. Requires that the environment variable ORACLE_SID has been set and that you have a valid username and password.
- ◆ OCIParse(). Parses a SQL statement.
- ◆ OCIExecute(). Executes the SQL statement.
- ◆ OCIFetchStatement(). Gets all the records as the result of a SQL statement and places them in a results buffer.
- ◆ OCIFreeStatement(). Frees the resources in use by the current statement.
- ◆ OCILogoff(). Closes the connection to Oracle.

First, you must have a valid username and password for the database defined by ORACLE_SID. In this example, the username is joeuser and your password is 34Nhjp. Start your PHP code by creating a connection variable:

```
$conn = OCILogon("joeuser","34Nhjp") or die("Couldn't logon.");
```

The die() function is used to print an error message and exit a script when the function cannot perform as required. In this case, die() would execute if the connection failed. The error message would be printed so you know where the error occurred ("Couldn't logon."), and no further actions would take place.

If you make it through the connection test, the next step is to create the SQL statement. Suppose that the FRIEND_INFO table, used in previous examples, exists in your Oracle database. Suppose you want to use the FRIEND_INFO table view your friends' names, birthdays, and favorite colors, ordered from oldest to youngest friend. Create a variable that holds your SQL statement:

```
$sql = "SELECT FULL_NAME, BIRTH_DATE, FAVE_COLOR FROM FRIEND_INFO ORDER BY
BIRTH_DATE ASC";
```

Next, use the OCIParse() function to parse the statement in the context of your database connection:

```
$sql_statement = OCIParse($conn,$sql) or die("Couldn't parse statement.");
```

The next step is to execute the statement:

```
OCIExecute($sql_statement) or die("Couldn't execute query.");
```

Now that you have executed the query, you'll want to format the results. As you have more than one record to loop through, first get all the records using the `OCIFetchStatement()` function:

```
$my_records = OCIFetchStatement($sql_statement, $results);
if ($my_records > 0) {
            // more code here...
}
```

The code within the `if` statement will execute as long as there are records in the result set, so let's put some code inside the loop!

This code assumes you'll want to format the results in a nice HTML table. First, you'll need to start the table:

```
echo "<TABLE BORDER=1>
<TR>";
```

Next, you'll look through the result set (which is an array) to gather the field names:

```
while (list($key, $val) = each($results)) {
echo "<TH>$key</TH>";
}
echo "</TR>";
```

With your labels printed, you'll want to create the rows for the data. Inside a `for` statement, you'll reset the `$results` array and then loop through the result set and print out the data:

```
for ($i = 0; $i < $my_records; $i++) {
      reset($results);
      echo "<TR>";
      while($row = each($results)) {
          $some_data = $row['value'];
          echo "<TD>$some_data[$i]</TD>";
      }
echo "</TR>";
}
```

Close up the HTML table and then print a message, if there are no records in your result set:

```
echo "</TABLE>";
} else {
    echo "No records selected.";
}
```

Finally, you'll want to free up the resources used to perform the query and close the database connection. Failing to do so could cause memory leaks and other nasty resource-hogging events to occur.

```
OCIFreeStatement($sql_statement);
OCILogoff($conn);
```

The full script to perform a simple connection and data selection from an Oracle database could look something like this:

```
<?php
// substitute your own username and password
$conn = OCILogon("joeuser","34Nhjp") or die("Couldn't logon.");

// create SQL statement
$sql = "SELECT FULL_NAME, BIRTH_DATE, FAVE_COLOR FROM FRIEND_INFO
ORDER BY BIRTH_DATE ASC";

// parse SQL statement
$sql_statement = OCIParse($conn,$sql) or die("Couldn't parse statement.");

// execute SQL query
OCIExecute($sql_statement) or die("Couldn't execute query.");
$my_records = OCIFetchStatement($sql_statement, $results);

if ($my_records > 0) {
            echo "<TABLE BORDER=1>
<TR>";
while (list($key, $val) = each($results)) {
echo "<TH>$key</TH>";
}
echo "</TR>";
```

```
        for ($i = 0; $i < $my_records; $i++) {
    reset($results);
    echo "<TR>";
        while($row = each($results)) {
            $some_data = $row['value'];
        echo "<TD>$some_data[$i]</TD>";
}
        echo "</TR>";
}
echo "</TABLE>";
} else {
        echo "No records selected.";
}


// free resources and close connection
OCIFreeStatement($sql_statement);
OCILogoff($conn);
?>
```

See the PHP Manual, at http://www.php.net/oci8, for the numerous other Oracle functions, and try using your own tables and SQL statements in place of the examples shown here. The basic idea of connecting, querying, and retrieving a result is fundamental to all other actions used in the code driving dynamic Web applications.

Connecting to Microsoft SQL Server

There are numerous PHP functions for Microsoft SQL Server connectivity, documented in detail in the PHP Manual at http://www.php.net/mssql. However, you need only a few of these functions in order to make a simple connection and select some data:

- ◆ `mssql_connect()`. Opens a connection to Microsoft SQL Server. Requires a server name, username, and password.
- ◆ `mssql_select_db()`. Selects a database on the Microsoft SQL Server.
- ◆ `mssql_query()`. Issues the SQL statement.
- ◆ `mssql_fetch_array()`. Puts a SQL statement result row in an array.

First, you must know the name of the server on which the database resides, as well as a valid username and password for that database. In this example, the database name is MyDB on localhost, your username is joeuser, and your password is 34Nhjp. Start your PHP code by creating a connection variable:

```
$conn = mssql_connect("localhost","joeuser","34Nhjp") or die("Couldn't connect
to the server.");
```

The die() function is used to print an error message and exit a script when the function cannot perform as required. In this case, die() would execute if the connection failed. The error message would be printed so that you'll know where the error occurred ("Couldn't connect to the server."), and no further actions would take place. Using die() properly will alleviate many headaches as you attempt to debug your code.

If you make it through the connection test, the next step is to select the database and create the SQL statement. Suppose that the FRIEND_INFO table, used in previous examples, exists in a database called MyDB. Create a database variable such as this:

```
$db = mssql_select_db("MyDB", $connection) or die("Couldn't select database.");
```

Up to this point, you've told PHP to connect to a server and select a database. If you've made it this far, you can issue a SQL statement and hopefully see some results!

Suppose you want use the FRIEND_INFO table to view your friends' names, birthdays, and favorite colors, ordered from oldest to youngest friend. Create a variable that holds your SQL statement:

```
$sql = "SELECT FULL_NAME, BIRTH_DATE, FAVE_COLOR FROM FRIEND_INFO ORDER BY
BIRTH_DATE ASC";
```

Next, create a variable to hold the result of the query, carried out by the mssql_query() function. The mssql_query() function takes two arguments: the connection and the SQL statement variables you just created.

```
$sql_result = mssql_query($sql,$conn) or die("Couldn't execute query.");
```

To format the results currently held in $sql_result, first separate the results by row, using the mssql_fetch_array() function:

```
while ($row = mssql_fetch_array($sql_result)) {
            // more code here...
}
```

The while loop creates an array called $row for each record in the result set. To get the individual elements of the record (FULL_NAME, BIRTH_DATE, FAVE_COLOR), create specific variables:

```
$full_name = $row["FULL_NAME"];
$birth_date = $row["BIRTH_DATE"];
$fave_color = $row["FAVE_COLOR"];
```

Suppose you want to print the results in a simple HTML table. Step back and place this statement before the while loop begins in order to open the table tag and create the row headings:

```
echo "<TABLE BORDER=1>
<TR>
<TH>Full Name</TH>
<TH>Birthday</TH>
<TH>Favorite Color</TH>
</TR>";
```

After defining the variables within the while loop, print them in table format:

```
echo "<TR>
<TD>$full_name</TD>
<TD>$birth_date</TD>
<TD>$fave_color</TD>
</TR>";
```

The new while loop looks like this:

```
while ($row = mssql_fetch_array($sql_result)) {
            $full_name = $row["FULL_NAME"];
            $birth_date = $row["BIRTH_DATE"];
            $fave_color = $row["FAVE_COLOR"];
            echo "<TR>
            <TD>$full_name</TD>
            <TD>$birth_date</TD>
```

```
              <TD>$fave_color</TD>
              </TR>";
}
```

After the while loop, close the HTML table:

```
echo "</TABLE>";
```

The full script to perform a simple connection and data selection from Microsoft SQL Server could look something like this:

```
<?php
// create connection; substitute your own information!
$conn = mssql_connect("localhost","joeuser","34Nhjp")
          or die("Couldn't connect to the server.")

// select database; substitute your own database name
$db = mysql_select_db("MyDB", $conn) or die("Couldn't select database.");

// create SQL statement
$sql = "SELECT FULL_NAME, BIRTH_DATE, FAVE_COLOR FROM FRIEND_INFO
ORDER BY BIRTH_DATE ASC";

// execute SQL query and get result
$sql_result = mssql_query($sql,$conn) or die("Couldn't execute query.");

// start results formatting
echo "<TABLE BORDER=1>
<TR>
<TH>Full Name</TH>
<TH>Birthday</TH>
<TH>Favorite Color</TH>
</TR>";

// format results by row
          while ($row = mssql_fetch_array($sql_result)) {
          $full_name = $row["FULL_NAME"];
          $birth_date = $row["BIRTH_DATE"];
          $fave_color = $row["FAVE_COLOR"];
          echo "<TR>
```

```
            <TD>$full_name</TD>
            <TD>$birth_date</TD>
            <TD>$fave_color</TD>
            </TR>";
}
echo "</TABLE>";
?>
```

This example didn't use the `mssql_result()` function, because `mssql_fetch_array()` is more useful for retrieving multiple records. If your SQL query was meant to select only one record, you could have used `mssql_result()`.

For example, say your SQL statement was

```
SELECT BIRTH_DATE FROM FRIEND_INFO WHERE ID = 1;
```

After issuing the query

```
$sql_result = mssql_query($sql,$conn) or die("Couldn't execute query.");
```

simply use `mssql_result()` like so:

```
$birthday = mssql_result($sql_result, 0, "BIRTH_DATE") or die("Couldn't get
result.");
```

The first argument used in the function is the resource result of the SQL statement. Next in the list comes the row (starting with number 0), and finally, there's the name of the field you selected.

See the PHP Manual, at http://www.php.net/mssql, for the numerous additional Microsoft SQL Server functions, and try using your own tables and SQL statements in place of the examples shown here. The basic idea of connecting, querying, and retrieving a result is fundamental to all other actions used in the code driving dynamic Web applications.

Using Other Databases with PHP

If you are using a database not referenced in previous sections, have no fear. PHP has extensions for numerous databases (dBase, Informix, and so on), and can also simply use ODBC connections to communicate with IBM DB2, Sybase, and others. Regardless of the type of database in use, the fundamentals you learned at the beginning of this chapter are still relevant.

If you're using Informix, or simply Microsoft Access, you'll still want to create the most efficient, relational tables possible. With SQL, you know that to retrieve data you use SELECT statements and to insert data you use INSERT statements. All of those rules remain the same in PHP; the only differences are in the names and types of functions used to execute your commands. For that specific information, simply peruse the PHP Manual online, at http://www.php.net/manual/.

Chapter 4

opefully, the previous chapter has given you a basic understanding of database connectivity with PHP. Now we'll move past the basic connection and use PHP and HTML forms to create database tables and populate these tables with data.

The following code examples use the MySQL database; however, each of the actions can be carried out on any supported database type. Check the PHP Manual at http://www.php.net/manual/ for the exact function name for your particular database—it won't be vastly different.

Create a Database Table

Essentially, to create a simple database table, you only need to give it a name. But that would make for a boring table, since it wouldn't contain any columns (fields) and couldn't hold any data. So, besides the name, you should know the number of fields and the types of fields you'd like to have in your table.

Suppose that you own a store, and you want to create a table to hold all your products. Think of the types of fields you might need: a product identification number, a title, a description, and the price of the item. Now, think of a name for the table, such as MY_PRODUCTS.

Next, you'll create a sequence of forms that will take your table information and send it to your MySQL database. In this first step, you'll submit the name of the table and the number of fields you want to include. The second step will display additional form fields so that you can define the properties of your table columns. Finally, the third step will send the request to MySQL, verify that the table was created, and display a "Success!" message.

Step 1: Basic Table Definition

To begin, open your favorite text editor, create a file called show_createtable1.html, and set up an HTML "shell":

```
<!DOCTYPE HTML PUBLIC "-//W3C//DTD HTML 4.0 Transitional//EN">
<HTML>
<HEAD>
```

```
<TITLE>Create a Database Table: Step 1</TITLE>
</HEAD>
<BODY>
                <!- your HTML form will go here -->
</BODY>
</HTML>
```

To create the form code, assume that step two in the sequence will be a PHP script called do_showfielddef.php and that your form will use the POST method:

```
<FORM method="POST" action="do_showfielddef.php">
```

Next, create two text fields to capture the values for $_POST[table_name] and $_POST[num_fields]—the name of the new table and the number of fields it contains:

```
<P>Table Name:<br><INPUT type="text" name="table_name" size=30></P>
<P>Number of Fields:<br><INPUT type="text" name="num_fields" size=5></P>
```

Finally, add the "Go to Step 2" button:

```
<INPUT type="submit" value="Go to Step 2">
```

Don't forget the closing </FORM> tag!

Your HTML source code should look something like this:

```
<!DOCTYPE HTML PUBLIC "-//W3C//DTD HTML 4.0 Transitional//EN">
<HTML>
<HEAD>
<TITLE>Create a Database Table: Step 1</TITLE>
</HEAD>
<BODY>
<FORM method="POST" action="do_showfielddef.php">
<P>Table Name:<br><INPUT type="text" name="table_name" size=30></p>
<P>Number of Fields:<br><INPUT type="text" name="num_fields" size=5></p>
<INPUT type="submit" value="Go to Step 2">
</FORM>
</BODY>
</HTML>
```

Place this file on your Web server, and access it with your browser at its URL, http://127.0.0.1/show_createtable1.html. In your browser window, you should now see what is shown in Figure 4.1.

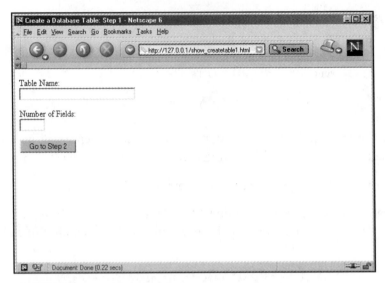

FIGURE 4.1 *Step 1: Name that table*

In Step 2, you'll dynamically create parts of the form based on the values sent through the form in Step 1.

Step 2: Field Definitions

In Step 1, you created variables to hold the name of the table ($_POST[table_name]) and the number of fields you want to place in the table ($_POST[num_fields]). In this step, you'll create a PHP script to display additional form elements needed for further definition of the fields. To begin, open your favorite text editor and create a file called do_showfielddef.php.

Before your script does anything else, you'll want to check that values were actually entered in the form in Step 1. Set up a statement that looks for these values and, if they don't exist, redirects the user to the form in Step 1:

```php
<?php
if ((!$_POST[table_name]) || (!$_POST[num_fields])) {
        header("Location: http://127.0.0.1/show_createtable1.html");
        exit;
}
?>
```

Next, add the HTML "shell" after the `if` statement:

```
<!DOCTYPE HTML PUBLIC "-//W3C//DTD HTML 4.0 Transitional//EN">
<HTML>
<HEAD>
<TITLE>Create a Database Table: Step 2</TITLE>
</HEAD>
<BODY>
            <!-- your HTML form will go here -->
</BODY>
</HTML>
```

Now you're ready to build the form. First, though, give the page a heading so that you know what you're doing:

```
<h1>Define fields for <?php echo "$_POST[table_name]"; ?></h1>
```

To create the form code, assume that Step 3 in the sequence will be a PHP script called do_createtable.php and that your form will use the `POST` method:

```
<FORM method="POST" action="do_createtable.php">
```

Next, add a hidden field to your form to ensure that the value of the `$_POST[table_name]` variable is passed along to Step 3:

```
<INPUT type="hidden" name="table_name" value="<?php echo "$_POST[table_name]";
?>">
```

The three basic field definitions are field name, field type, and field length. To create the table, you'll need to know these three elements for each field you want to create. For example, to create the `MY_PRODUCTS` table with four fields (product identification number, product title, product description, and product price), you'll need to provide a field name, field type, and field length for each of those four fields.

Create the beginning of an HTML table to display the three form fields:

```
<table cellspacing=5 cellpadding=5>
<tr>
<th>FIELD NAME</th><th>FIELD TYPE</th><th>FIELD LENGTH</th></tr>
```

Now you'll learn a tricky bit of PHP, which will create enough form fields to cover the number of fields you need to define in your database table.

Remember the $_POST[num_fields] variable from the first step? Create a for statement that will loop until that number is reached:

```
for ($i = 0 ; $i < $_POST[num_fields]; $i++) {
            // more code here
}
```

The goal is to display three form fields for each field you want to create in your database table. First, open the echo statement, and then start the table row and print the first input field, remembering to escape your double quotes with a backslash:

```
echo "<tr>
<td align=center>
<input type=\"text\" name=\"field_name[]\" size=\"30\">
</td>
```

Note the use of [] after field_name. The [] indicates the presence of an array. For each field in your database table, you'll be adding a value to the $_POST[field_name] array. An array holds many scalar variables in numbered slots, beginning with 0. Slots are added automatically as the array needs to grow.

For example, if you are creating a database table with six fields, the $_POST[field_name] array would be made up of six field name variables:

```
$field_name[0] // first field name
$field_name[1] // second field name

...

$field_name[5] // sixth field name
```

After creating the first input field, create a drop-down list containing a few field types. The field types used in this example (float, int, text, varchar) are very common field types and are all that's needed for this example. A complete list of valid field types can be found in your database documentation.

```
<td align=center>
<select name=\"field_type[]\">
            <option value=\"float\">float</option>
            <option value=\"int\">int</option>
            <option value=\"text\">text</option>
            <option value=\"varchar\">varchar</option>
</select>
</td>
```

The last field definition is field length. Create a text field for this value, and close your table row as well as the `for` statement:

```
<td align=center>
<input type=\"text\" name=\"field_length[]\" size=\"5\">
</td>
</tr>";
}
```

Putting it all together, your `for` statement should look something like this:

```
for ($i = 0 ; $i < $_POST[num_fields]; $i++) {
         echo "
         <tr>
         <td align=center>
         <input type=\"text\" name=\"field_name[]\" size=\"30\">
         </td>

         <td align=center>
         <select name=\"field_type[]\">
             <option value=\"float\">float</option>
             <option value=\"int\">int</option>
             <option value=\"text\">text</option>
             <option value=\"varchar\">varchar</option>
         </select>
         </td>

         <td align=center>
         <input type=\"text\" name=\"field_length[]\" size=\"5\">
         </td>
         </tr>";
}
```

To finish this step, create the submit button and close the form and the HTML table:

```
<tr>
<td align=center colspan=3>
<INPUT type="submit" value="Create Table"></td>
</tr>
</table>
```

```
</FORM>
</BODY>
</HTML>
```

All in all, the do_showfielddef.php file should look something like this:

```php
<?php
if ((!$_POST[table_name]) || (!$_POST[num_fields])) {
        header("Location: http://127.0.0.1/show_createtable1.html");
        exit;
}
?>
<!DOCTYPE HTML PUBLIC "-//W3C//DTD HTML 4.0 Transitional//EN">
<HTML>
<HEAD>
<TITLE>Create a Database Table: Step 2</TITLE>
</HEAD>
<BODY>
<h1>Define fields for <?php echo "$_POST[table_name]"; ?></h1>
<FORM method="POST" action="do_createtable.php">
<INPUT type="hidden" name="table_name" value="<?php echo "$_POST[table_name]";
?>">
<table cellspacing=5 cellpadding=5>
<tr>
<th>FIELD NAME</th><th>FIELD TYPE</th><th>FIELD LENGTH</th></tr>
<?php
for ($i = 0 ; $i <$num_fields; $i++) {
        echo "
        <tr>
        <td align=center>
        <input type=\"text\" name=\"field_name[]\" size=\"30\">
        </td>

        <td align=center>
        <select name=\"field_type[]\">
        <option value=\"float\">float</option>
            <option value=\"int\">int</option>
            <option value=\"text\">text</option>
            <option value=\"varchar\">varchar</option>
        </select>
```

```
        </td>

        <td align=center>
        <input type=\"text\" name=\"field_length[]\" size=\"5\">
        </td>
        </tr>";
}
?>
<tr>
<td align=center colspan=3>
<INPUT type="submit" value="Create Table">
</td>
</tr>
</table>
</FORM>
</BODY>
</HTML>
```

Place this file on your Web server, and go back and access the form in Step 1 at its URL, http://127.0.0.1/show_createtable1.html. Enter MY_PRODUCTS for a table name and 4 for the number of fields. In your browser window, you should now see what is shown in Figure 4.2.

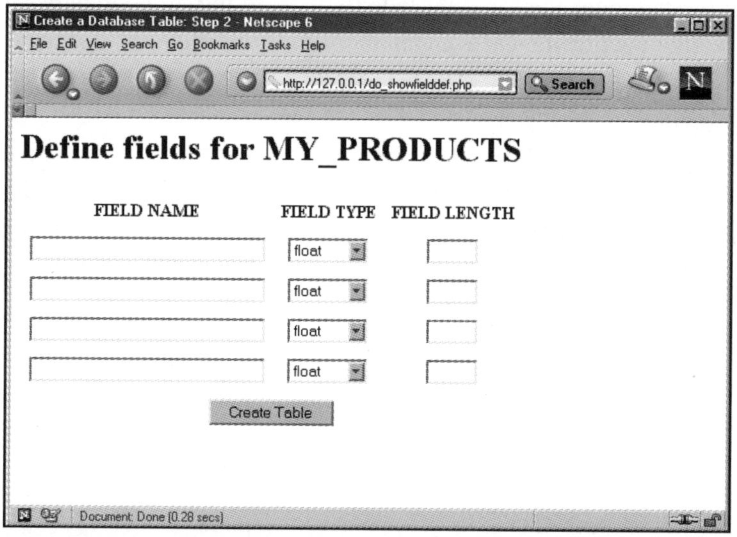

FIGURE 4.2 *Step 2: Form field definition table*

Step 3: Connect to MySQL and Create the Table

Before you fill out the form created in Step 2, let's create the PHP script that will make it "go." Since the action of the form in Step 2 is do_createtable.php, open your favorite text editor and create a file called do_createtable.php, then add the HTML "shell":

```
<!DOCTYPE HTML PUBLIC "-//W3C//DTD HTML 4.0 Transitional//EN">
<HTML>
<HEAD>
<TITLE>Create a Database Table: Step 3</TITLE>
</HEAD>
<BODY>
            <!-- your HTML form will go here -->
</BODY>
</HTML>
```

Give the page a heading so that you know what you're doing:

```
<h1>Adding table <?php echo "$_POST[table_name]"; ?></h1>
```

The next section of PHP code will build the SQL statement that will be sent to MySQL. Remember, the CREATE syntax is

```
CREATE TABLE [table name] [(field_name field_data_type,...)] [options]
```

Hold the SQL statement in a variable called $sql, and initially populate this variable with the first part of the CREATE statement plus the value of $table_name:

```
$sql = "CREATE TABLE $table_name (";
```

Now create the loop that will populate the remainder of the SQL statement. The loop should repeat for as many fields as you want to add to the table, or the number of fields that you defined in Step 2. Since each field definition was placed in an array, you can count the number of elements in the $_POST[field_name] array to get the number of times to run the loop:

```
for ($i = 0; $i < count($_POST[field_name]); $i++) {
// more code here
}
```

For each new field, you'll need to add the field name, type, and length to the SQL statement using this syntax:

```
field_name field_type (field_length)
```

 NOTE

A comma must separate multiple field definitions.

Immediately inside the loop, add this statement to begin adding to the value of the $sql variable:

```
$sql .= $_POST[field_name][$i]." ".$_POST[field_type][$i];
```

Before adding the field length, check to see that a length has been specified, add to the $sql variable accordingly, and then close the loop:

```
if ($_POST[field_length][$i] != "") {
            $sql .= " (".$_POST [field_length][$i]."),";
} else {
            $sql .= ",";
}
}
```

This if...else statement looks for a value for $_POST[field_length] and prints it inside a set of parentheses if it's found. Then it adds a comma to separate the value from the next field waiting to be added. If no value is found, just the comma is added to the SQL statement.

The entire loop should look something like this:

```
for ($i =0;$i < count($_POST[field_name]);$i++){
            $sql .= $_POST[field_name][$i]." ".$_POST[field_type][$i];
            if ($_POST[field_length][$i] != "") {
                $sql .= " (".$_POST [field_length][$i]."),";
            } else {
                $sql .= ",";
            }
}
```

However, there's still a bit of work to do on the SQL statement: it has an extraneous comma at the end, and the parentheses have yet to be closed. To get rid of the extra comma at the end, use the substr() function to return only part of the string. In this case, you'll be returning the entire string, with the exception of the last character:

```
$sql = substr($sql, 0, -1);
```

The 0 in the argument list tells the function to begin at the first character, and the −1 tells the function to stop at the next-to-last character.

The final step in the creation of the SQL statement is to close the parentheses:

```
$sql .= ")";
```

Now use the basic connection code to connect to and query the MySQL database using your table-creation SQL statement:

```
// create connection; substitute your own information
$conn = mysql_connect("localhost","joeuser","34Nhjp") or die(mysql_error())";

// select database; substitute your own database name
$db = mysql_select_db("MyDB", $conn) or die(mysql_error());

// execute SQL query and get result
$sql_result = mysql_query($sql,$conn) or die(mysql_error());
```

Print a nice message upon success:

```
if ($sql_result) {
        echo "<P>$_POST[table_name] has been created!</p>";
}
```

From start to finish, the file do_createtable.php should look something like this:

```
<!DOCTYPE HTML PUBLIC "-//W3C//DTD HTML 4.0 Transitional//EN">
<HTML>
<HEAD>
<TITLE>Create a Database Table: Step 3</TITLE></HEAD>
<BODY>
<h1>Adding table <?php echo "$_POST[table_name]"; ?></h1>
<?php
$sql = "CREATE TABLE $_POST[table_name] (";
```

```
for ($i =0;$i < count($_POST[field_name]);$i++){
            $sql .= $_POST[field_name][$i]." ".$_POST[field_type][$i];
            if ($_POST[field_length][$i] != "") {
                $sql .= " (".$_POST [field_length][$i]."),";
            } else {
                $sql .= ",";
            }
}
$sql = substr($sql, 0, -1);
$sql .= ")";

// create connection; substitute your own information
$conn = mysql_connect("localhost","joeuser","34Nhjp") or die(mysql_error());

// select database; substitute your own database name
$db = mysql_select_db("MyDB", $conn) or die(mysql_error());

// execute SQL query and get result
$sql_result = mysql_query($sql,$conn) or die(mysql_error());

//print success message
if ($sql_result) {
            echo "<P>$_POST[table_name] has been created!</p>";
}
?>
</BODY>
</HTML>
```

Place this file on your Web server, and then go back to your Web browser and the form staring back at you from Step 2. You should see four sets of form fields. Create the following fields:

```
FIELD NAME    FIELD TYPE    FIELD SIZE
ITEM_ID       int  5
ITEM_TITLE    varchar       50
ITEM_DESC     text
ITEM_PRICE    float
```

Before you submit the form, it should look something like what is shown in Figure 4.3.

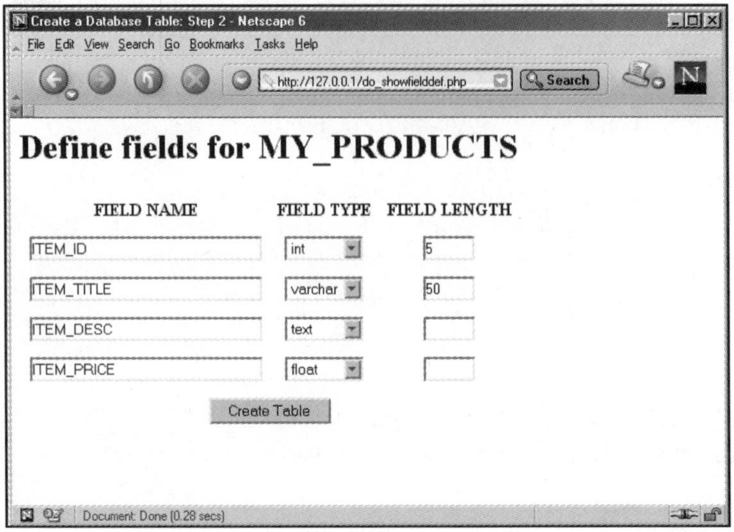

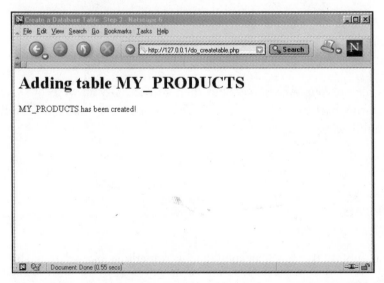

FIGURE 4.3 *Preparing to submit the form*

Go ahead and click on the Create Table button to execute the do_createtable.php script. You should see a results page like the one shown in Figure 4.4.

In the next section, you'll create a form and accompanying PHP script to populate the table. Tables aren't much fun without any data in them!

FIGURE 4.4 *Successful table creation*

Inserting Data

The series of forms for adding records to the MY_PRODUCTS table is much simpler than the three-step table-creation sequence—it has only two steps.

To begin, open your favorite text editor, create a file called show_addrecord.html, and set up an HTML "shell":

```
<!DOCTYPE HTML PUBLIC "-//W3C//DTD HTML 4.0 Transitional//EN">
<HTML>
<HEAD>
<TITLE>Add a Record</TITLE>
</HEAD>
<BODY>
          <!-- your HTML form will go here -->
</BODY>
</HTML>
```

Give the page a heading so that you know what you're doing:

```
<h1>Adding a Record to MY_PRODUCTS</h1>
```

To create the form code, assume that step two in the sequence will be a PHP script called do_addrecord.php and that your form will use the POST method:

```
<FORM method="POST" action="do_addrecord.php">
```

Next, create three text fields and a text area to capture the values for $_POST[item_id], $_POST[item_title], $_POST[item_desc], and $_POST[item_price]—the names of the columns in MY_PRODUCTS. The following sample form uses an HTML table to display the form fields, but feel free to display the form however you'd like:

```
<FORM method="POST" action="do_addrecord.php">
<table cellspacing=5 cellpadding=5>
<tr>
<td valign=top><strong>Item ID:</strong></td>
<td valign=top><INPUT type="text" name="item_id" size=5 maxlength=5></td>
</tr>
<tr>
<td valign=top><strong>Item Title:</strong></td>
<td valign=top><INPUT type="text" name="item_title" size=30 maxlength=50></td>
</tr>
```

```
<tr>
<td valign=top><strong>Item Description:</strong></td>
<td valign=top><TEXTAREA name="item_desc" cols=30 rows=5></TEXTAREA></td>
</tr>
<tr>
<td valign=top><strong>Item Price:</strong></td>
<td valign=top>$ <INPUT type="text" name="item_price" size=10></td>
</tr>
```

Finally, add the Add Record button:

```
<tr>
<td align=center colspan=2><INPUT type="submit" value="Add Record"></td>
</tr>
```

Don't forget the closing `</FORM>` and `</TABLE>` tags!

Your HTML source code should look something like this:

```
<!DOCTYPE HTML PUBLIC "-//W3C//DTD HTML 4.0 Transitional//EN">
<HTML>
<HEAD>
<TITLE>Add a Record</TITLE>
</HEAD>
<BODY>
<h1>Adding a Record to MY_PRODUCTS</h1>
<FORM method="POST" action="do_addrecord.php">
        <table cellspacing=5 cellpadding=5>
        <tr>
        <td valign=top><strong>Item ID:</strong></td>
        <td valign=top><INPUT type="text" name="item_id"
        size=5 maxlength=5></td>
        </tr>
        <tr>
        <td valign=top><strong>Item Title:</strong></td>
        <td valign=top><INPUT type="text" name="item_title"
        size=30 maxlength=50></td>
        </tr>
        <tr>
        <td valign=top><strong>Item Description:</strong></td>
```

```
        <td valign=top><TEXTAREA name="item_desc" cols=30
        rows=5></TEXTAREA></td>
        </tr>
        <tr>
        <td valign=top><strong>Item Price:</strong></td>
        <td valign=top>$ <INPUT type="text" name="item_price" size=10></td>
        </tr>
        <tr>
        <td align=center colspan=2><INPUT type="submit" value="Add
        Record"></td>
        </tr>
        </table>
        </FORM>
</BODY>
</HTML>
```

Place this file on your Web server, and access it with your browser at its URL, http://127.0.0.1/show_addrecord.html. In your browser window, you should now see something like what is shown in Figure 4.5.

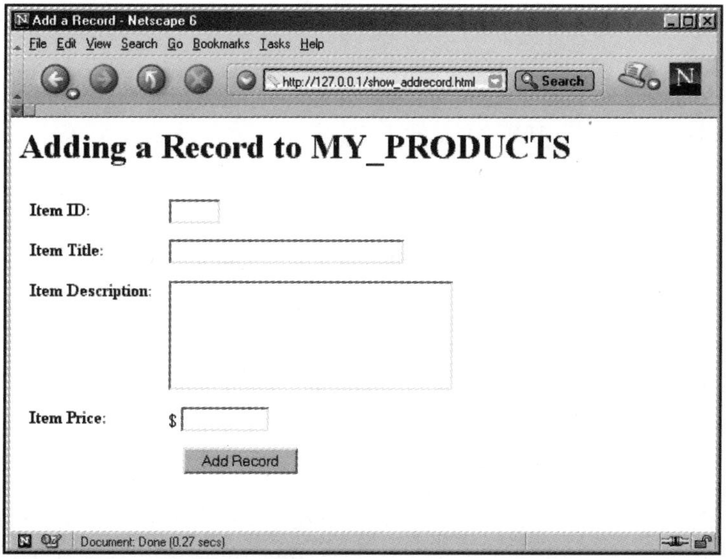

FIGURE 4.5 *The form to add a record*

Next, you'll create the PHP script that takes your form input, creates a proper SQL statement, creates the record, and displays the record for you as a confirmation. It's not as difficult as it sounds. Since the form action in show_addrecord.html is do_addrecord.php, open your favorite text editor and create a file called do_addrecord.php.

Before your script does anything else, you'll want to check that values were actually entered in the form. Set up a statement that looks for these values. If they don't exist, redirect the user to the form:

```php
<?php
if ((!$_POST[item_id]) || (!_POST[$item_title]) || (!$_POST[item_desc]) ||
(!$_POST[item_price])) {
            header("Location: http://127.0.0.1/show_addrecord.html");
            exit;
}
?>
```

Next, add the HTML "shell" after the if statement:

```
<!DOCTYPE HTML PUBLIC "-//W3C//DTD HTML 4.0 Transitional//EN">
<HTML>
<HEAD>
<TITLE>Add a Record</TITLE>
</HEAD>
<BODY>
            <!-- your HTML form will go here -->
</BODY>
</HTML>
```

Give the page a heading so that you know what you're doing:

```
<h1>Adding a record to MY_PRODUCTS</h1>
```

The next section of PHP code will build the SQL statement that will be sent to MySQL. Remember, the INSERT syntax is

```
INSERT INTO [table name] (column1, column2) VALUES ('value1', 'value2');
```

When you initially created the MY_PRODUCTS table, the field order was ITEM_ID, ITEM_TITLE, ITEM_DESC, and ITEM_PRICE. Use this same order in the INSERT statement used to create a record. Hold the SQL statement in a variable called $sql, and build the VALUES list using the variable names from the form:

```
$sql = "INSERT INTO MY_PRODUCTS (ITEM_ID, ITEM_TITLE, ITEM_DESC, ITEM_PRICE)
VALUES ('$_POST[item_id]', '$_POST[item_title]', '$_POST[item_desc]',
'$_POST[item_price]')";
```

After the SQL statement, simply add the connection and query code you used earlier. Next, add an if statement to print the full text of the record that was successfully added. One trick, though—use the stripslashes() function on the strings to remove any slashes that were automatically added by PHP. You want to use the original strings during the insertion into the database, as all elements will be properly escaped. However, you don't need to see the slashes when displaying the results to the screen.

```
if ($sql_result) {
echo "
            <P>Record added!</p>
            <table cellspacing=5 cellpadding=5>
            <tr>
            <td valign=top><strong>Item ID:</strong></td>
            <td valign=top>".stripslashes($_POST[item_id])."</td>
            </tr>
            <tr>
            <td valign=top><strong>Item Title:</strong></td>
            <td valign=top>".stripslashes($_POST[item_title])."</td>
            </tr>
            <tr>
            <td valign=top><strong>Item Description:</strong></td>
            <td valign=top>".stripslashes($_POST[item_desc]."</td>
            </tr>
            <tr>
            <td valign=top><strong>Item Price:</strong></td>
            <td valign=top>\$ ".stripslashes($_POST[item_price]."</td>
            </tr>
            </table>";
}
?>
```

That's all there is to it. Your source code should look something like this:

```php
<?php
if ((!$_POST[item_id]) || (!$_POST[item_title]) || (!$_POST[item_desc])
            || (!$_POST[item_price])) {
            header("Location: http://127.0.0.1/show_addrecord.html");
            exit;
}
?>
<!DOCTYPE HTML PUBLIC "-//W3C//DTD HTML 4.0 Transitional//EN">
<HTML>
<HEAD>
<TITLE>Add a Record</TITLE>
</HEAD>
<BODY>
<h1>Adding a Record to MY_PRODUCTS</h1>
<?php
$sql = "INSERT INTO MY_PRODUCTS (ITEM_ID, ITEM_TITLE, ITEM_DESC, ITEM_PRICE)
VALUES ('$_POST[item_id]', '$_POST[item_title]', '$_POST[item_desc]',
'$_POST[item_price]')";

// create connection; substitute your own information
$conn = mysql_connect("localhost","joeuser","34Nhjp") or die (mysql_error())";

// select database; substitute your own database name
$db = mysql_select_db("MyDB", $conn) or die(mysql_error());

// execute SQL query and get result
$sql_result = mysql_query($sql,$conn) or die (mysql_error());

if ($sql_result) {
            echo "
            <P>Record added!</p>
            <table cellspacing=5 cellpadding=5>
            <tr>
            <td valign=top><strong>Item ID:</strong></td>
            <td valign=top>".stripslashes($_POST[item_id])."</td>
            </tr>
            <tr>
```

```
            <td valign=top><strong>Item Title:</strong></td>
            <td valign=top>".stripslashes($_POST[item_title])."</td>
            </tr>
            <tr>
            <td valign=top><strong>Item Description:</strong></td>
            <td valign=top>".stripslashes($_POST[item_desc]."</td>
            </tr>
            <tr>
            <td valign=top><strong>Item Price:</strong></td>
            <td valign=top>\$ ".stripslashes($_POST[item_price]."</td>
            </tr>
            </table>";
}
?>
</BODY>
</HTML>
```

Place this file on your Web server, and go back to the form at http://127.0.0.1/show_addrecord.html. Create a sample product such as the one shown in Figure 4.6.

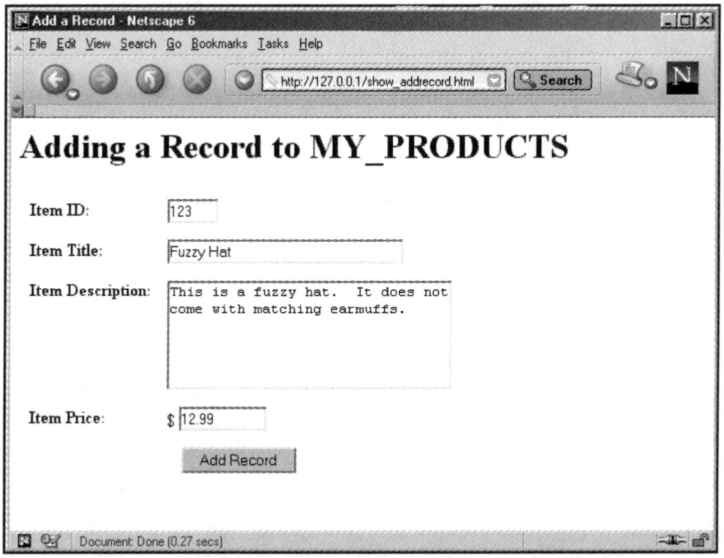

FIGURE 4.6 *Adding a sample product*

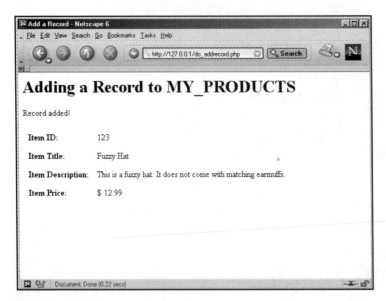

FIGURE 4.7 *Successful record addition*

Go ahead and click on the Add Record button to execute the do_addrecord.php script. If the query is successful, you should see a results page like the one shown in Figure 4.7.

Use this form to add several more products to the MY_PRODUCTS table. In the next section, you'll select some records to display (it won't be any fun with just one record!).

Select and Display Data

The most difficult part of selecting and displaying data is deciding the order in which you want to see it! Remember, the SELECT syntax is

```
SELECT [field names] FROM [table] WHERE [expression] ORDER BY [fields];
```

To view all the records in the MY_PRODUCTS table ordered by ITEM_ID, the SQL statement would look something like this:

```
$sql = "SELECT ITEM_ID, ITEM_TITLE, ITEM_DESC, ITEM_PRICE FROM MY_PRODUCTS ORDER
BY ITEM_ID ASC";
```

To view the records in MY_PRODUCTS ordered by ITEM_PRICE, from highest price to lowest, use this SQL statement:

```
$sql = "SELECT ITEM_ID, ITEM_TITLE, ITEM_DESC, ITEM_PRICE FROM MY_PRODUCTS ORDER
BY ITEM_PRICE DESC";
```

To view all the records in MY_PRODUCTS that have a price greater than $10.00, use a WHERE clause in your SQL statement:

```
$sql = "SELECT ITEM_ID, ITEM_TITLE, ITEM_DESC, ITEM_PRICE FROM MY_PRODUCTS WHERE
ITEM_PRICE > 10.00 ORDER BY ITEM_ID ASC ";
```

Using the basic connection code found earlier in this chapter, create a PHP script called display_products.php and use any of the sample SQL statements just shown as the value of the variable $sql.

Here's a complete sample script, using a SQL statement that shows all records in the MY_PRODUCTS table ordered by ITEM_ID:

```php
<?php
// create connection; substitute your own information
$conn = mysql_connect("localhost","joeuser","34Nhjp") or die(mysql_error())";

// select database; substitute your own database name
$db = mysql_select_db("MyDB", $conn) or die(mysql_error());

// create SQL statement
$sql = "SELECT ITEM_ID, ITEM_TITLE, ITEM_DESC, ITEM_PRICE FROM MY_PRODUCTS ORDER
BY ITEM_ID ASC";

// execute SQL query and get result
$sql_result = mysql_query($sql,$conn) or die(mysql_error());

// start results formatting
echo "<TABLE BORDER=1>
<TR>
<TH>Item ID</TH>
<TH>Item Title</TH>
<TH>Item Description</TH>
<TH>Item Price</TH>
```

```
</TR>";

// format results by row
while ($row = mysql_fetch_array($sql_result)) {
            $item_id = $row["ITEM_ID"];
            $item_title = $row["ITEM_TITLE"];
            $item_desc = $row["ITEM_DESC"];
            $item_price = $row["ITEM_PRICE"];
            echo "<TR>
            <TD>$item_id</TD>
            <TD>$item_title</TD>
            <TD>$item_desc</TD>
            <TD align=right>$item_price</TD>
            </TR>";
}
echo "</TABLE>";
?>
```

Some sample results are shown in Figures 4.8 through 4.10. Your results will differ, depending on the products you inserted into your table.

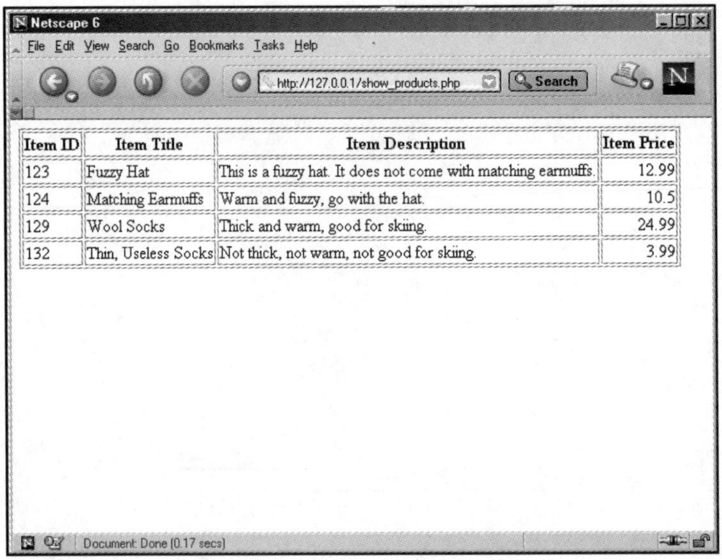

FIGURE 4.8 *View records ordered by ITEM_ID (ascending)*

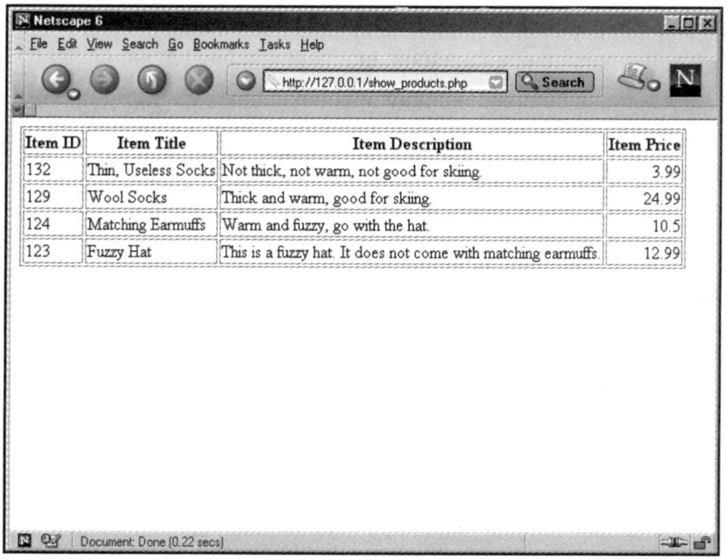

FIGURE 4.9 *View records ordered by ITEM_PRICE (descending)*

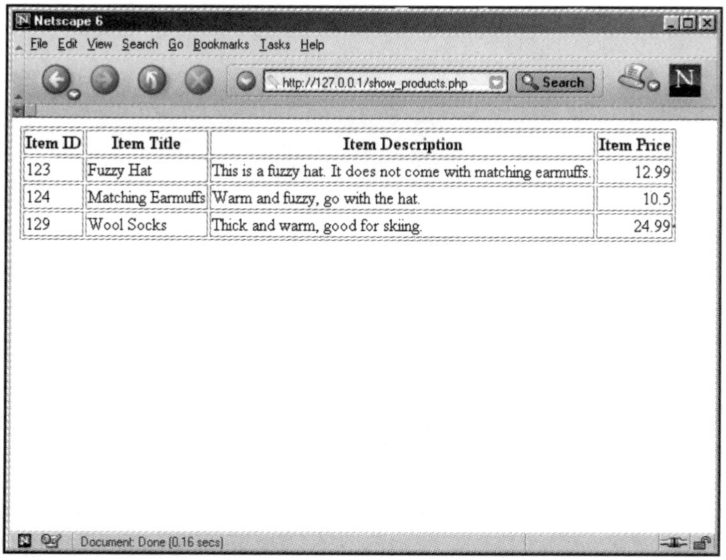

FIGURE 4.10 *View records with ITEM_PRICE greater than $10.00*

This chapter has provided you with the basics of database connectivity, table and record creation, and record display. Part of Chapter 7, "Advanced PHP Techniques: e-Commerce," is devoted to taking these processes one step further. In that chapter, you'll learn to add record update and deletion functions in the context of creating your own database administration system.

Chapter 5

User
Authentication

User authentication methods are used to verify that a user has permission to access certain content on a Web site. When initially developing a Web site, you may want to restrict access to only certain members of your development team. Or, if your corporate Web site contains sensitive financial data, you may want to restrict your financial statements to a particular list of investors.

Web developers usually employ one of the following types of user authentication for reasons ranging from ease of installation and ease of maintenance to how the authentication scheme works within their overall application development:

- **Basic HTTP authentication.** This method of authentication is built right into your Web server, and it limits access to documents and entire directories. The popularity of this scheme stems from the fact that any site developer, whether he controls his own server or houses his site with an Internet service provider, has the ability to use basic HTTP authentication within his document directories.

- **Database-driven authentication.** Using this method, usernames and passwords are kept in a database table and accessed via a script. The script determines whether or not you're allowed to see a certain item.

- **Limit by IP address.** With this method, be it server-based or script-based, access is limited to a specific IP or IP range.

In this chapter, you'll learn how to use various forms of user authentication in your PHP-enabled Web sites.

Basic HTTP Authentication

Basic HTTP authentication uses a *challenge/response scheme* to authenticate users. The process begins when the user requests a file from a Web server. If the file is within a protected area, the server responds with a 401 (Unauthorized User) error, and the browser displays the familiar username/password dialog box. The user then enters a username and password and clicks on OK, which sends the information to the server for authentication. If the username and password pair is valid, the server displays the requested file. Otherwise, the dialog box appears and prompts the user to try again.

To use basic HTTP authentication, you must have available two elements: an authentication-enabled Web server and a list of usernames and passwords. However, authentication configuration varies from one Web server to the next. While Microsoft IIS has a graphical user interface for creating and administering a username and password list, the Apache Web server uses the "old school" method that requires a user to manually modify the server configuration and password files.

The next section will show you how to use basic HTTP authentication with Apache. For information on configuring basic HTTP authentication with Microsoft IIS, consult your server documentation, and ensure that you have installed all updates and service packs before starting the process.

Configuring HTTP Authentication on Apache

The first step in configuring basic HTTP authentication on Apache is to create the file containing usernames and passwords. This file contains a list of all valid users for a particular protected area (or *realm*), along with the matching password for each user. You can place this file anywhere on your Web server, preferably in a private directory above the document root. If your password file is kept under the document root, anyone with Web access can access your password file via a URL. For example, if your file is called passwordfile and it is located directly in the document root directory, its URL would be http://www.yourserver.com/passwordfile. Obviously, this is not a good idea.

Creating the Users and Groups Files

Use the htpasswd program included in the Apache distribution (in the bin directory) to create the username/password file. To create a username/password file called users with an entry for the user jane, issue the following command:

1. Type **/usr/local/bin/apache/bin/htpasswd −c /usr/local/apache/users jane**. The -c flag alerts the program that the file /usr/local/apache/users must be created.

2. You are prompted to add a password for user jane. Enter the password and press Enter.

3. You are prompted to confirm the password. Type the password again, exactly as before, and press Enter.

Open the /usr/local/apache/users file to see the username you just entered, followed by a colon, followed by the encrypted version of the password you just entered. For example:

jane:Hsyn78/dQdr9

To add additional users, such as joe, bob, and mary, follow the preceding steps, omitting the -c flag because the /usr/local/apache/users file already exists.

Categorizing your users into groups makes your life much easier, because you'll be able to grant access rights to an entire group rather than to 10 or 12 (or 200!) individual users. By granting access to an entire group, you won't have to manually list each individual member of that group in the corresponding access file.

To create a group file, manually create the file /usr/local/apache/groups. To define the friends group, which contains the users jane, joe, bob, and mary (who are already defined in your users file), type the following in the /usr/local/apache/groups file:

```
friends: jane joe bob mary
```

In the next section, you'll learn to configure Apache to allow members of the friends group to access a protected directory.

Configuring the Web Server

Configuration directives can be inserted either in the Apache httpd.conf file (found in /usr/local/apache/conf/) or in a separate .htaccess file, placed in the protected directory. For example:

- ◆ To protect http://www.yourdomain.com/privatestuff/ using an .htaccess file, place the file in /usr/local/apache/htdocs/privatestuff/.

- ◆ To protect http://www.yourdomain.com/privatestuff/ using httpd.conf, create a section in httpd.conf beginning with `<Directory /usr/local/apache/htdocs/privatestuff/>` and ending with `</Directory>`. The directives will go between these start and end tags, as you'll soon see.

One drawback to using multiple .htaccess files is that you must keep track of all of them! When issuing directives in the httpd.conf file, all of the directives are in one place and are easier to maintain. Whether you put the directives in an .htaccess file or within a `<Directory>` `</Directory>` section of the httpd.conf file, the information is the same.

- ◆ **AuthName.** The name of the protected area, or *realm*, such as "My Private Stuff" or "Jane's Development Area."

- ◆ **AuthType.** The authentication protocol in use, usually basic. Digest authentication also exists, in which the usernames and passwords are encrypted as they pass between browser and server. Digest authentication is unsupported by some older browsers, limiting its use in applications.

- ◆ **AuthUserFile.** The full path to the file containing the usernames and passwords.

- ◆ **AuthGroupFile.** The full path to the file containing the list of groups, if any.

- ◆ **require.** Specifies which users and/or groups have access to the protected area. Can be valid users, just jane, just the friends group, or a combination.

A sample set of directives might look like this:

```
AuthName "My Private Stuff"
AuthType Basic
AuthGroup /usr/local/apache/groups
require group friends
```

In this example, anyone accessing the privatestuff directory will be met with the username/password dialog box. If the user is a member of the friends group and enters the correct username and password, the protected information is displayed.

However, imagine the amount of server processing that is necessary for a Web site that has more visitors than just your friends. As your user base increases and Web server performance begins to erode, consider moving the usernames and passwords to a separate database table (which can be parsed by the Web server faster than a simple text file) and creating your own authentication systems.

Working with PHP Authentication Variables

A custom PHP script can mimic the HTTP authentication challenge/response system by setting HTTP headers that cause the automatic display of the username/password dialog box. PHP stores the information entered in the dialog box in twp variables ($_SERVER[PHP_AUTH_USER] and $_SERVER[PHP_AUTH_PW]) that can be used to validate input.

To become familiar with sending authorization headers via the header() function, first create a PHP script that pops up the username/password dialog box without validating a username/password pair.

The following script (call it authorize1.php) checks for the existence of a value for $_SERVER[PHP_AUTH_USER] , displays the username/password dialog box if a value does not exist, and then exits:

```php
<?php
// Check to see if $_SERVER[PHP_AUTH_USER] already contains info
if (!isset($_SERVER[PHP_AUTH_USER])) {
        // If empty, send header causing dialog box to appear
        header('WWW-Authenticate: Basic realm="My Private Stuff"');
        header('HTTP/1.0 401 Unauthorized');
        echo 'Authorization Required.';
        exit;
} else {
        // If not empty, display values for variables
        echo "<P>You have entered this username: $_SERVER[PHP_AUTH_USER]<br>";
        echo "You have entered this password: $_SERVER[PHP_AUTH_PW]</p>";
}
?>
```

In this case, if any value exists, the script assumes that the username and password are valid and returns the value of the three PHP authorization variables as directed in the else statement. Absolutely no authentication is performed in this example, because the script does not check the values against a master list of allowable users.

The header() function is key to this script; the HTTP header is the first output from the script to the browser. When a user enters a username and password in the dialog box and clicks on OK, the page reloads and sends another HTTP header to the server, this time with the variables populated.

Since $_SERVER[PHP_AUTH_USER] now contains a value, the if statement returns false and the script skips to the else statement, which contains code to print the variable information to the screen.

Now that you know how to create the dialog box, write some code that validates these values. The easiest method is to hard-code acceptable values in the script, as shown in the following script (call it authorize2.php):

```php
<?php
// Check to see if $_SERVER[PHP_AUTH_USER] already contains info
if (!isset($_SERVER[PHP_AUTH_USER])) {
        // If empty, send header causing dialog box to appear
        header('WWW-Authenticate: Basic realm="My Private Stuff"');
        header('HTTP/1.0 401 Unauthorized');
        echo 'Authorization Required.';
        exit;
} else {
        // If not empty, do something else
        // Try to validate against hard-coded values
        if (($_SERVER[PHP_AUTH_USER] == "jane") && ($_SERVER[PHP_AUTH_PW] ==
"mypassword")) {
                echo "<P>Since you have entered a username of
$_SERVER[PHP_AUTH_USER] and a password of $_SERVER[PHP_AUTH_PW], you are
authorized to be here!</P>";
        } else {
                echo "You are not authorized!";
        }
}
?>
```

But who wants to hard-code all valid usernames and passwords into their authentication script? It's an awful lot of work. Furthermore, if you carry your authentication routine through numerous pages, each of those pages must contain the entire list. If you have to make a change in the list, you have to make it on every single page containing the list. It's better to carry through only an authorization routine, which accesses a database containing all the usernames and passwords.

Not surprisingly, you'll learn about this method next!

Database-Driven Authentication

Validating against a database alleviates the need for additional Web server configuration and increases Web server response times. Using the PHP authentication variables, you can still present the familiar username/password dialog box. Or, create a short HTML login form that requests a username and password. Whichever method you choose, you need to have access to a users table that holds username and password information.

Your table can be as simple or as complex as you want to make it. For the following examples, I've created a four-field users table in a MySQL database. The fields are id, real_name, username, and password.

> **NOTE**
>
> You can use any database type to create and access a users table. See Chapter 3, "Working with Databases," for instructions on creating a table and accessing it via PHP for your specific database type.

Using PHP Authentication Variables to Validate Users

With a few minor additions to the authorize2.php script, you can validate the input from your authentication dialog box against usernames and passwords in the users table. Assume that the users table has been populated with the following information, where username is a unique field and password contains a hash of the actual passwords ("mypassword", "passme", and "gopass", respectively):

```
+----+-----------+----------+------------------+
| id | real_name | username | password         |
+----+-----------+----------+------------------+
|  1 | Jane Smith | jane    | 162eebfb6477e5d3 |
|  2 | Mary Smith | mary    | 7bbdc9837f055863 |
|  3 | John Smith | john    | 26de36bb5818d066 |
+----+-----------+----------+------------------+
```

The steps taken by the authorize3.php script, shown below, will:

1. Display the username/password dialog box
2. Accept the values.
3. Open the database connection.
4. Validate the values.
5. Display the appropriate information.

```php
<?php
// Check to see if $_SERVER[PHP_AUTH_USER] already contains info
if (!isset($_SERVER[PHP_AUTH_USER])) {
    // If empty, send header causing dialog box to appear
    header('WWW-Authenticate: Basic realm="My Private Stuff"');
header('HTTP/1.0 401 Unauthorized');
    echo 'Authorization Required.';
    exit;
} else {
    // If not empty, do something else
    // create connection; substitute your own information!
    $conn = mysql_connect("localhost","joeuser","34Nhjp") or
die(mysql_error());
    // select database; substitute your own database name
    $db = mysql_select_db("MyDB", $conn) or die(mysql_error());
    // formulate and execute the query
    $sql = "SELECT id FROM users WHERE
username='$_SERVER[PHP_AUTH_USER]' and password=
password('$_SERVER[PHP_AUTH_PW]')";
    $result = mysql_query($sql) or die (mysql_error());

// Present results based on validity, by counting rows.
    if (mysql_num_rows($result) == 1) {
        echo "<P>You are a valid user!<br>";
echo "You entered a username of $_SERVER[PHP_AUTH_USER] and a password
of $_SERVER[PHP_AUTH_PW]</P>";
    } else {
```

```
            echo "You are not authorized!";
        }
    }
?>
```

There are limitations to sending and receiving HTTP headers and PHP authentication variables. For example, once a user is authorized, a different user can't attempt to authorize himself within the current browser session. After processing the script and validating a user within the current browser session, the browser will not display the username/password dialog box again, because the browser doesn't know whether or not a different person is sitting in front of the machine. You must end the browser session, then restart the browser and access the protected area again in order to validate a different user. An additional problem is that no "global" authentication directive exists, such that which exists when you use an .htaccess file in a protected directory or create a `<Directory></Directory>` block in the Apache configuration file. When using PHP-based authentication, the authentication routine must be included at the beginning of each file you want to protect.

If you are querying a database for valid users, these additional requests will cause some slowdown in your server response times. Using an HTML form as a front-end to an authentication system has proven to be the most successful user authentication method in my own commercial applications. The database is queried on-demand, which provides accurate results as well as a consistently speedy server connection.

Using HTML Forms to Validate Users

Instead of sending HTTP authorization headers and displaying the username/password dialog box, create a simple form, called login.html, that asks for a username and password.

```
<HTML>
<HEAD>
<TITLE>My Login Form</TITLE>
</HEAD>
<!-- Configure the form -->
<FORM ACTION="login.php" METHOD="post">
<!-- Create the form fields in a pretty table -->
```

```
<table border=0>
<tr>
<td><strong>Username</strong></td>
<td><input type="text" name="username" size="10" maxsize="10"></td>
</tr>
<tr>
<td><strong>Password</strong></td>
<td><input type="password" name="password" size="10" maxsize="10"></td>
</tr>
<tr>
<td colspan="2" align="center">
<input type="submit" value="Validate Me">
</td>
</tr>
</table>
</FORM>
</BODY>
</HTML>
```

When the user types values in the form fields and clicks on the Validate Me button, the values are sent to the login.php script (shown next). This script must hold the values, connect to the database, validate the user, and display the appropriate information. Essentially, only a few variable names will change from the authorize3.php script used earlier in this chapter. Instead of storing the username and password in $_SERVER[PHP_AUTH_USER] and $_SERVER[PHP_*AUTH_PW*], the values are stored in $_POST[username] and $_POST[password], as named by the form field names.

```
<?php
// create connection; substitute your own information!
$conn = mysql_connect("localhost","joeuser","34Nhjp") or die(mysql_error());
// select database; substitute your own database name
$db = mysql_select_db("MyDB", $conn) or die(mysql_error());

// formulate and execute the query
$sql = "SELECT id FROM users WHERE username='$_POST[username]' and password=
password('$_POST[password]')";
$result = mysql_query($sql) or die (mysql_error());
```

```
// Present results based on validity.
if (mysql_num_rows($result) == 1) {
           echo "<P>You are a valid user!<br>";
           echo "Your username is $_POST[username]<br>";
           echo "Your password is $_POST[password]</P>";
} else {
           echo "You are not authorized!";
}
?>
```

To take this process a step further, you can combine the HTML form and PHP script into one file using the include() function. By telling the script when to include the file containing the login form, you can display the form again without leaving this one script, should a user enter invalid entries (or none at all).

First, create a file called login_form.inc containing the following code:

```
<!-- Configure the form -->
<FORM ACTION="login2.php" METHOD="post">
<input type="hidden" name="do" value="authenticate">
<!-- Create the form fields in a pretty table -->
<table border=0>
<tr>
<td><strong>Username</strong></td>
<td><input type="text" name="username" size="10" maxlength="10"></td>
</tr>
<tr>
<td><strong>Password</strong></td>
<td><input type="password" name="password" size="10" maxlength="10"></td>
</tr>
<tr>
<td colspan="2" align="center">
<input type="submit" value="Validate Me">
</td>
</tr>
</table>
```

This code is simply the snippet of HTML that displays the form fields. The surrounding HTML will already be in the login2.php file, as you can intertwine HTML and PHP code in the same file.

```html
<HTML>
<HEAD>
<TITLE>My Login Form</TITLE>
</HEAD>
<!-- Now we start our PHP code -->
<?php
// Continue a process, depending on the value of the $_POST[do] variable.
// If this is the first time to access this script, the $_POST[do] variable
// has no value.

switch ($_POST['do']) {
        // if the value of $_POST[do] is "authenticate", continue this process
        case "authenticate":

        // create connection; substitute your own information!
        $conn = mysql_connect("localhost","root","3Kb7a*#1") or die(mysql_error());
        // select database; substitute your own database name
        $db = mysql_select_db("thickbook_com", $conn) or die(mysql_error());

        // formulate and execute the query
        $sql = "SELECT id FROM users WHERE username='$_POST[username]' and password= password('$_POST[password]')";
        $result = mysql_query($sql) or die (mysql_error());

        // Present results based on validity.
        if (mysql_num_rows($result) == 1) {
                echo "<P>You are a valid user!<br>";
                echo "Your username is $_POST[username]<br>";
                echo "Your password is $_POST[password]</P>";
        } else {
                unset($_POST['do']);
                echo "<P>You are not authorized! Please try again.</P>";
```

```
                    // The next command automatically places the contents of
                    // login_form.inc at this position; the HTML form fields will
                       display.
                    include("login_form.inc");

            }

            break;

            default:
            // The default case, in this instance, means "if no value
            // exists for $_POST[do], or if no other case matches a value
            // for $_POST[do], display the login form."
            include("login_form.inc");

    }
    ?>
    <!-- We have exited out of PHP code and are back in HTML -->
    </BODY>
    </HTML>
```

It's that simple to combine PHP and HTML into one comprehensive file that contains all the routines for querying a database, displaying error messages to unauthorized users, and providing custom content to valid users.

If you need to indicate to a subsequent script whether or not a user has been authenticated, it's not a good idea to pass the username and password in the URL using the GET method. Using the GET method would create a URL such as http://www.yourcompany.com/login2.php?username=jane&password=mypassword.

If a friend or coworker (or a random person off the street) looks over the user's shoulder at the browser, he will see the full URL in the Location area and will then know a valid username and password pair. Similarly, if the user bookmarks the page after a successful login, he will have bookmarked the complete URL, with the username and password. If the user shares a terminal with someone, or if a friend or coworker (or random person off the street) opens the browser and uses that bookmark, that person will have access to everything a correct username and password pair grants him.

In the next chapter, you'll learn to use cookies, those powerful little bits of text stored on a user's hard drive, to set and store variables and values you may need later, such as authentication variables. But right now, let's look at another simple method of restricting access.

Limit by IP Address

Another method of protecting sensitive data is to limit the display to users accessing from a specific IP or IP range. Although this is a very simple process, it's not the most effective. Most users do not have static IP addresses, and those who do are usually behind a firewall and access the Web via a proxy. When you access via a *proxy*, a kind of gateway that filters traffic out to the Internet, the remote address is always the same value because it belongs to the proxy and not the specific user attempting to access a Web site.

However, if you're creating a site in a closed environment, adding the following few lines at the beginning of your PHP script will determine the remote IP address and will limit access based on the result it finds:

```php
<?php //limitbyIP.php
$userIP = $_SERVER[REMOTE_ADDR];
if ($userIP != "127.0.0.1") {
        echo "It's not me, it's $userIP!";
} else {
        echo "User is authorized, it's me!";
}
?>
```

You can use regular expressions to match a block of IP addresses, in this case, any IP address that begins with 63.196.7. This script actually looks for something that does not match 63.196.7., as evidenced by the use of the ! before the function name.

```php
<?php //limitbyIPrange.php
$userIP = $_SERVER[REMOTE_ADDR];
if (!preg_match("/63.196.7./", "$userIP")) {
        echo "You're not in my neighborhood...";
```

```
} else {
        echo "Welcome, neighbor!";
}
?>
```

$_SERVER[REMOTE_ADDR] contains a standard environment variable that is always sent by the machine making the request. The limitbyIP.php script uses 127.0.0.1, or the default value for localhost, as the only authorized IP address. In that script, if the remote address *is not* 127.0.0.1 or localhost, the user *is not* shown any content, and instead the message "It's not me, it's [some IP]" is displayed in the browser.

Although this is a neat trick—and quite speedy, as the script doesn't connect to a database to validate specific users—it loses its value in a production environment given the prevalence of non-static IPs and proxy servers.

In the next chapter, you'll learn how to store information in cookies and sessions, and retrieve that information to provide customized user environments.

Chapter 6

User Tracking
and Session
Management

You can't effectively track visitors on a Web site without a little intervention. Every Web server tracks basic accesses, meaning that for each "hit," it keeps a log of at least the date and time, the IP or domain name of the user making the request, and the name of the file that was sent. This type of log isn't very helpful when you want to track buying trends or user preferences, and it doesn't give you any real insight into your user base. The solution to this problem requires definite planning, but it is easy to implement using cookies or full-blown user sessions.

Cookies

Cookies are little pieces of text that are sent to a user's browser along with the pretty pictures and well-worded content of a good Web site. They can help you create shopping carts, user communities, and personalized sites. For example, say you've planned to assign an identification variable to a user so that you can track what he does when he visits your site. First, the user logs in, and you send a cookie with variables designed to say, "This is Joe, and Joe is allowed to be here." While Joe is surfing around your site, you can say "Hello, Joe!" on each and every page. If Joe clicks through your catalog and chooses 14 different items to buy, you can keep track of these items and display them all in a bunch when Joe clicks on Checkout. But what happens when a user doesn't accept cookies? Are your well-laid plans all for naught? Will Joe ever get to buy those 14 items?

These sorts of identification cookies are valuable in e-commerce sites, when you're creating a shopping system that allows the user to store selected items until he's ready to pay for them. You can use cookies for all sorts of things, but because e-commerce sites are popular, we'll go with that example.

Setting Cookies

Before you go around setting cookies, determine how you will use them and at what point you will set them. Do you want to check for a cookie on every page of your site, and set one if it doesn't exist? How will you use the cookie data?

Whatever cookies you decide to use, remember that you absolutely must set a cookie before sending any other content to the browser. If you remember this, you won't spend hours wondering why you're getting "Can't send additional information, header already sent" errors from your scripts.

PHP has a built-in function for setting cookies called `setcookie()`, which expects six arguments:

- **Name.** Holds the name of the variable that will be kept in the `$_COOKIE` superglobal, and will be accessible by subsequent scripts.

- **Value.** The value of the variable passed in the Name argument.

- **Expiration.** Sets a specific time at which the cookie value will no longer be accessible. Cookies without a specific expiration time will expire when the Web browser closes.

- **Path.** Determines for which directories the cookie is valid. If a single slash is in the path parameter, the cookie is valid for all files and directories on the Web server. If a specific directory is named, this cookie is valid only for pages within that directory.

- **Domain.** Cookies are valid only for the host and domain that set them. If no domain is specified, the default value is the host name of the server that generated the cookie. The domain parameter must have at least two periods in the string in order to be valid.

- **Security.** If the security parameter is 1, the cookie will only be transmitted via HTTPS, which is to say, over a secure Web server.

The following snippet of code shows how to set a cookie called `id` with a value of `55sds809892jjsj2`. This particular cookie will expire in four hours (the current time plus 14,400 seconds), and it is valid for any page below the document root on the domain yourdomain.com.

```
setcookie("id", "55sds809892jjsj2", time()+14400, "/" ,".yourdomain.com",0);
```

Reading Cookies

There's an element to using cookies that most people forget about (until they spend a few hours trying to debug something that isn't even wrong), and that's the fact that when a Web browser accepts a cookie, you can't extract its value until the next HTTP request is made.

In other words, if you set a cookie called name with a value of Jane on page 1, you can't extract that value until the user reaches page 2 (or page 5 or page 28—just some other page that isn't the page on which the cookie is initially set).

When it is time to extract a value from a cookie, simply extract the value from the $_COOKIE superglobal. If you set a cookie like the one described above, where name is the name of the cookie, you would print the value like this:

```
<? echo "$_COOKIE[name]"; ?>
```

Hopefully, it would print the string "Jane" to the screen.

Session Handling

If the question is "How do I maintain user-specific information without setting multiple cookies and making numerous calls to a database?", then the answer is to use session management functions. In terms of time, a *session* is the amount of time during which a user visits a site. In the programming world, a session is kind of like a big blob that can hold all sorts of variables and values.

This blob of stuff, also known as a *session object*, has an identification string. This identification string, such as 940f8b05a40d5119c030c9c7745aead9, is automatically sent to the user when a session is initiated, via a cookie referred to as $_COOKIE[PHPSESSID]. On the server side, a matching temporary file is created with the same name—940f8b05a40d5119c030c9c7745aead9.

With your session object in place, you have a container that can hold all sorts of data, and generally make your life as an application developer much easier!

Understanding Session Variables

Each session object has variables registered with it, such as count or valid. Inside the session file on the server, the registered variables and their values are kept safe and sound. Since these values and variables are not kept in a database, no additional system resources are required to connect to and extract information from database tables.

For example, the session file might look like this:

```
count|s:7:"76";
valid|s:7:"yes";
```

where `count` and `valid` are the names of the registered variables, and `76` and `yes` are their respective values.

When you register a session variable, you eliminate the need to send additional cookies to the user. To assign values for `count` and `valid` to a user without using sessions, you'd have to send two separate cookies, like so:

```
setcookie("count","1",time()+14400,"/",".yourdomain.com",0);
setcookie("valid","yes",time()+14400,"/",".yourdomain.com",0);
```

To access session variables, just reference their position in the `$_SESSION` super-global, like this: `$_SESSION[count]` or `$_SESSION[valid]`. When you use something like the following in your code:

```
echo "<P>$_SESSION[count]</p>";
```

the PHP engine takes the value of `$_COOKIE[PHPSESSID]` (the unique user session ID, stored in a cookie), matches it to a temporary session file, looks for `count`, finds its value (say, "76"), and returns it to your script.

Starting a Session and Registering Variables

We'll use a simple access counter to get used to the idea of sessions and session variables. At the beginning of your page, call the `session_start()` function. This function serves two purposes. First, it checks to see if a session has been started for this user and starts one if necessary. Second, it alerts the PHP engine that session variables and other session-related functions will be used within the specific script.

Open your favorite text editor, create a file called count_me.php, and type the following:

```
<?php
// if a session does not yet exist for this user, start one
session_start();
```

Next, register the `count` variable inside your session object:

```
session_register('count');
```

Now, for as long as this session exists, a variable referred to as `$_SESSION[count]` also exists. Currently, the variable has no value. However, if you increment it, it will have a value of "1":

```
$_SESSION[count]++;
```

Put these pieces together, and you'll have started a session if it hasn't already been started, assigned a session ID to a user if one doesn't exist, and registered the variable referred to as $_SESSION[count] and incremented it by 1 to represent the initial time the user has accessed the page.

Next, to display the value of the $_SESSION[count] session variable and show the user how many times he has accessed this page in his current session, just print the variable's value within a string:

```
echo "<P>You've been here $_SESSION[count] times. Thanks!</p>";
```

The entire access count code should look something like this:

```
<?php
// if a session does not yet exist for this user, start one
session_start();
session_register('count');
$_SESSION[count]++;
echo "<P>You've been here $_SESSION[count] times. Thanks!</p>";
?>
```

Reload the page a number of times, and watch the value of $_SESSION[count] increment by 1 each time. Though this may not be the most exciting example, you should now understand the basics of sessions.

Managing User Preferences with Sessions

Moving beyond the simple access counter, you can use sessions to manage your users' preferences when they visit your site. For example, you can have your users select their favorite font ($_SESSION[font_family]) and font size ($_SESSION[font_size]) for displaying site content.

In this example, you'll start a session, ask a user for his display preferences, display those preferences on subsequent pages, and allow the user to change his mind and reset the values.

For the first step, create a file called session1.php and start the session:

```
<?php
// if a session does not yet exist for this user, start one
session_start();
```

Immediately, begin an `if...else` construct that checks for any previously registered values:

```
if ((!$_SESSION[font_family]) || (!$_SESSION[font_size])) {
        $font_family = "sans-serif";
        $font_size = "10";
        $_SESSION[font_family] = $font_family;
        $_SESSION[font_size] = $font_size;
} else {
        $font_family = $_SESSION[font_family];
        $font_size = $_SESSION[font_size];
}
?>
```

This construct is important because it takes into consideration that, as the user must come back to this screen to reset his display preferences, the values of the variables must always be extracted from the session itself.

With the initial session-related code out of the way, create a simple HTML form that asks the user to select his font preferences:

```
<HTML>
<HEAD>
<TITLE>My Display Preferences</TITLE>
<style type="text/css">
BODY, P, A {font-family:<? echo "$_SESSION[font_family]"; ?>;font-size:<? echo
"$_SESSION[font_size]"; ?>pt;font-weight:normal;}
H1 {font-family:<? echo "$_SESSION[font_family]"; ?>;font-size:<? echo $_SES-
SION[font_size] + 4; ?>pt;font-weight:normal;}
</style>
</HEAD>
<BODY>
<H1>Set Your Display Preferences</h1>
<FORM METHOD="POST" ACTION="session2.php">
<P>Pick a Font Family:<br>
<input type="radio" name="sel_font_family" value="serif" checked> serif
<input type="radio" name="sel_font_family" value="sans-serif"> sans-serif
<input type="radio" name="sel_font_family" value="Courier"> Courier
<input type="radio" name="sel_font_family" value="Wingdings"> Wingdings
```

```
<P>Pick a Font Size:<br>
<input type="radio" name="sel_font_size" value="8" checked> 8pt
<input type="radio" name="sel_font_size" value="10"> 10pt
<input type="radio" name="sel_font_size" value="12"> 12pt
<input type="radio" name="sel_font_size" value="14"> 14pt

<P><input type="submit" name="submit" value="Set Display Preferences"></p>
</FORM>
</BODY>
</HTML>
```

Note that the style sheet contains in-line PHP code, to take into consideration the user's preferred (or default) font family and size. If you place this file on your Web server and access it with your browser, you should see something like that in Figure 6.1, with the default values in use.

In the next step, which creates the form action script (session2.php), we'll assign to the appropriate session variables the values selected by the user. Open your text editor and create a file called session2.php. Create a session in your code if one

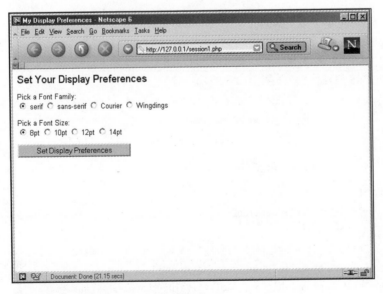

FIGURE 6.1 *The Display Preferences form*

doesn't exist, and then check for values posted from the form. Next, check for previously stored values—but only if no values have been posted from the form. Finally, use default values if, for some reason, there are no values from the form or in a previous user session.

```php
<?php
// if a session does not yet exist for this user, start one
session_start();
//check for registered values, or set defaults
if (($_POST[sel_font_family]) || ($_POST[sel_font_size])) {
        $font_family = $_POST[sel_font_family];
        $font_size = $_POST[sel_font_size];
        $_SESSION[font_family] = $font_family;
        $_SESSION[font_size] = $font_size;
} else if ((((!$_POST[sel_font_family]) && (!$_POST[sel_font_size])) &&
(($_SESSION[font_family]) && ($_SESSION[font_size]))) {
        $font_family = $_SESSION[font_family];
        $font_size = $_SESSION[font_size];
        $_SESSION[font_family] = $font_family;
        $_SESSION[font_size] = $font_size;
} else {
        $font_family = "sans-serif";
        $font_size = "10";
        $_SESSION[font_family] = $font_family;
        $_SESSION[font_size] = $font_size;
}
?>
```

With the PHP code out of the way, move on to the HTML, including the dynamic stylesheet.

```html
<HTML>
<HEAD>
<TITLE>My Display Preferences</TITLE>
<style type="text/css">
BODY, P, A {font-family:<? echo "$_SESSION[font_family]"; ?>;font-size:<? echo
"$_SESSION[font_size]"; ?>pt;font-weight:normal;}
H1 {font-family:<? echo "$_SESSION[font_family]"; ?>;font-size:<? echo $_SES-
```

```
SION[font_size] + 4; ?>pt;font-weight:normal;}
</style>
</HEAD>
<BODY>
<H1>Your Preferences Have Been Set</h1>
<P>As you can see, your selected font family is <strong><? echo
"$_SESSION[font_family]"; ?></strong> and your font size is <strong><? echo
"$_SESSION[font_size]"; ?></strong>.</p>
<P>Please feel free to <a href="session1.php">change your preferences</a>
again.</p>
</BODY>
</HTML>
```

Save this file and place it on your Web server. If you go back and forth between session1.php and session2.php, changing your preferences as much as you like, you may end up with display preferences such as those shown in Figures 6.2 and 6.3.

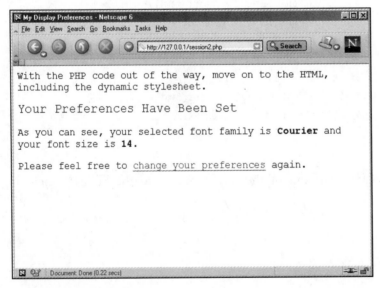

FIGURE 6.2 *Using Courier as a font preference*

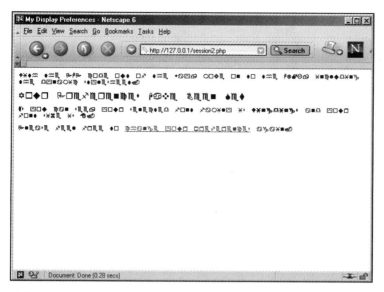

FIGURE 6.3 *Using Wingdings as a font preference*

This simple exercise shows how easy it is to use sessions to create dynamic, user-based Web sites.

Chapter 7

Advanced PHP Techniques: Web-Based Database Administration

The previous chapters were designed to give you a solid foundation for developing applications with PHP. Many dynamic and user-friendly Web sites are simply several basic concepts put together to form one cohesive unit. For example, a successful shopping system may use an underlying product catalog, a method for maintaining the catalog, some sort of order tracking, and a method to order products securely. In this chapter, you'll learn the basics of performing these tasks.

While the term *Web-based database administration* might seem daunting, don't be afraid—it's just a fancy label for "data goes in, data comes out." The goal of this section is to create a product catalog for an online shopping system, which will be fully functional by the end of this chapter. By breaking down the elements piece by piece, before you know it you'll have created a graphical user interface to a product catalog in a MySQL database. You can repeat the same steps for any type of database-driven system you want to develop: news articles, address books, your mother's recipe collection, whatever you want. If you're not using the MySQL database, just substitute the functions for your particular database for the MySQL database functions.

Planning Your Product Catalog

This sample shopping site will be called XYZ Company, and it will sell books. The first step in creating this site is developing the product catalog. Because we're creating only a simple example for this site, intending only to get the basics down, we'll use one table called MASTER_PRODUCTS. At the end of this chapter, I'll provide pointers for normalizing a set of tables for this type of catalog.

Think about the basic information you'll need to know in order to give the user an accurate description of a product:

- An ID for the record
- ISBN (a standard publishing identification number)
- Book title
- Author's name
- Publisher

- ◆ Category
- ◆ Type (hardcover or paperback)
- ◆ A paragraph of information about the book
- ◆ Number of pages in the book
- ◆ Price of the book

You can use the three-step process from Chapter 3, "Working with Databases," to create the MASTER_PRODUCTS table for XYZ Company, or you can manually type a CREATE TABLE command through your MySQL interface of choice (I personally prefer the command line).

This MASTER_PRODUCTS table will have 10 fields, as defined in Table 7.1.

Table 7.1 MASTER_PRODUCTS Table Fields

Field Name	Field Type	Field Length
ID	int	
ISBN	varchar	25
TITLE	varchar	150
AUTHOR	varchar	75
PUBLISHER	varchar	75
CATEGORY	varchar	50
TYPE	varchar	25
INFO_BLURB	text	
PAGE_NUM	smallint	
PRICE	float	

The ID field will be a primary key, automatically incremented by MySQL when a new record is inserted.

The actual SQL command for the MASTER_PRODUCTS table is as follows:

```
CREATE TABLE MASTER_PRODUCTS (
        ID int not null primary key auto_increment,
        ISBN varchar(25),
        TITLE varchar(150),
```

```
      AUTHOR varchar(75),
      PUBLISHER varchar(75),
      CATEGORY varchar(50),
      TYPE varchar(25),
      INFO_BLURB text,
      PAGE_NUM smallint,
      PRICE float
);
```

If you look at the description of the table using the MySQL DESCRIBE command, it looks like this:

```
+-------------+---------------+------+-----+---------+----------------+
| Field       | Type          | Null | Key | Default | Extra          |
+-------------+---------------+------+-----+---------+----------------+
| ID          | int(11)       |      | PRI | NULL    | auto_increment |
| ISBN        | varchar(25)   | YES  |     | NULL    |                |
| TITLE       | varchar(150)  | YES  |     | NULL    |                |
| AUTHOR      | varchar(75)   | YES  |     | NULL    |                |
| PUBLISHER   | varchar(75)   | YES  |     | NULL    |                |
| CATEGORY    | varchar(50)   | YES  |     | NULL    |                |
| TYPE        | varchar(25)   | YES  |     | NULL    |                |
| INFO_BLURB  | text          | YES  |     | NULL    |                |
| PAGE_NUM    | smallint(6)   | YES  |     | NULL    |                |
| PRICE       | float         | YES  |     | NULL    |                |
+-------------+---------------+------+-----+---------+----------------+
```

In the next sections, you'll create sequences of HTML forms and PHP scripts to add, modify, and delete records in your MASTER_PRODUCTS table.

Developing an Administration Menu

Somewhere on the Web site for XYZ Company, you'll want to have a special series of "admin" pages, which only you (or whomever has the correct password) can access to make changes to the product catalog. The main elements of the administration menu will be as follows:

- ◆ Add a New Product
- ◆ Modify an Existing Product
- ◆ Delete an Existing Product

We'll use a PHP-based authentication scheme, which you learned about in Chapter 5, "User Authentication."

The XYZ Company administration area will be accessible by anyone who knows the username and password pair—in this case, "admin" and "abc123." At the top of every page in the administration sequence, use the following code, which should look very familiar to you if you've read Chapter 5:

```php
<?php
// Check to see if $_SERVER[PHP_AUTH_USER] already contains info
if (!isset($_SERVER[PHP_AUTH_USER])) {
        // If empty, send header causing dialog box to appear
        header('WWW-Authenticate: Basic realm="XYZ Company Admin"');
        header('HTTP/1.0 401 Unauthorized');
        echo 'Authorization Required.';
        exit;
} else {
        // If not empty, do something else
// Try to validate against hard-coded values
        if (($_SERVER[PHP_AUTH_USER] != "admin") ||
                ($_SERVER[PHP_AUTH_PW] != "abc123")) {
                header('WWW-Authenticate: Basic realm="XYZ Company Admin"');
                header('HTTP/1.0 401 Unauthorized');
                echo 'Authorization Required.';
                exit;
        } else {
                // Display code here.
        }
}
?>
```

If you add this to the top of every page in the XYZ Company administration area, the PHP script will always look for a valid entry for $_SERVER[PHP_AUTH_USER] and $_SERVER[PHP_AUTH_PW]. You will only need to enter the login information the first time you see the pop-up box. From that point forward, the proper values will exist for $_SERVER[PHP_AUTH_USER] and $_SERVER[PHP_AUTH_PW], and will be carried along wherever you go, until you exit your browser. The code comment // Display code here will be replaced by the content you want to display to the valid user. For the first screen (the administration menu), this content can be three bullet items, linking to admin_addrecord.php, admin_modrecord.php, and admin_delrecord.php.

When you put a section of HTML within an echo statement, remember to escape the quotation marks! The entire administration menu code should look something like this:

```
<?
// Check to see if $_SERVER[PHP_AUTH_USER] already contains info
if (!isset($_SERVER[PHP_AUTH_USER])) {
        // If empty, send header causing dialog box to appear
        header('WWW-Authenticate: Basic realm="XYZ Company Admin"');
        header('HTTP/1.0 401 Unauthorized');
        echo 'Authorization Required.';
        exit;
} else {
        // If not empty, do something else
// Try to validate against hard-coded values
        if (($_SERVER[PHP_AUTH_USER] != "admin") ||
            ($_SERVER[PHP_AUTH_PW] != "abc123")) {
            header('WWW-Authenticate: Basic realm="XYZ Company Admin"');
            header('HTTP/1.0 401 Unauthorized');
            echo 'Authorization Required.';
            exit;
        } else {
            echo "<HTML>
            <HEAD>
            <TITLE>XYZ Company Administration Menu</TITLE>
            </HEAD>
            <BODY>
            <h1>XYZ Company Administration Menu</h1>
            <p>Select an option:</p>
            <ul>
            <li><a href=\"admin_addrecord.php\">Add a New Product</a>
            <li><a href=\"admin_modrecord.php\">Modify an Existing Product</a>
            <li><a href=\"admin_delrecord.php\">Delete an Existing Product</a>
            </ul>
            </BODY>
            </HTML>";
        }
    }
?>
```

Save this file and place it on your Web server. Access it at its URL and enter the correct username and password when prompted. If you are authorized, you should see a menu such as the one shown in Figure 7.1.

Now that you've built the menu, it's time to build the pages behind it, starting with "Add a New Product."

Adding Records to the Product Catalog

Of the three menu options, adding a product is the simplest to execute. Using a two-step system, you'll create the addition form, and then you'll create the PHP script to insert the contents into the MASTER_PRODUCTS table. The link in the administration menu says admin_addrecord.php, so create a file with that name and add your PHP authentication code, leaving room for the "show" portion of the form. The "show" portion will begin with the title and main topic heading, followed by the form. The form will contain fields for each of the fields in the MASTER_PRODUCTS table, with the exception of ID.

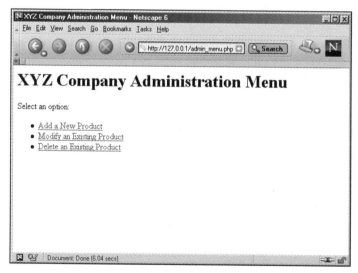

FIGURE 7.1 *XYZ Company administration menu*

> **NOTE**
>
> In this example, the values of the drop-down menus are hard-coded into the HTML. You could also put these values in separate PUBLISHER, CATEGORY, and TYPE tables, and use PHP to extract the data and dynamically create your drop-down menus.

While not the most aesthetically pleasing form, an example admin_addrecord.php script could look something like this:

```
<?
// Check to see if $_SERVER[PHP_AUTH_USER] already contains info
if (!isset($_SERVER[PHP_AUTH_USER])) {
        // If empty, send header causing dialog box to appear
        header('WWW-Authenticate: Basic realm="XYZ Company Admin"');
        header('HTTP/1.0 401 Unauthorized');
        echo 'Authorization Required.';
        exit;
} else {
        // If not empty, do something else
        // Try to validate against hard-coded values
        if (($_SERVER[PHP_AUTH_USER] != "admin") ||
                ($_SERVER[PHP_AUTH_PW] != "abc123")) {
                header('WWW-Authenticate: Basic realm="XYZ Company Admin"');
                header('HTTP/1.0 401 Unauthorized');
                echo 'Authorization Required.';
                exit;
        } else {
                echo "
                <HTML>
                <HEAD>
                <TITLE>XYZ Company: Add a Product</TITLE>
                </HEAD>
                <BODY>
                <h1>Add a product to the XYZ Company Catalog</h1>
                <FORM method=\"POST\" action=\"admin_doaddrecord.php\">
                <P><strong>ISBN:</strong>
                <INPUT type=\"text\" name=\"isbn\" size=35 maxlength=25>
                <P><strong>Title:</strong>
                <INPUT type=\"text\" name=\"title\" size=35 maxlength=150>
```

```
<P><strong>Author:</strong>
<INPUT type=\"text\" name=\"author\" size=35 maxlength=75>
<P><strong>Publisher:</strong>
<SELECT name=\"publisher\">
<OPTION value=\"\">-- Select One --</OPTION>
<OPTION value=\"Premier Press\">Premier Press</OPTION>
<OPTION value=\"Course Technology\">Course Technology</OPTION>
</SELECT>
<strong>Category:</strong>
<SELECT name=\"category\">
<OPTION value=\"\">-- Select One --</OPTION>
<OPTION value=\"Applications\">Applications</OPTION>
<OPTION value=\"Operating Systems\">Operating Systems</OPTION>
<OPTION value=\"Programming\">Programming</OPTION>
</SELECT>
<strong>Type:</strong>
<SELECT name=\"type\">
<OPTION value=\"\">-- Select One --</OPTION>
<OPTION value=\"hardcover\">hardcover</OPTION>
<OPTION value=\"paperback\">paperback</OPTION>
</SELECT>
<P><strong>Description:</strong><br>
<TEXTAREA name=\"info_blurb\" cols=35 rows=3></TEXTAREA>
<P><strong>Page Count:</strong>
<INPUT type=\"text\" name=\"page_num\" size=5 maxlength=5>
<P><strong>Price:</strong>
<INPUT type=\"text\" name=\"price\" size=5 maxlength=5><br>
<p align=center><INPUT type=\"submit\"
value=\"Add New Product\"></p>
</FORM>
</BODY>
</HTML>";
        }
    }
?>
```

Place this file on your Web server, and click on the Add a New Product link on
the initial administration menu. If you are authorized, you should see a product
addition form like that shown in Figure 7.2.

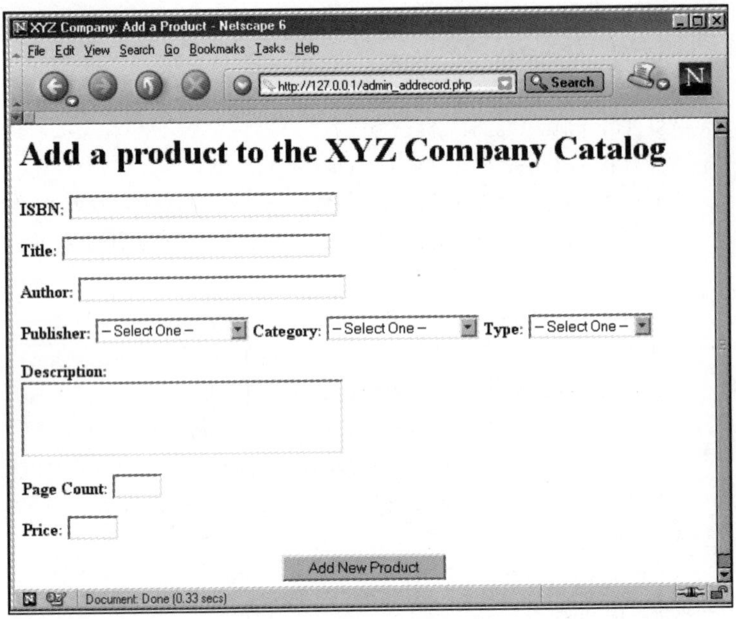

FIGURE 7.2 *Add a new product to the XYZ Company product catalog*

Next, you'll create the PHP script that takes your form input, creates a proper SQL statement, creates the record, and displays the record to you as a confirmation. It's not as difficult as it sounds. As the form action in admin_addrecord.php is admin_doaddrecord.php, open your favorite text editor and create a file called admin_doaddrecord.php. Add the PHP authentication code, as you've done in the previous scripts. However, in this script, you'll want to do a bit more than just echo HTML back to the browser. First, you'll want to check for some required fields. Then, if all the necessary fields aren't complete, you'll redirect the user to the form.

In this catalog, suppose the required fields are ISBN, book title, and book price. Check that a value has been entered for their matching variable names: $_POST[isbn], $_POST[title], and $_POST[price]:

```
if ((!$_POST[isbn]) || (!$_POST[title]) || (!$_POST[price])) {
        header("Location: http://www.yourserver.com/admin_addrecord.php");
        exit;
}
```

If your script makes it past the required-field check, the next step is to build the SQL statement used to insert the data into the MASTER_PRODUCTS table. Hold the SQL statement in a variable called $sql, and build the VALUES list using the variable names from the form:

```
$sql = "INSERT INTO MASTER_PRODUCTS VALUES ('', '$_POST[isbn]', '$_POST[title]',
'$_POST[author]', '$_POST[publisher]', '$_POST[category]', '$_POST[type]',
'$_POST[info_blurb]', '$_POST[page_num]', '$_POST[price]')";
```

Use the basic connection code described in Chapter 3, "Working with Databases," to connect to and query the MySQL database using the SQL statement above. Upon success, echo a copy of the record to the screen, just for validation. If an error occurs, the die() function will let you know where!

The admin_doaddrecord.php script could look something like this (substitute your own database connectivity code):

```
<?
if ((!$_POST[isbn]) || (!$_POST[title]) || (!$_POST[price])) {
        header("Location: http://www.yourserver.com/admin_addrecord.php");
        exit;
}
// Check to see if $_SERVER[PHP_AUTH_USER] already contains info
if (!isset($_SERVER[PHP_AUTH_USER])) {
        // If empty, send header causing dialog box to appear
        header('WWW-Authenticate: Basic realm="XYZ Company Admin"');
        header('HTTP/1.0 401 Unauthorized');
        echo 'Authorization Required.';
        exit;
} else {
        // If not empty, do something else
        // Try to validate against hard-coded values
        if (($_SERVER[PHP_AUTH_USER] != "admin") ||
                ($_SERVER[PHP_AUTH_PW] != "abc123")) {
                header('WWW-Authenticate: Basic realm="XYZ Company Admin"');
                header('HTTP/1.0 401 Unauthorized');
                echo 'Authorization Required.';
                exit;
        } else {
```

```php
// create connection; substitute your own information!
$conn = mysql_connect("localhost","joeuser","34Nhjp")
        or die(mysql_error());
        // select database; substitute your own database name
$db = mysql_select_db("MyDB", $conn) or die(mysql_error());

// formulate and execute the query
$sql = "INSERT INTO MASTER_PRODUCTS VALUES
('', '$_POST[isbn]', '$_POST[title]', '$_POST[author]',
'$_POST[publisher]',        '$_POST[category]', '$_POST[type]',
'$_POST[info_blurb]', '$_POST[page_num]', '$_POST[price]')";
$result = mysql_query($sql) or die (mysql_error());
if (isset($result)) {
        echo "
        <HTML>
        <HEAD>
        <TITLE>XYZ Company: Add a Product</TITLE>
        </HEAD>
        <BODY>
        <h1>The following was added to the XYZ
        Company Catalog:</h1>
        <P><strong>ISBN:</strong> ".stripslashes($_POST[isbn])."
        <P><strong>Title:</strong>
        ".stripslashes($_POST[title])."
        <P><strong>Author:</strong>
        ".stripslashes($_POST[author])."
        <P><strong>Publisher:</strong>
        ".stripslashes($_POST[publisher])."
        <strong>Category:</strong>
        ".stripslashes($_POST[category])."
        <strong>Type:</strong> ".stripslashes($_POST[type])."
        <P><strong>Description:</strong><br>
        ".stripslashes($_POST[info_blurb])."
        <P><strong>Page Count:</strong>
         ".stripslashes($_POST[page_num])."
        <P><strong>Price:</strong>
        ".stripslashes($_POST[price])."
```

```
                    <P align=center><a href=\"admin_menu.php\">Return to
                    Menu</a></p>
                    </BODY>
                    </HTML>";
            } else {
                    echo "Some sort of error has occurred!</p>";
            }
       }
   }
?>
```

Note the use of the stripslashes() function, used with the text displayed to the user. This function simply removes the slashes that are automatically added to POSTed data, escaping any special characters.

Place this file on your Web server and go back to the form used to add a record. Complete the form to add a product. If the query is successful, you should see a results page like the one shown in Figure 7.3.

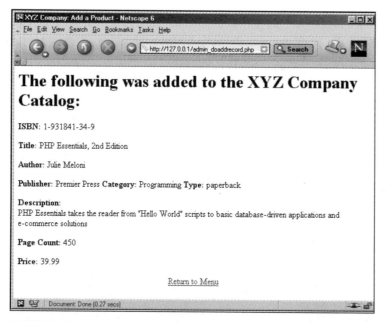

FIGURE 7.3 *Successful record addition*

Use this sequence of forms to continue adding several more products to the MAS-TER_PRODUCTS table. In the next sections, you'll modify and delete some of these records. In the next chapter, you'll use the MASTER_PRODUCTS table to create a functioning online bookstore.

Modifying Records in the Product Catalog

If you really were an online bookseller, at some point you'd probably want to modify the information in your product catalog. You've already got the link in your administration menu, so let's make it work. Before you modify a product's information, you need to select a single record to work with. So, the first step in the modification sequence is to select a record to modify.

As with just about everything related to programming, there are several ways to display the selection screen. You could display the title of each book in a list, along with a radio button, to select the record you want to edit. If you have a long list of products, you could limit the display to groups of 10 or 15 or some other number and use Next and Previous links to display each group. The goal is to pick one record whose modifiable contents will be displayed in the next step. My sample product catalog has only a few items, so I'm going to populate a drop-down list box with each book's ISBN and title.

Open your text editor and create a file called admin_modrecord.php. As the product selection form is also part of the administration area, add the basic PHP authentication code you used in previous scripts in this chapter. The selection form itself is quite basic: it's just one drop-down list box and a submit button. The trick is to populate that list box with elements in the MASTER_PRODUCTS table. As you'll soon see, it's not that tricky!

All you really need in order to populate the <OPTION> elements of the <SELECT> box are the book's ISBN and title. You can order the results any way you'd like, but I've chosen to order the books alphabetically, in ascending order (numbers first, then A, B, C, and so on). The following code snippet shows the basic connectivity function and query that will perform this task:

```
// create connection; substitute your own information!
$conn = mysql_connect("localhost","joeuser","34Nhjp") or die(mysql_error());

// select database; substitute your own database name
$db = mysql_select_db("MyDB", $conn) or die(mysql_error());
```

```
//SQL statement to select the ID, ISBN and title
$sql = "SELECT ID, ISBN, TITLE FROM MASTER_PRODUCTS ORDER BY TITLE ASC";

// execute SQL query and get result
$sql_result = mysql_query($sql,$connection) or die (mysql_error());

if (!$sql_result) {
        echo "<P>Couldn't get list!";
} else {
        // Display code here
}
```

The code comment // Display code here will be replaced by the HTML used
to create the product addition form. Start by echoing the title and main topic
heading:

```
echo "
<HTML>
<HEAD>
<TITLE>XYZ Company: Modify a Product</TITLE>
</HEAD>
<BODY>
<h1>Select a Product from the XYZ Company Catalog</h1>
```

Assume that the PHP script for the next step is called
admin_showmodrecord.php and add the following file name to the form action:

```
<FORM method=\"POST\" action=\"admin_showmodrecord.php\">
```

Next, start the HTML for the drop-down list box. Go so far as to open the
<SELECT> tag, which will have a name of sel_record, and add an empty Select an
Item <OPTION> tag:

```
<P>Select a Product:</strong><br>
<select name=\"sel_record\">
<option value=\"\"> -- Select an Item -- </option>";
```

This first echo statement ends here because the next section of code will dynamically create additional <OPTION> elements based on the number of rows in the
MASTER_PRODUCTS table. As a result of the SQL query, the following while loop
continues to execute for as long as there are rows waiting for retrieval. For each

row that is retrieved, the value of the ID column is assigned to the variable $id, the ISBN column is assigned to the variable $isbn, and the value of the TITLE column is assigned to the variable $title. The loop then creates the <OPTION> element for the product retrieved, placing the value of $id in the value attribute of the <OPTION> field.

```
while ($row = mysql_fetch_array($sql_result)) {
        $id = $row["ID"];
        $isbn = $row["ISBN"];
        $title = $row["TITLE"];
        echo "<option value=\"$id\">$title (ISBN: $isbn)</option>";
}
```

After the while loop runs its course, begin another echo statement and print the rest of the page, closing all open tags and sticking in a form submission button where appropriate. That's all that's involved in dynamically populating a <SELECT> list as part of a form. The entire admin_addrecord.php script could look something like this:

```
<?
// Check to see if $_SERVER[PHP_AUTH_USER] already contains info
if (!isset($_SERVER[PHP_AUTH_USER])) {
        // If empty, send header causing dialog box to appear
        header('WWW-Authenticate: Basic realm="XYZ Company Admin"');
        header('HTTP/1.0 401 Unauthorized');
        echo 'Authorization Required.';
        exit;
} else {
        // If not empty, do something else
        // Try to validate against hard-coded values
        if (($_SERVER[PHP_AUTH_USER] != "admin") ||
                ($_SERVER[PHP_AUTH_PW] != "abc123")) {
                header('WWW-Authenticate: Basic realm="XYZ Company Admin"');
                header('HTTP/1.0 401 Unauthorized');
                echo 'Authorization Required.';
                exit;
        } else {
                // create connection; substitute your own information!
                $conn = mysql_connect("localhost","joeuser","34Nhjp")
                        or die(mysql_error());
```

```php
// select database; substitute your own database name
$db = mysql_select_db("MyDB", $conn) or die(mysql_error());
//SQL statement to select ID, ISBN and title
$sql = "SELECT ID, ISBN, TITLE FROM MASTER_PRODUCTS
ORDER BY TITLE ASC";
// execute SQL query and get result
$sql_result = mysql_query($sql) or die (mysql_error());
if (!$sql_result) {
        echo "Something has gone wrong!";
} else {
        echo "<HTML>
        <HEAD>
        <TITLE>XYZ Company: Modify a Product</TITLE>
        </HEAD>
        <BODY>
        <h1>Select a Product from the XYZ Company Catalog</h1>
        <FORM method=\"POST\" action=\"admin_showmodrecord.php\">
        <p><strong>Select a Product:</strong><br>
        <select name=\"sel_record\">
        <option value=\"\"> -- Select an Item -- </option>";
        while ($row = mysql_fetch_array($sql_result)) {
                $id = $row["ID"];
                $isbn = $row["ISBN"];
                $title = $row["TITLE"];
                echo "<option value=\"$id\">$title
                (ISBN: $isbn)</option>";
        }
        echo "
        </select>
        <P align=center><INPUT type=\"submit\" value=\"Modify
        this Product\"></p>
        </FORM>
        </BODY>
        </HTML>";
    }
        }
}
?>
```

Place this file on your Web server, and click on the Modify an Existing Product link on the initial administration menu. If you are authorized, you should see the product selection form, shown in Figure 7.4.

The next step will create the PHP script used to display the selected record. The information currently in the database will be used to pre-populate the modification form. The modification form is exactly the same as the addition form, so its structure should be familiar to you.

The action of the form in step one is admin_showmodrecord.php, so open your text editor and create a file with that name. As the product modification form is also part of the administration area, add the basic PHP authentication code you used in previous scripts in this chapter. But before any of that, add an if statement that checks for the one required field: $_POST[sel_record]. If a record hasn't been selected, you won't have anything to do with the modification and, therefore, authenticating yourself won't really make a difference.

```
if (!$_POST[sel_record]) {
        header("Location: http://www.yourcompany.com/admin_modrecord.php");
        exit;
}
```

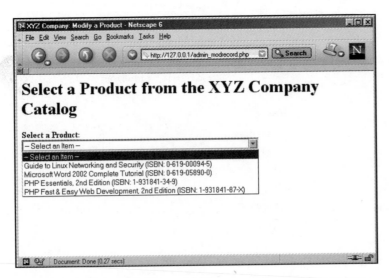

FIGURE 7.4 *Select the product to modify*

If your script makes it past the required-field check and you authenticate yourself properly, the next step is to connect to the database and issue the SQL statement used to retrieve the selected record. The goal is to pull all of the information for a record with a matching ISBN, so issue the following SQL statement within your basic connection code:

```
$sql = "SELECT * FROM MASTER_PRODUCTS WHERE ID = '$_POST[sel_record]'";
```

After issuing the query and retrieving a result, you'll use the `mysql_fetch_array()` function to grab all of the data for the selected record and assign meaningful variable names to the columns in the table. These values will go into the HTML form for modifying the product.

The form for modifying a product looks suspiciously like the form for adding a product, only with a different form action and a string holding the current value of the input field in the `value` attribute of each text field.

Within the form for modifying a product you have some drop-down list boxes. Instead of using multiple `if...else` statements to determine selected elements in a drop-down list box, we'll put the possible `<OPTION>` elements in an array and loop through it.

 NOTE

If the elements existed in a separate table, such as in a normalized database, then the same looping concept would hold true. The difference would be that the array would be obtained from the database and not from a hard-coded entry, as is the case here.

An example admin_showmodrecord.php script could look something like this:

```
<?
//check for required field
if (!$_POST[sel_record]) {
        header("Location: http://www.yourcompany.com/admin_modrecord.php");
        exit;
}
// Made it trhough, so authenticate.
// Check to see if $_SERVER[PHP_AUTH_USER] already contains info
```

```php
if (!isset($_SERVER[PHP_AUTH_USER])) {
        // If empty, send header causing dialog box to appear
        header('WWW-Authenticate: Basic realm="XYZ Company Admin"');
        header('HTTP/1.0 401 Unauthorized');
        echo 'Authorization Required.';
        exit;
} else {
        // If not empty, do something else
        // Try to validate against hard-coded values
        if (($_SERVER[PHP_AUTH_USER] != "admin") ||
                ($_SERVER[PHP_AUTH_PW] != "abc123")) {
                header('WWW-Authenticate: Basic realm="XYZ Company Admin"');
                header('HTTP/1.0 401 Unauthorized');
                echo 'Authorization Required.';
                exit;
        } else {
                // create connection; substitute your own information!
                $conn = mysql_connect("localhost","joeuser","34Nhjp")
                or die(mysql_error());
                // select database; substitute your own database name
                $db = mysql_select_db("MyDB", $conn) or die(mysql_error());
                //SQL statement to select information
                $sql = "SELECT * FROM MASTER_PRODUCTS WHERE
                ID = '$_POST[sel_record]'";
                // execute SQL query and get result
                $sql_result = mysql_query($sql) or die (mysql_error());
                if (!$sql_result) {
                        echo "Something has gone wrong!";
                } else {
                        //loop through record and get values
                        while ($record = mysql_fetch_array($sql_result)) {
                                $id = $record['ID'];
                                $isbn = stripslashes($record['ISBN']);
                                $title = stripslashes($record['TITLE']);
                                $author = stripslashes($record['AUTHOR']);
                                $publisher = $record['PUBLISHER'];
```

```
            $category = $record['CATEGORY'];
            $type = $record['TYPE'];
            $info_blurb = stripslashes($record['INFO_BLURB']);
            $page_num = stripslashes($record['PAGE_NUM']);
            $price = stripslashes($record['PRICE']);
}
echo "<HTML>
<HEAD>
<TITLE>XYZ Company: Modify a Product</TITLE>
</HEAD>
<BODY>
<h1>Modify this product from the XYZ Company Catalog</h1>
<FORM method=\"POST\" action=\"admin_domodrecord.php\">
<INPUT TYPE=\"hidden\" name=\"id\" value=\"$id\">
<P><strong>ISBN:</strong>
<INPUT type=\"text\" name=\"isbn\" value=\"$isbn\"
size=35 maxlength=25>
<P><strong>Title:</strong>
<INPUT type=\"text\" name=\"title\" value=\"$title\"
size=35 maxlength=150>
<P><strong>Author:</strong> <INPUT type=\"text\"
name=\"author\" value=\"$author\"  size=35 maxlength=75>
<P><strong>Publisher:</strong>
<SELECT name=\"publisher\">
<OPTION value=\"\">-- Select One --</OPTION>";
$pub_array = array("Premier Press", "Course Technology");
foreach ($pub_array as $pub) {
        if ($pub == "$publisher") {
                echo "<OPTION value=\"$pub\"
                selected>$pub</OPTION>";
        } else {
                echo "<OPTION value=\"$pub\">$pub</OPTION>";
        }
}
echo "</SELECT>
<strong>Category:</strong>
```

```
<SELECT name=\"category\">
<OPTION value=\"\">-- Select One --</OPTION>";
$cat_array = array("Applications", "Operating Systems",
"Programming");
foreach ($cat_array as $cat) {
        if ($cat == "$category") {
                echo "<OPTION value=\"$cat\"
                selected>$cat</OPTION>";
        } else {
                echo "<OPTION
                value=\"$cat\">$cat</OPTION>";
        }
}

echo "</SELECT>
<strong>Type:</strong>
<SELECT name=\"type\">
<OPTION value=\"\">-- Select One --</OPTION>";
$type_array = array("hardcover", "paperback");
foreach ($type_array as $book_type) {
        if ($type_array == "$type") {
                echo "<OPTION value=\"$book_type\"
                selected>$book_type</OPTION>";
        } else {
                echo "<OPTION
                value=\"$book_type\">$book_type</OPTION>";
        }
}
echo "</SELECT>
<P><strong>Description:</strong><br>
<TEXTAREA name=\"info_blurb\"
cols=35 rows=3>$info_blurb</TEXTAREA>
<P><strong>Page Count:</strong> <INPUT type=\"text\"
name=\"page_num\" value=\"$page_num\" size=5 maxlength=5>
<P><strong>Price:</strong> <INPUT type=\"text\"
name=\"price\" value=\"$price\" size=5 maxlength=5><br>
<p align=center><INPUT type=\"submit\" value=\"Modify
```

```
                Product\"></p>
                </FORM>
                </BODY>
                </HTML>";
            }
        }
    }
?>
```

Place this file on your Web server and choose a product by selecting an option via the admin_modrecord.php form. The modification form should now appear, pre-populating with the proper data from your MASTER_PRODUCTS table. Figure 7.5 shows an example.

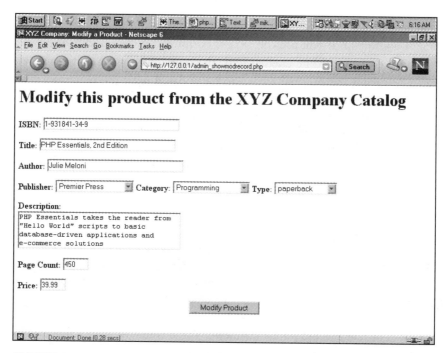

FIGURE 7.5 *Product information pre-populates the modification form*

The final step in the modification sequence is to update the fields in the table with their new values and return a confirmation to the user. This script is nearly identical to the admin_doaddrecord.php script created earlier in this chapter. In fact, just copy admin_doaddrecord.php to admin_domodrecord.php and open it in your text editor. I'll explain the minor changes, and you'll be on your way to the next section.

The first modification is the `if` statement that checks required fields. The redirection that occurs if a required value is not present should look something like this (adding a check for the value of `$_POST[id]`):

```
if ((!$_POST[id]) || (!$_POST[isbn]) || (!$_POST[title]) || (!$_POST[price])) {
        header("Location: http://www.yourserver.com/admin_addrecord.php");
        exit;
}
```

The next difference is in the SQL statement. The Add Product script uses the `INSERT` command. If you use the `INSERT` command in the modification sequence, a second record would be created with the new information. This isn't what you want. You want the original record to be updated with the new information. In this case, you can use the `UPDATE` command and `SET` the fields to the new values:

```
$sql = "UPDATE MASTER_PRODUCTS SET ISBN = '$_POST[isbn]', TITLE = '$_POST[title]',
AUTHOR = '$_POST[author]', PUBLISHER = '$_POST[publisher]', CATEGORY =
'$_POST[category]', TYPE = '$_POST[type]', INFO_BLURB = '$_POST[info_blurb]',
PAGE_NUM = '$_POST[page_num]', PRICE = '$_POST[price]' where ID = '$_POST[id]'";
```

 NOTE

Since you have a primary key in the ID field, you could also use the `REPLACE` command, which will `INSERT` a record in place of a record with a matching unique field.

The final differences are purely cosmetic. You'll want the page's title and heading to reflect your actions:

```
<TITLE>XYZ Company: Modify a Product</TITLE>
```

and

```
<h1>The new record looks like this:</h1>
```

The entire admin_domodrecord.php script could look something like this:

```php
<?
if ((!$_POST[isbn]) || (!$_POST[title]) || (!$_POST[price])) {
    header("Location: http://www.yourserver.com/admin_addrecord.php");
    exit;
}
// Check to see if $_SERVER[PHP_AUTH_USER] already contains info
if (!isset($_SERVER[PHP_AUTH_USER])) {
    // If empty, send header causing dialog box to appear
    header('WWW-Authenticate: Basic realm="XYZ Company Admin"');
    header('HTTP/1.0 401 Unauthorized');
    echo 'Authorization Required.';
    exit;
} else {
    // If not empty, do something else
    // Try to validate against hard-coded values
    if (($_SERVER[PHP_AUTH_USER] != "admin") ||
        ($_SERVER[PHP_AUTH_PW] != "abc123")) {
        header('WWW-Authenticate: Basic realm="XYZ Company Admin"');
        header('HTTP/1.0 401 Unauthorized');
        echo 'Authorization Required.';
        exit;
    } else {
        // create connection; substitute your own information!
        $conn = mysql_connect("localhost","joeuser","34Nhjp")
            or die(mysql_error());
        // select database; substitute your own database name
        $db = mysql_select_db("MyDB", $conn) or die(mysql_error());
        // formulate and execute the query
        $sql = "UPDATE MASTER_PRODUCTS SET ISBN = '$_POST[isbn]',
        TITLE = '$_POST[title]', AUTHOR = '$_POST[author]',
        PUBLISHER = '$_POST[publisher]', CATEGORY = '$_POST[category]',
        TYPE = '$_POST[type]', INFO_BLURB = '$_POST[info_blurb]',
        PAGE_NUM = '$_POST[page_num]', PRICE = '$_POST[price]'
        WHERE ID = '$_POST[id]'";
        $result = mysql_query($sql) or die (mysql_error());
```

```
        if (isset($result)) {
            echo "<HTML>
            <HEAD>
            <TITLE>XYZ Company: Modify a Product</TITLE>
            </HEAD>
            <BODY>
            <h1>The new record looks like this:</h1>
            <P><strong>ISBN:</strong> ".stripslashes($_POST[isbn])."
            <P><strong>Title:</strong> ".stripslashes($_POST[title])."
            <P><strong>Author:</strong>
            ".stripslashes($_POST[author])."
    <P><strong>Publisher:</strong>
            ".stripslashes($_POST[publisher])."
            <strong>Category:</strong>
            ".stripslashes($_POST[category])."
            <strong>Type:</strong> ".stripslashes($_POST[type])."
            <P><strong>Description:</strong><br>
            ".stripslashes($_POST[info_blurb])."
            <P><strong>Page Count:</strong>
             ".stripslashes($_POST[page_num])."
            <P><strong>Price:</strong>  ".stripslashes($_POST[price])."
            <P align=center><a href=\"admin_menu.php\">Return to M
            enu</a></p>
            </BODY>
            </HTML>";
        } else {
            echo "Some sort of error has occurred!</p>";
        }
    }
}
?>
```

Place this file on your Web server and go back to the form at http://www.
yourserver.com/admin_modrecord.php. Select a product to modify, and make
some changes to its record. If successful, you should see a verification screen such
as the one shown in Figure 7.6.

Use this sequence of forms to modify any records you need to change in the
MASTER_PRODUCTS table. The next section shows you the final step in a basic product administration menu: deleting a record.

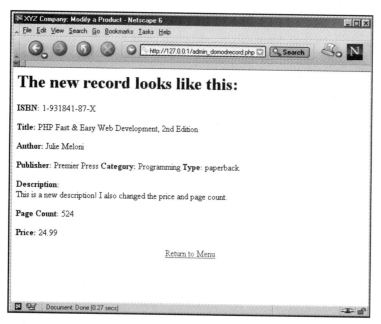

FIGURE 7.6 *Verification of product modifications*

Deleting Records from the Product Catalog

During the course of business, products are sometimes discontinued for one reason or another. A good administration menu will account for this by offering a Delete Product option. The following three-step sequence gives you that option in your administration menu.

The first step is to select a product for deletion, using virtually the same code you used to select a product for modification. Copy admin_modrecord.php to admin_delrecord.php, and open it in your text editor. The very basic changes are as follows:

Change the title to

```
<TITLE>XYZ Company: Delete a Product</TITLE>
```

and change the form action to

```
<FORM method=\"POST\" action=\"admin_showdelrecord.php\">
```

and change the button to

```
<P align=center><INPUT type=\"submit\" value=\"Select this Product\"></p>
```

Those are the only changes you'll need to make, so I won't repeat all that code here. Place this file on your Web server, and click on the Delete an Existing Product link on the initial administration menu. If you are authorized, you should see the product selection form in Figure 7.7, which you've seen before.

The next step in the form sequence will display the selected record as a confirmation before acting on a delete command. The script, admin_showdelrecord.php, is very similar to admin_showmodrecord.php in that it selects the contents of the record and displays them to the user. The difference lies in the fact that the information does not prepopulate a form. Instead, the script just displays the information on the screen.

Copy admin_showmodrecord.php to admin_showdelrecord.php, and open it in your text editor. The first modification is part of the if statement that checks required fields. The redirection that occurs if a required value is not present should be something like this:

```
//check for required field
if (!$_POST[sel_record]) {
        header("Location: http://www.yourcompany.com/admin_delrecord.php");
        exit;
}
```

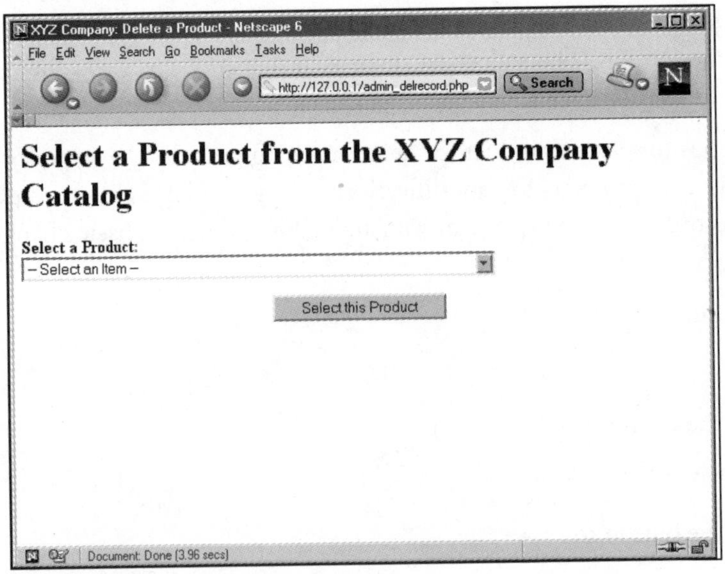

FIGURE 7.7 *Select an item to delete*

The next changes are in the HTML. Change the title to

```
<TITLE>XYZ Company: Delete a Product</TITLE>
```

and the heading to

```
<h1>Do you wish to delete this product?</h1>
```

and the form action to

```
<FORM method=\"POST\" action=\"admin_dodelrecord.php\">
```

Add a hidden field to identify the record to be deleted:

```
<input type=\"hidden\" name=\"id\" value=\"$id\">
```

Next, instead of printing a form with input fields, simply print the item headings followed by the values from the database for that particular item. Finish up by changing the form submission button to

```
<p align=center><INPUT type=\"submit\" value=\"Delete Product\"></p>
```

The entire code for admin_dodelrecord.php should look something like this:

```
<?
//check for required field
if (!$_POST[sel_record]) {
        header("Location: http://www.yourcompany.com/admin_delrecord.php");
        exit;
}
// Made it trhough, so authenticate.
// Check to see if $_SERVER[PHP_AUTH_USER] already contains info
if (!isset($_SERVER[PHP_AUTH_USER])) {
        // If empty, send header causing dialog box to appear
        header('WWW-Authenticate: Basic realm="XYZ Company Admin"');
        header('HTTP/1.0 401 Unauthorized');
        echo 'Authorization Required.';
        exit;
} else {
        // If not empty, do something else
        // Try to validate against hard-coded values
        if (($_SERVER[PHP_AUTH_USER] != "admin") ||
        ($_SERVER[PHP_AUTH_PW] != "abc123")) {
```

```php
        header('WWW-Authenticate: Basic realm="XYZ Company Admin"');
        header('HTTP/1.0 401 Unauthorized');
        echo 'Authorization Required.';
        exit;
} else {
        // create connection; substitute your own information!
        $conn = mysql_connect("localhost","joeuser","34Nhjp")
                or die(mysql_error());
        // select database; substitute your own database name
        $db = mysql_select_db("MyDB", $conn) or die(mysql_error());
        //SQL statement to select information
        $sql = "SELECT * FROM MASTER_PRODUCTS WHERE
                ID = '$_POST[sel_record]'";
        // execute SQL query and get result
        $sql_result = mysql_query($sql) or die (mysql_error());
        if (!$sql_result) {
                echo "Something has gone wrong!";
        } else {
                //loop through record and get values
                while ($record = mysql_fetch_array($sql_result)) {
                        $id = $record['ID'];
                        $isbn = stripslashes($record['ISBN']);
                        $title = stripslashes($record['TITLE']);
                        $author = stripslashes($record['AUTHOR']);
                        $publisher = $record['PUBLISHER'];
                        $category = $record['CATEGORY'];
                        $type = $record['TYPE'];
                        $info_blurb = stripslashes(
                        $record['INFO_BLURB']);
                        $page_num = stripslashes($record['PAGE_NUM']);
                        $price = stripslashes($record['PRICE']);
                }
                echo "<HTML>
                <HEAD>
                <TITLE>XYZ Company: Delete a Product</TITLE>
                </HEAD>
```

```
<BODY>
<h1>Do you wish to delete this product?</h1>
<FORM method=\"POST\"
action=\"admin_dodelrecord.php\">
<input type=\"hidden\" name=\"id\" value=\"$id\">
<P><strong>ISBN:</strong> $isbn
<P><strong>Title:</strong> $title
<P><strong>Author:</strong> $author
<P><strong>Publisher:</strong> $publisher
<strong>Category:</strong> $category
<strong>Type:</strong> $type
<P><strong>Description:</strong><br>
$info_blurb
<P><strong>Page Count:</strong> $page_num
<P><strong>Price:</strong> $price
<p align=center><INPUT type=\"submit\"
value=\"Delete Product\"></p>
</FORM>
</BODY>
</HTML>";
            }
        }
    }
?>
```

Place this file on your Web server and choose a product by selecting an option in admin_delrecord.php and clicking on the Select Product button. The confirmation should appear, as shown in Figure 7.8.

The final step in the deletion sequence is to actually issue the DELETE command and return a confirmation to the user. This script, called admin_dodelrecord.php, has all the trappings of other scripts in this series, the only difference being in the SQL statement and the HTML displayed on the screen.

Copy admin_delrecord.php to admin_dodelrecord.php and open it in your text editor. The first modification is to the SQL statement. Instead of using the SELECT command, you'll use DELETE:

```
$sql = "DELETE FROM MASTER_PRODUCTS WHERE ID = \"$_POST[id]\"";
```

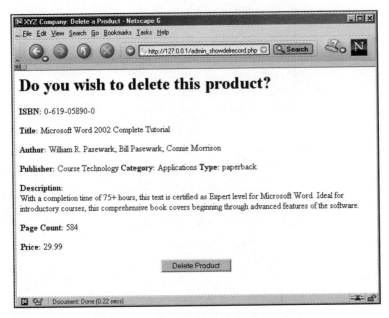

FIGURE 7.8 *Display product information to verify deletion*

The final difference is the confirmation that's returned to the user. Change the heading to something like this:

```
<h1>Product deleted.</h1>
```

and remove the form-related code, so that the entire code looks something like this:

```
<?
// Check to see if $_SERVER[PHP_AUTH_USER] already contains info
if (!isset($_SERVER[PHP_AUTH_USER])) {
    // If empty, send header causing dialog box to appear
    header('WWW-Authenticate: Basic realm="XYZ Company Admin"');
    header('HTTP/1.0 401 Unauthorized');
    echo 'Authorization Required.';
    exit;
} else {
    // If not empty, do something else
```

```
// Try to validate against hard-coded values
if (($_SERVER[PHP_AUTH_USER] != "admin") ||
        ($_SERVER[PHP_AUTH_PW] != "abc123")) {
        header('WWW-Authenticate: Basic realm="XYZ Company Admin"');
        header('HTTP/1.0 401 Unauthorized');
        echo 'Authorization Required.';
        exit;
} else {
        // create connection; substitute your own information!
        $conn = mysql_connect("localhost","joeuser","34Nhjp")
        or die(mysql_error());
        // select database; substitute your own database name
        $db = mysql_select_db("MyDB", $conn) or die(mysql_error());
        //SQL statement to delete item
        $sql = "DELETE FROM MASTER_PRODUCTS WHERE ID = \"$_POST[id]\"";
        // execute SQL query and get result
        $sql_result = mysql_query($sql) or die (mysql_error());
        if (!$sql_result) {
                echo "Something has gone wrong!";
        } else {
                echo "<HTML>
                <HEAD>
                <TITLE>XYZ Company: Delete a Product</TITLE>
                </HEAD>
                <BODY>
                <h1>Product deleted.</h1>
                </BODY>
                </HTML>";
        }
    }
}
?>
```

Place this file on your Web server and go back to the selection form. Select a product to delete, confirm your action, then press the button to delete the record once and for all. You should see a result screen such as the one shown in Figure 7.9.

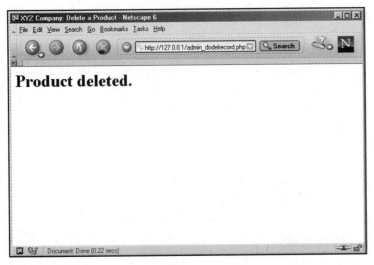

FIGURE 7.9 *Deletion confirmed!*

You now have the ability to perform basic administration tasks within a product catalog. Now you can move on to creating a functioning e-commerce Web site with the catalog.

Safe and Secure Shopping

It should be obvious that no matter how large or small your storefront might be, if it operates in an insecure environment, you have a problem. The legal liability aspects differ from country to country, but without a doubt, the bulk of the responsibility lies with you, the site designer, to develop a safe and secure application. For example, any transaction of personal information—especially credit card information—should be performed over a secure connection. Similarly, try to make use of real-time credit card processing rather than storing information (which would then necessitate encryption of that information) on your own system.

Let's take a moment from the development of your shopping system to talk about security. In this environment, you should know all the ins and outs of SSL, or Secure Sockets Layer, before you even think about creating a working storefront.

Becoming SSL-Enabled

When using SSL, you specify that you want to connect to a server using SSL by replacing http with https in the protocol component of a URL. What happens from that point on is essentially a lot of great mathematics, or encryption.

Encryption is the process of converting a plain text message into a new, encrypted message, or *ciphertext*. This activity usually involves a key; if both sender and recipient have different, complementary keys (as in SSL-based transactions), the process is called *asymmetric* or *public key* cryptography. The SSL protocol uses public key cryptography in an initial handshake phase to securely exchange symmetric keys that can then be used to encrypt the communication.

SSL uses digital certificates to authenticate both parties participating in the communication—in this case the browser and the server. Such certificates are signed by a trusted third party authority, which certifies that the information is correct. Examples of such third party authorities are Thawte (http://www.thawte.com/) and Verisign (http://www.verisign.com/).

Enabling SSL

Enabling SSL on the server side does entail some modifications to your server setup that are not covered in this book. For instance, to enable SSL support in Apache, you must compile the mod_ssl Apache module in addition to installing the OpenSSL libraries. You can find more information about these items at http://www.modssl.org/ and http://www.openssl.org/, respectively.

To enable SSL on other Web servers, consult your server documentation. But remember, enabling SSL is only one piece of the puzzle—you need that SSL certificate!

Credit Card Processing and Store Checkout Procedures

As this chapter deals with the fundamental aspects of building an online shopping system, the "How do I get paid?" portion is obviously important. Several commerce methods exist with which users can pay for the purchases in their shopping cart, and the "right" method for you will depend on how your business is structured. For example, merchant credit card accounts through banking institutions often require you to have a business license, a reseller's permit, and other documentation proving you're a legitimate business. If you're simply a person who has a few items to sell, you may not want to go through all of that paperwork. In that case, you do still have options, such as using a third-party method like PayPal for completing monetary transactions.

But for the most part, a legitimate business performing online commerce-based transactions will be doing so with merchant credit card accounts. If you have obtained a merchant account through your bank, you can use real-time payment services such as Verisign's PayFlo Pro. PHP has a built-in set of functions that, when used with the PayFlo libraries from Verisign, allows you to create a simple script to handle credit card transactions. You can learn more about PayFlo Pro at the Verisign Web site, at http://www.verisign.com/products/payflow/pro/index.html. The PHP manual section for PayFlo functions is at http://www.php.net/manual/en/ref.pfpro.php.

Creating a Basic Shopping System

With inventory items happily existing in the database tables created previously in this chapter, you can now display your products online within a shopping environment, and allow people to put these items in a shopping cart. The remainder of this chapter will take you through the process of creating storefront menus and tracking selected items, in preparation for checkout.

Displaying Your Product Catalog

Unlike with the administration menu created in the previous chapter, you don't have to worry about PHP authentication code at the beginning of every page of your store. However, as you'll be tracking, per user, items in a shopping cart, you'll want to start/enable a session using session_start() at the beginning of each script.

Let's jump right into creating the storefront menu. For the sake of brevity, we'll use two types of pre-sorted user views:

- ◆ View Products by Category
- ◆ View Products Alphabetically By Title

You can present user views of your catalog, based on any information found in your table. For example, you could show all items sorted alphabetically by author, publisher, price, and so forth.

Open your text editor, create a file called shop_menu.php, and add the session_start() function at the beginning. Next, create a basic HTML menu containing the two menu items. Use the file name shop_viewbycat.php for the first link and shop_viewalpha.php for the second link.

The code for this little menu should look something like this:

```
<? session_start(); ?>
<HTML>
<HEAD>
<TITLE>XYZ Company Shopping Menu</TITLE>
</HEAD>
<BODY>
<h1>XYZ Company Shopping Menu</h1>
<p>Select an option:</p>
<ul>
<li><a href="shop_viewbycat.php">View Products by Category</a>
<li><a href="shop_viewalpha.php">View All Products Alphabetically</a>
</ul>
</BODY>
</HTML>
```

Now that you've built the menu, it's time to build the pages behind it, starting with View Products by Category. Create a file called shop_viewbycat.php and add the session_start() function, followed by the basic MySQL connection code you've been using throughout the book.

The goal of this script is to display the name of each category that contains books, followed by links to the books themselves. The PHP code snippet, with SQL query, for this portion of the script would look something like this:

```
// formulate and execute the query
$getCats = "SELECT DISTINCT CATEGORY FROM MASTER_PRODUCTS ORDER BY CATEGORY"
$getCats_res = mysql_query($getCats) or die (mysql_error());

if (@mysql_num_rows($getCats_res) < 1)) {
        $display_block = "<P>Sorry, no categories exist!</p>";
} else {
        //categories exist, so get them and then get information
        while ($cat_row = @mysql_fetch_array($getCats_res)) {
```

```
$category = stripslashes($cat_row['CATEGORY']);

//now start the display_block and then get items
$display_block  .= "<P><strong>$category</strong></p>
<ul>";

$getItems = "SELECT ID, TITLE, AUTHOR FROM MASTER_PRODUCTS WHERE
CATEGORY = '$category' ORDER BY TITLE";
$getItems_res = @mysql_query($getItems_res)  or die (mysql_error());

while ($item_row = @mysql_fetch_array($getItems_res)) {
        $id = $item_row['ID'];
        $title = stripslashes($item_row['TITLE']);
        $author = stripslashes($item_row['AUTHOR']);
        $display_block .= "<li><a href=\"shop_iteminfo.php?id=$id\">
        <strong>$title</strong></a> <em>(by $author)</em>";
}
$display_block .= "</ul>";
}
}
```

If you follow along with the code, you'll see that it performs two basic looping actions, both of which you've seen before. The result of these actions is a text string called $display_block, which you will stick in the middle of your basic HTML template:

```
<HTML>
<HEAD>
<TITLE>XYZ Company Shopping Menu: View by Category</TITLE>
</HEAD>
<BODY>
<h1>XYZ Company Shopping : Category List</h1>
<? echo "$display_block"; ?>
</BODY>
</HTML>
```

Put all of your code together and you have something like this:

```
<?
//start a session
session_start();

// create connection; substitute your own information!
$conn = mysql_connect("localhost","joeuser","34Nhjp") or die(mysql_error());

// select database; substitute your own database name
$db = mysql_select_db("MyDB", $conn) or die(mysql_error());

// formulate and execute the query
$getCats = "SELECT DISTINCT CATEGORY FROM MASTER_PRODUCTS ORDER BY CATEGORY";
$getCats_res = mysql_query($getCats) or die (mysql_error());

if (@mysql_num_rows($getCats_res) < 1) {
        $display_block = "<P>Sorry, no categories exist!</p>";
} else {
        //categories exist, so get them and then get information
        while ($cat_row = @mysql_fetch_array($getCats_res)) {
                $category = stripslashes($cat_row['CATEGORY']);

                //now start the display_block and then get items
                $display_block  .= "<P><strong>$category</strong></p>
                <ul>";

                $getItems = "SELECT ID, TITLE, AUTHOR FROM MASTER_PRODUCTS
                        WHERE CATEGORY = '$category' ORDER BY TITLE";
                $getItems_res = @mysql_query($getItems)
                        or die (mysql_error());

                while ($item_row = @mysql_fetch_array($getItems_res)) {
                        $id = $item_row['ID'];
                        $title = stripslashes($item_row['TITLE']);
                        $author = stripslashes($item_row['AUTHOR']);
                        $display_block .= "<li>
```

```
                          <a href=\"shop_iteminfo.php?id=$id\">
                          <strong>$title</strong></a> <em>(by $author)</em>";
               }
               $display_block .= "</ul>";
       }
}
?>
<HTML>
<HEAD>
<TITLE>XYZ Company Shopping Menu: View by Category</TITLE>
</HEAD>
<BODY>
<h1>XYZ Company Shopping : Category List</h1>
<? echo "$display_block"; ?>
</BODY>
</HTML>
```

Save this file and place it on your Web server. Go to the main shopping menu and click on the View Products by Category link. You should see something like that in Figure 7.10.

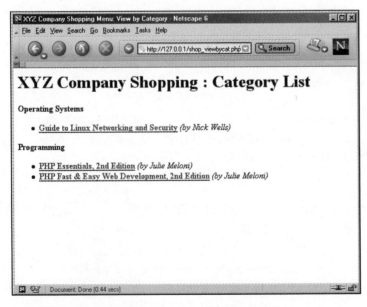

FIGURE 7.10 *XYZ Company products listed by category*

The second link on the main shopping menu goes to the View Products Alphabetically By Title script. This script looks a lot like the shop_viewbycat.php script, minus the outer loop. The "guts" of this script look something like this:

```
// formulate and execute the query
$getItems = "SELECT ID, TITLE, AUTHOR FROM MASTER_PRODUCTS ORDER BY TITLE";
$getItems_res = @mysql_query($getItems) or die (mysql_error());

if (@mysql_num_rows($getItems_res) < 1) {
        $display_block = "<P>Sorry, no items exist!</p>";
} else {
        //now start the display_block and then get items
        $display_block  .= "<ul>";
        while ($item_row = @mysql_fetch_array($getItems_res)) {
                $id = $item_row['ID'];
                $title = stripslashes($item_row['TITLE']);
                $author = stripslashes($item_row['AUTHOR']);
                $display_block .= "<li>
                        <a href=\"shop_iteminfo.php?id=$id\">
                        <strong>$title</strong></a> <em>(by $author)</em>";
        }
}
```

There's no need for an outer loop, as all you're doing is retrieving information on all records alphabetically, regardless of category. The entire script looks something like this:

```
<?
session_start();

// create connection; substitute your own information!
$conn = mysql_connect("localhost","joeuser","34Nhjp") or die(mysql_error());

// select database; substitute your own database name
$db = mysql_select_db("MyDB", $conn) or die(mysql_error());

// formulate and execute the query
$getItems = "SELECT ID, TITLE, AUTHOR FROM MASTER_PRODUCTS ORDER BY TITLE";
$getItems_res = @mysql_query($getItems) or die (mysql_error());
```

```php
if (@mysql_num_rows($getItems_res) < 1) {
        $display_block = "<P>Sorry, no items exist!</p>";
} else {
        //now start the display_block and then get items
        $display_block  .= "<ul>";

        while ($item_row = @mysql_fetch_array($getItems_res)) {
                $id = $item_row['ID'];
                $title = stripslashes($item_row['TITLE']);
                $author = stripslashes($item_row['AUTHOR']);
                $display_block .= "<li>
                        <a href=\"shop_iteminfo.php?id=$id\">
                        <strong>$title</strong></a> <em>(by $author)</em>";
        }
}
?>
<HTML>
<HEAD>
<TITLE>XYZ Company Shopping Menu: View Items Alphabetically</TITLE>
</HEAD>
<BODY>
<h1>XYZ Company Shopping : Alphabetical List</h1>
<? echo "$display_block"; ?>
</BODY>
</HTML>
```

Save this file and place it on your Web server. Go to the main shopping menu and click on the View All Products Alphabetically link. You should see something like that in Figure 7.11.

The last step in your catalog display code is the product details template, called shop_iteminfo.php. Open a text file with that name, start a session, and check for the all-important value for ID, which is passed in the query string of the link.

```php
<?
session_start();

if (!($_GET[id])) {
        header("Location: http://www.yourcompany.com/show_menu.php");
        exit;
}
```

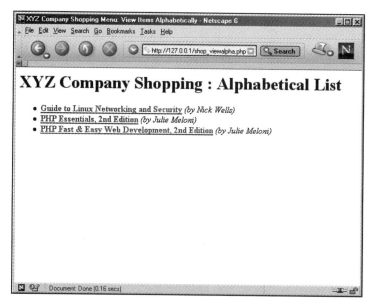

FIGURE 7.11 *All XYZ Company products listed alphabetically*

Next, add the database connectivity code and issue the following query, which is used to retrieve all fields for the selected record:

```
$sql = "SELECT * FROM MASTER_PRODUCTS WHERE ID = '$_GET[id]'";
```

Loop through the result set for this record, assigning names to the extracted information. You'll use these values to populate a display template, such as the following one:

```
<h1>XYZ Company Shopping : Book Details</h1>
<h2><? echo "$title"; ?></h2>
<P><? echo "$info_blurb"; ?></p>
<ul>
<li><strong>Author:</strong> <? echo "$author"; ?>
<li><strong>Publisher:</strong> <? echo "$publisher"; ?>
<li><strong>ISBN:</strong> <? echo "$isbn"; ?>
<li><strong>Category:</strong> <? echo "$category"; ?>
<li><strong>Type:</strong> <? echo "$type"; ?>
<li><strong>Number of Pages:</strong> <? echo "$page_num"; ?>
</ul>
<h3><font color="red">Only <? echo "\$ $price"; ?>!</font></h3>
```

As this is a shopping system, you'll want people to be able to purchase this item, so include the Add to Shopping Cart form for this item. Assume that the form action is called shop_addtocart.php, and use this as the form action:

```
<form method="post" action="shop_addtocart.php">
```

You'll also need to track the item, item title, item price, and quantity, so create hidden fields for the values you know (ID, title, price) and a text field for the value completed by the user (quantity):

```
<input type="hidden" name="sel_item" value="<? echo "$id"; ?>">
<input type="hidden" name="sel_item_title" value="<? echo "$title"; ?>">
<input type="hidden" name="sel_item_price" value="<? echo "$price"; ?>">
<em>Quantity:</em> <input type="text" name="sel_item_qty" value="1" size=3>
```

Add the submit button, and close the form:

```
<P><input type="submit" name="submit" value="Add to Shopping Cart"></p>
</form>
```

From start to finish, the product details template looks something like this:

```
<?
session_start();

if (!($_GET[id])) {
        header("Location: http://www.yourcompany.com/show_menu.php");
        exit;
}


// create connection; substitute your own information!
$conn = mysql_connect("localhost","joeuser","34Nhjp") or die(mysql_error());

// select database; substitute your own database name
$db = mysql_select_db("MyDB", $conn) or die(mysql_error());

// formulate and execute the query
$sql = "SELECT * FROM MASTER_PRODUCTS WHERE ID = '$_GET[id]'";
$result = @mysql_query($sql) or die(mysql_error());
```

```
if (@mysql_num_rows($result) < 1) {
        header("Location: http://www.yourcompany.com/show_menu.php");
        exit;
} else {
        while ($rec = @mysql_fetch_array($result)) {
                $isbn = $rec['ISBN'];
                $title = stripslashes($rec['TITLE']);
                $author = stripslashes($rec['AUTHOR']);
                $publisher = stripslashes($rec['PUBLISHER']);
                $category = stripslashes($rec['CATEGORY']);
                $type = stripslashes($rec['TYPE']);
                $info_blurb = stripslashes($rec['INFO_BLURB']);
                $page_num = $rec['PAGE_NUM'];
                $price = $rec['PRICE'];
        }
}
?>
<HTML>
<HEAD>
<TITLE>XYZ Company Shopping : Book Details</TITLE>
</HEAD>
<BODY>
<h1>XYZ Company Shopping : Book Details</h1>
<h2><? echo "$title"; ?></h2>
<P><? echo "$info_blurb"; ?></p>
<ul>
<li><strong>Author:</strong> <? echo "$author"; ?>
<li><strong>Publisher:</strong> <? echo "$publisher"; ?>
<li><strong>ISBN:</strong> <? echo "$isbn"; ?>
<li><strong>Category:</strong> <? echo "$category"; ?>
<li><strong>Type:</strong> <? echo "$type"; ?>
<li><strong>Number of Pages:</strong> <? echo "$page_num"; ?>
</ul>
<h3><font color="red">Only <? echo "\$ $price"; ?>!</font></h3>
<form method="post" action="shop_addtocart.php">
```

```
<input type="hidden" name="sel_item" value="<? echo "$id"; ?>">
<input type="hidden" name="sel_item_title" value="<? echo "$title"; ?>">
<input type="hidden" name="sel_item_price" value="<? echo "$price"; ?>">
<em>Quantity:</em> <input type="text" name="sel_item_qty" value="1" size=3>
<P><input type="submit" name="submit" value="Add to Shopping Cart"></p>
</form>
</BODY>
</HTML>
```

Save this file and place it on your Web server. Go back to your shopping menu and select an individual product to view. You should see something like Figure 7.12.

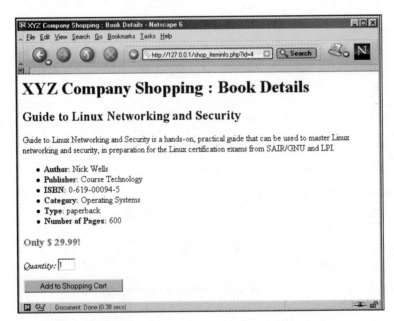

FIGURE 7.12 *Individual product display template*

The next section details how you can hold on to the items users add to their shopping carts, ultimately resulting in numerous orders, wealth, and fame. Well, maybe.

Tracking Your Users' Shopping Carts

To keep track of your users' shopping carts, first create a database table called something like USER_TRACK, with the following field attributes:

- ◆ ID int. A basic record ID.
- ◆ USER_ID varchar (32). Used to associate the entry with a user. The value is the session ID.
- ◆ SEL_ITEM int. The ID of the book added to the cart.
- ◆ SEL_ITEM_TITLE varchar (150). The title of the book added to the cart.
- ◆ SEL_ITEM_QTY tinyint. The quantity the user wants to purchase.
- ◆ SEL_ITEM_PRICE float. The single-item price of the item the user has added to the cart.
- ◆ DATE_ADDED date. The date the item was added to the cart.

You can use the three-step process from Chapter 3 to create the USER_TRACK table for XYZ Company, or you can manually type a CREATE TABLE command through your MySQL interface of choice. The ID field will be a primary key, automatically incremented by MySQL when a new record is inserted. The actual SQL command for the USER_TRACK table would be.

```
CREATE TABLE USER_TRACK (
        ID int not null primary key auto_increment,
        USER_ID varchar(32),
        SEL_ITEM int,
        SEL_ITEM_TITLE varchar(150),
        SEL_ITEM_QTY tinyint,
        SEL_ITEM_PRICE float,
        DATE_ADDED date
);
```

If you look at the description of the table using the MySQL DESCRIBE command, it looks like this:

```
+-----------------+----------------+------+------+----------+-----------------+
| Field           | Type           | Null | Key  | Default  | Extra           |
+-----------------+----------------+------+------+----------+-----------------+
| ID              | int(11)        |      | PRI  | NULL     | auto_increment  |
| USER_ID         | varchar(32)    | YES  |      | NULL     |                 |
| SEL_ITEM        | int(11)        | YES  |      | NULL     |                 |
| SEL_ITEM_TITLE  | varchar(150)   | YES  |      | NULL     |                 |
| SEL_ITEM_QTY    | tinyint(4)     | YES  |      | NULL     |                 |
| SEL_ITEM_PRICE  | float          | YES  |      | NULL     |                 |
| DATE_ADDED      | date           | YES  |      | NULL     |                 |
+-----------------+----------------+------+------+----------+-----------------+
```

With your table all ready and waiting, you can make the script called shop_addtocart.php, which will insert records into this table. Open your text editor, start a session, and check for required fields:

```
if ((!($_POST[sel_item])) || (!($_POST[sel_item_title])) ||
(!($_POST[sel_item_qty])) || (!($_POST[sel_item_price]))) {
        header("Location: http://www.yourcompany.com/show_menu.php");
        exit;
}
```

Add the standard database connection code, and then issue the SQL statement for inserting the shopping cart item:

```
$sql = "INSERT INTO USER_TRACK VALUES('', '$_SERVER[PHPSESSID]',
'$_POST[sel_item]', '$_POST[$sel_item_title]', '$_POST[sel_item_qty]',
'$_POST[sel_item_price]', now())";
@mysql_query($sql) or die(mysql_error());
```

 NOTE

The MySQL now() function is for adding the current date to the given field.

Finally, display a confirmation to the user:

```
<HTML>
<HEAD>
<TITLE>XYZ Company Shopping: Product Added to Cart</TITLE>
</HEAD>
<BODY>
<h1>XYZ Company Shopping : Product Added to Cart</h1>
<p><strong>You have added the following item to your shopping cart:</strong></p>
<P><strong>Item:</strong> <? echo "$_POST[sel_item_title]"; ?><br>
<strong>Quantity:</strong> <? echo "$_POST[sel_item_qty]"; ?><br>
<strong>Single Unit Price:</strong> <? echo "$_POST[sel_item_price]"; ?><br>
<strong>Total Price:</strong> <?echo ($_POST[sel_item_price] *
$_POST[sel_item_qty]); ?></p>
<P><a href="shop_menu.php">Continue Shopping</a></p>
</BODY>
</HTML>
```

Put it all together, and you have a script something like this:

```
<?
session_start();

if ((!($_POST[sel_item])) || (!($_POST[sel_item_title])) ||
(!($_POST[sel_item_qty])) || (!($_POST[sel_item_price]))) {
        header("Location: http://www.yourcompany.com/show_menu.php");
        exit;
}


// create connection; substitute your own information!
$conn = mysql_connect("localhost","joeuser","34Nhjp") or die(mysql_error());

// select database; substitute your own database name
$db = mysql_select_db("MyDB", $conn) or die(mysql_error());

$sql = "INSERT INTO USER_TRACK VALUES('', '$_SERVER[PHPSESSID]',
'$_POST[sel_item]', '$_POST[$sel_item_title]', '$_POST[sel_item_qty]',
'$_POST[sel_item_price]', now())";
@mysql_query($sql) or die(mysql_error());
```

```
?>
<HTML>
<HEAD>
<TITLE>XYZ Company Shopping: Product Added to Cart</TITLE>
</HEAD>
<BODY>
<h1>XYZ Company Shopping : Product Added to Cart</h1>
<p><strong>You have added the following item to your shopping cart:</strong></p>
<P><strong>Item:</strong> <? echo "$_POST[sel_item_title]"; ?><br>
<strong>Quantity:</strong> <? echo "$_POST[sel_item_qty]"; ?><br>
<strong>Single Unit Price:</strong> <? echo "$_POST[sel_item_price]"; ?><br>
<strong>Total Price:</strong> <?echo ($_POST[sel_item_price] *
$_POST[sel_item_qty]); ?></p>
<P><a href="shop_menu.php">Continue Shopping</a></p>
</BODY>
</HTML>
```

Go through the shopping menu system again, and use the Add to Shopping Cart button on an individual product page. You should see something like what is shown in Figure 7.13.

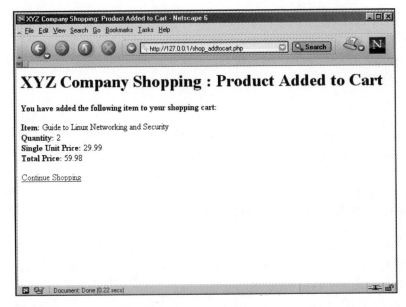

FIGURE 7.13 *Product added to cart: user confirmation*

Users can now continue through your shopping site, merrily adding items. But why should you leave it up to your consumers to remember how many items they've put in their shopping carts, when you have those handy SQL mathematical functions? The next section provides a short piece of code that will make your site look cool by always showing the number of items in the cart. Plus, you'll add the link to the checkout form.

Counting the Cart Items

If you plan to show the current user's shopping cart count on every page, be sure to place this sort of query *after* any code that adds to the cart.

The SQL statement and query functions are pretty straightforward:

```
$item_count = "SELECT SUM(SEL_ITEM_QTY) AS cart_total FROM USER_TRACK WHERE
USER_ID = '$_SERVER[PHPSESSID]'";
$item_result = @mysql_query($item_count) or die(mysql_error());
$item_count_total = @mysql_result($item_result,0,"cart_total");
```

Note the use of the sum() function instead of the count() function. You could use count(), but what if a user has ordered two copies of one book? Instead of showing two items in the cart, count() would return 1, as it's two copies of one item.

It may be tricky to find a space on your page in which to show the total number of items in the cart, but when you do, you could just say this:

```
<P>Your cart contains
<?
if ($item_count_total == "1") {
        echo "1 item.";
} else {
        echo "$item_count_total items.";
}
?>
```

Add a link to the checkout form, called shop_checkout.php

```
You can <a href="shop_checkout.php">checkout</a> at any time.</p>
```

The shop_addtocart.php script from the previous section, with the shopping cart count and display code added, looks something like this:

```
<?
session_start();

if ((!($_POST[sel_item])) || (!($_POST[sel_item_title])) ||
(!($_POST[sel_item_qty])) || (!($_POST[sel_item_price]))) {
        header("Location: http://www.yourcompany.com/show_menu.php");
        exit;
}

// create connection; substitute your own information!
$conn = mysql_connect("localhost","joeuser","34Nhjp") or die(mysql_error());

// select database; substitute your own database name
$db = mysql_select_db("MyDB", $conn) or die(mysql_error());

$sql = "INSERT INTO USER_TRACK VALUES('', '$_SERVER[PHPSESSID]',
'$_POST[sel_item]', '$_POST[$sel_item_title]', '$_POST[sel_item_qty]',
'$_POST[sel_item_price]', now())";
@mysql_query($sql) or die(mysql_error());

$item_count = "SELECT SUM(SEL_ITEM_QTY) AS cart_total FROM USER_TRACK WHERE
USER_ID = '$_SERVER[PHPSESSID]'";
$item_result = @mysql_query($item_count) or die(mysql_error());
$item_count_total = @mysql_result($item_result,0,"cart_total");
?>
<HTML>
<HEAD>
<TITLE>XYZ Company Shopping: Product Added to Cart</TITLE>
</HEAD>
<BODY>
<h1>XYZ Company Shopping : Product Added to Cart</h1>
<p><strong>You have added the following item to your shopping cart:</strong></p>
<P><strong>Item:</strong> <? echo "$_POST[sel_item_title]"; ?><br>
<strong>Quantity:</strong> <? echo "$_POST[sel_item_qty]"; ?><br>
<strong>Single Unit Price:</strong> <? echo "$_POST[sel_item_price]"; ?><br>
```

```
<strong>Total Price:</strong> <?echo ($_POST[sel_item_price] *
$_POST[sel_item_qty]); ?></p>
<P>Your cart contains
<?
if ($item_count_total == "1") {
        echo "1 item.";
} else {
        echo "$item_count_total items.";
}
?>
<br>You can <a href="shop_checkout.php">checkout</a> at any time.</p>
<P><a href="shop_menu.php">Continue Shopping</a></p>
</BODY>
</HTML>
```

Now, when you add a product to your shopping cart, the page looks something like Figure 7.14.

If you can successfully add products to your shopping cart, there's only one more step to go before fame and fortune is yours: checking out!

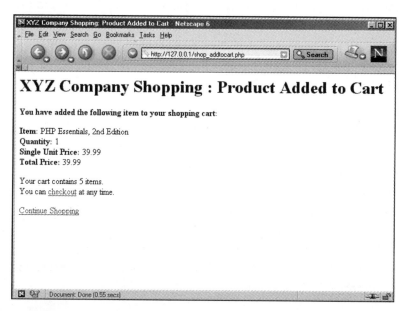

FIGURE 7.14 *Product added to cart: show total cart items*

When It's Checkout Time

In the previous section, you added a checkout link called shop_checkout.php. You're on your own when it comes to creating that file, but rest assured that you already know enough about PHP to make something work. The reason this book does not go into detail and provide code for performing the checkout process from your online store is because there are simply too many variables (and no best way) to make a generic script that works for everyone in all situations. However, your checkout script might very well follow a path like this:

1. Total the items, then add tax (if applicable) and shipping costs. This gives you the total amount to authorize from the user's credit card.

2. Perform credit card authorization for the total amount. Note that you are not storing the card number anywhere on your own system!

3. You will receive either a success or failure response from your card processing routine. If the response is a failure, then print a message to the user and end the transaction. If the response is a success, continue to Step 4.

4. Write the basic order information to a database table created to hold such information. Include the authorization code you will receive upon the successful authorization, and get the ID value of this record using the mysql_insert_id() function.

5. For each item in the order, insert a record into a database table designed to hold line items. Each record will reference the ID of the master order, gathered in the previous step.

6. Delete the shopping cart items for this user.

7. Display the order information—with authorization code in place of the credit card information—on the screen, so that the user can print it and hold it as a receipt. You can also send this information via e-mail to the user.

Each of the steps listed above—with the exception of the actual payment authorization code—contain the same simple bits of PHP code you've been using throughout this book. No matter which processing method you decide on, you already know the basic code needed to make the method work—you simply have to bring it all together on your own.

Chapter 8

**Advanced PHP
Techniques:
Working with
Images**

You can use the built-in image-related functions of PHP to do marvelous and myriad things with images, whether it's creating new images on-the-fly or manipulating static images you already have on your system. The many, many image-related functions are well documented in the PHP Manual, at http://www.php.net/manual/en/ref.image.php.

In this chapter, you'll learn the basics of creating and manipulating images using PHP functions.

Installation and Configuration Requirements

Beginning with version 4.3.0, PHP includes a bundled version of Thomas Boutell's GD graphics library. This eliminates one step in the installation and configuration process, but if you're using an earlier version of PHP, you will have to do a little more work before tackling the scripts in this chapter.

If you are using a version of PHP earlier than 4.3.0, go to the Boutell Web site at http://www.boutell.com/gd/ and download the source of the GD library. Follow the instructions included with that software, and consult its manual if you have difficulties with the installation.

To enable GD, Linux/UNIX users must add the following to the `configure` parameters:

```
--with-gd=[path to GD directory]
```

 NOTE

If you are using the bundled version, you can omit the `[path to GD directory]` portion of the parameter.

After running the configure program again, go through the `make` and `make install` process as you did in Chapter 1. Windows users who want to enable GD simply have to activate php_gd2.dll as an extension in the php.ini file.

After making changes to PHP or the php.ini file, restart your Web server and look at the output of the `phpinfo()` function. You should see a section called "gd", and you're looking for something that says "GD support enabled."

By simply installing GD, or using the bundled library, you are limited to working with files in GIF format. However, by installing additional libraries, you can work with JPEG and PNG files as well.

◆ Find JPEG library information at ftp://ftp.uu.net/graphics/jpeg/.

◆ Find PNG library information at http://www.libpng.org/pub/png/libpng.html. To work with PNG files, you also need to install the zlib library, found at http://www.gzip.org/zlib/.

Follow the instructions at these sites to install the libraries. Then Linux/ UNIX users must re-configure PHP by adding the following to the `configure` parameters:

```
--with-jpeg-dir=[path to jpeg directory]
```

and/or

```
--with-png-dir=[path to PNG directory]
--with-zlib=[path to zlib directory]
```

After running the `configure` program again, go through the `make` and `make install` process, then restart your Web server so the new PHP module is activated. Look again at your `phpinfo()` output, and you should see that your additional libraries have been enabled. For instance, in the "gd" section, you'll see "JPEG support enabled" if you successfully used `--with-jpeg-dir` at configuration time.

With GD and its accompanying libraries installed, you can move on to learning about the basic image functions in PHP.

Creating New Images

With a function called imagecreate() in its repertoire, you might imagine that creating a new image with PHP is just a one-line program. Unfortunately it isn't, but it's not an exceptionally difficult process, either. Building an image is a stepwise process, using a few different functions. If you think about what an image contains—a size, a shape, colors, and so forth—you can deduce that the steps used to programmatically create an image are along those lines.

In this lesson, you'll just create some basic images with different colors and text—nothing too dramatic. Creating an image does begin with the imagecreate() function, but all this function does is set aside a canvas area for your new image. For example, to create an image that is 250 pixels wide by 100 pixels high, use

```
$im = imagecreate(250,100);
```

Having a canvas ready for you is all well and good, but next you have to define your colors and actually do some filling. Colors are defined through the imgcolorallocate() function using the RGB (red, green, blue) values. For example:

```
$black = imagecolorallocate ($im, 0, 0, 0);
$white = imagecolorallocate ($im, 255, 255, 255);
$red = imagecolorallocate ($im, 255, 0, 0);
$green = imagecolorallocate ($im, 0, 255, 0);
$blue = imagecolorallocate ($im, 0, 0, 255);
```

 NOTE

The first allocated color is used as the background color of the image. In this case, the background color will be black.

You now have a palette of five colors you can use on the $im canvas. Next, you can use one or more of the many drawing functions to indicate an area that should then be filled with one of the pre-defined colors.

◆ imagearc() is used to draw a partial ellipse.

◆ imageellipse() is used to draw an ellipse.

◆ imageline() is used to draw a line.

- `imagepolygon()` is used to draw a polygon.
- `imagerectangle()` is used to draw a rectangle.

These functions use x and y coordinates as indicators of where to start drawing on your canvas. To draw a red rectangle on your canvas beginning at the point (0, 0) and going for 20 pixels horizontally and 25 pixels vertically, you would use the `imagerectangle()` function like so:

```
imagerectangle($im, 0, 0, 20, 25, $red);
```

Next, draw another rectangle of the same size and in white, beginning at the x,y point where the previous rectangle stopped:

```
imagerectangle($im, 20, 25, 40, 50, $white);
```

To output this stream of image data to the screen, you must first send the appropriate `header()` function, using the mime type of the image being created. Then, use the `imagegif()`, `imagejpeg()`, or `imagepng()` functions as appropriate to output the data stream. For example:

```
header ("Content-type: image/jpeg");
imagejpeg ($im);
```

Finally, use the `imagedestroy()` function just to clear up the memory used by the `imagecreate()` function. You should now have a little script that looks something like this:

```
<?
$im = imagecreate (50, 100);

$black = imagecolorallocate ($im, 0, 0, 0);
$white = imagecolorallocate ($im, 255, 255, 255);
$red = imagecolorallocate ($im, 255, 0, 0);
$green = imagecolorallocate ($im, 0, 255, 0);
$blue = imagecolorallocate ($im, 0, 0, 255);

imagerectangle($im, 0, 0, 20, 25, $red);
imagerectangle($im, 20, 25, 40, 50, $white);

header ("Content-type: image/jpeg");
imagejpeg ($im);
```

```
imagedestroy($im);
?>
```

You're not yet using the other allocated colors in this particular image, but you will be shortly. For now, if you save this script as image1.php and access it with your Web browser, you'll see something like Figure 8.1 (except it'll be in color!).

You may notice that these rectangles are simply outlines. In fact, PHP has image functions called imagefilledarc(), imagefilledellipse(), imagefilledpolygon(), and imagefilledrectangle(), which are used exactly like their non-filled counterparts. The difference is in the output, as you'll see in Figure 8.2. The script resulting in this output uses imagefilledrectangle() in place of imagerectangle().

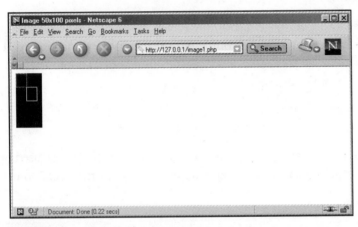

FIGURE 8.1 *Basic rectangles*

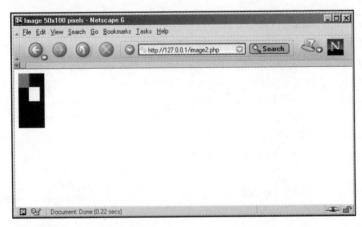

FIGURE 8.2 *Filled rectangles*

Pie Chart Example

Granted, the previous examples were somewhat boring, but think of the process that is in place—all the shapes that are created and filled are delineated by numbers, as well as by starting and ending points. You can also use this same sequence of events (define boundaries, fill shapes) to create charts and graphs from sets of data. For example, you can create pie charts, as shown in this code:

```
<?
$im = imagecreate (100, 100);

$white = imagecolorallocate($im, 255, 255, 255);
$red = imagecolorallocate($im, 255, 0, 0);
$green = imagecolorallocate($im, 0, 255, 0);
$blue = imagecolorallocate($im, 0, 0, 255);

imagefilledarc ($im, 50, 50, 100, 50, 0, 90, $red, IMG_ARC_PIE);
imagefilledarc ($im, 50, 50, 100, 50, 91, 180 , $green, IMG_ARC_PIE);
imagefilledarc ($im, 50, 50, 100, 50, 181, 360 , $blue, IMG_ARC_PIE);

header ("Content-type: image/jpg");
imagejpg ($im);
imagedestroy($im);
?>
```

With the exception of the `imagefilledarc()` function calls, this should look very familiar to you. Looking closely at the `imagefilledarc()` function, you can see that it takes several arguments:

- Image identifier
- Partial ellipse centered at x
- Partial ellipse centered at y
- Partial ellipse width
- Partial ellipse height
- Partial ellipse start point
- Partial ellipse end point
- Color
- Style

Check out the following code:

```
imagefilledarc ($im, 50, 50, 100, 50, 181, 360 , $blue, IMG_ARC_PIE);
```

This code says to begin the arc at point (50,50) and give it a width of 100 and a height of 50. The start point (think of degrees) is 181 and the end is 360. The arc should be filled with the defined color $blue and use the IMG_ARC_PIE style. IMG_ARC_PIE is one of several built-in styles that are used in the display; this one says to create a rounded edge.

All of this code produces the example you see in Figure 8.3.

Now, to get really tricky and give the pie a 3D appearance, define three more colors (for the edge), which can be either lighter or darker, as long as they contrast. For example:

```
$lt_red = imagecolorallocate($im, 255, 100, 100);
$lt_green = imagecolorallocate($im, 100, 255, 100);
$lt_blue = imagecolorallocate($im, 100, 100, 255);
```

Next, add a for loop, which makes a bunch of little arcs at the points (50,60) to (50,51), using the lighter colors as fill colors.

```
for ($i = 60;$i > 50;$i--) {
        imagefilledarc ($im, 50, $i, 100, 50, 0, 90, $lt_red, IMG_ARC_PIE);
        imagefilledarc ($im, 50, $i, 100, 50, 91, 180, $lt_green, IMG_ARC_PIE);
        imagefilledarc ($im, 50, $i, 100, 50, 181, 360, $lt_blue, IMG_ARC_PIE);
}
```

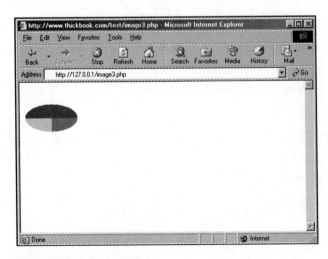

FIGURE 8.3 *Basic pie chart*

Your new code might look like this:

```
<?
$im = imagecreate (100, 100);

$white = imagecolorallocate($im, 255, 255, 255);
$red = imagecolorallocate($im, 255, 0, 0);
$green = imagecolorallocate($im, 0, 255, 0);
$blue = imagecolorallocate($im, 0, 0, 255);
$lt_red = imagecolorallocate($im, 255, 100, 100);
$lt_green = imagecolorallocate($im, 100, 255, 100);
$lt_blue = imagecolorallocate($im, 100, 100, 255);

for ($i = 60;$i > 50;$i--) {
        imagefilledarc ($im, 50, $i, 100, 50, 0, 90, $lt_red, IMG_ARC_PIE);
        imagefilledarc ($im, 50, $i, 100, 50, 91, 180, $lt_green, IMG_ARC_PIE);
        imagefilledarc ($im, 50, $i, 100, 50, 181, 360, $lt_blue, IMG_ARC_PIE);
}

imagefilledarc ($im, 50, 50, 100, 50, 0, 90, $red, IMG_ARC_PIE);
imagefilledarc ($im, 50, 50, 100, 50, 91, 180 , $green, IMG_ARC_PIE);
imagefilledarc ($im, 50, 50, 100, 50, 181, 360 , $blue, IMG_ARC_PIE);

header ("Content-type: image/jpg");
imagejpg ($im);
imagedestroy($im);
?>
```

Save this file and place it on your Web server, and then load the file in your browser. Figure 8.4 shows the output of this script, and you can see the 3D effect in the image.

These examples are just very basic examples that show the power of the image drawing and filling functions. In the next section, you'll learn how to slice and dice existing images.

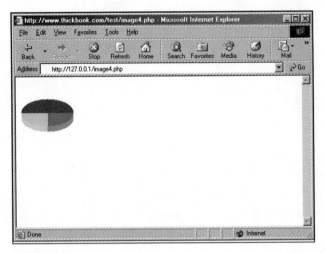

FIGURE 8.4 *A 3D pie chart*

Working with Existing Images

The process of creating images from other images follows the same essential steps as creating a new image—the difference lies in what acts as the image canvas. In the previous section, you created a new canvas using the imagecreate() function. When creating an image from a new image, you'll use the imagecreatefrom...() functions.

You can create images from existing GIFs, JPEGs, PNGs, and plenty of other image types. The functions used to create images from these formats are called imagecreatefromgif(), imagecreatefromjpg(), imagecreatefrompng(), and so forth. In the next example you'll see how easy it is to create a new image from an existing one. The base image is shown in Figure 8.5.

The following code shows you how to create the new canvas from the base image, allocate the color $white to the image, and draw three filled ellipses at a point on the image, as shown in Figure 8.6.

```
<?
$im = imagecreatefromjpeg ("baseimage.jpg");

$white = imagecolorallocate ($im, 255, 255, 255);

imagefilledellipse($im, 75, 70, 20, 20, $white);
```

```
imagefilledellipse($im, 150, 70, 20, 20, $white);
imagefilledellipse($im, 225, 70, 20, 20, $white);

header("Content-type: image/jpeg");
imagejpeg($im);
?>
```

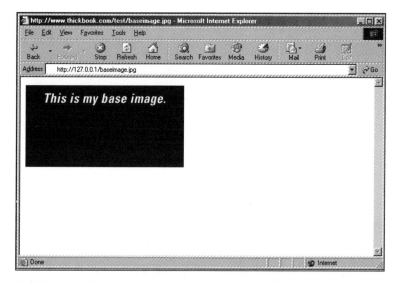

FIGURE 8.5 *The base image from which you'll create other images*

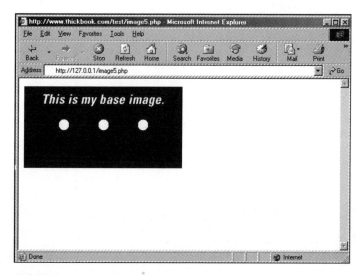

FIGURE 8.6 *New image with ellipses*

If you can contain your excitement, take a look at the next code, which takes this process a few steps forward and utilizes some different image modification functions.

In Figure 8.7, you can see four PNG images—differently colored (just take my word for it) triangular slices on a gray background.

In this example, the gray was defined as an alpha channel when the PNG was created (not using PHP, although you could). The goal of this code is to stack these slices on top of one another, blending them together at each step so that the alpha channel becomes transparent and the bottom image shows through.

First, select one image as a base image, in this case `sqaure1a.png`:

```
$baseimage = ImageCreateFromPNG("square1a.png");
```

Next, blend the bottom image:

```
ImageAlphaBlending($baseimage, true);
```

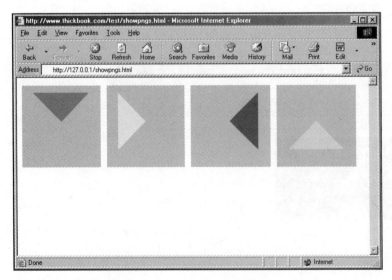

FIGURE 8.7 *PNG slices*

Repeat the process for the second sqaure:

```
$image2 = ImageCreateFromPNG("square1b.png");
ImageAlphaBlending($image2, true);
```

But now copy this second image stream to the first image stream:

```
ImageCopy($baseimage, $image2, 0, 0, 0, 0, 150, 150);
```

Repeat the process with the remaining two slices, and then output the image stream. Your code should look something like this:

```
<?
$baseimage = ImageCreateFromPNG("square1a.png");
ImageAlphaBlending($baseimage, true);

$image2 = ImageCreateFromPNG("square1b.png");
ImageAlphaBlending($image2, true);
ImageCopy($baseimage, $image2, 0, 0, 0, 0, 150, 150);

$image3 = ImageCreateFromPNG("square1c.png");
ImageAlphaBlending($image3, true);
ImageCopy($baseimage, $image3, 0, 0, 0, 0, 150, 150);

$image4 = ImageCreateFromPNG("square1d.png");
ImageAlphaBlending($image4, true);
ImageCopy($baseimage, $image4, 0, 0, 0, 0, 150, 150);

header("Content-type: image/png");
ImagePNG($baseimage);
?>
```

The resulting image is shown in Figure 8.8, you'll note that it doesn't have the gray background surrounding the colored areas, as those have been alpha-blended away.

If you had instead plopped these images on top of each other without blending the alpha channel, you would have ended up with what's shown in Figure 8.9, which is just the fourth image sitting on top of the others. You can't see the others, as they're obscured by the top image, which has no transparent parts.

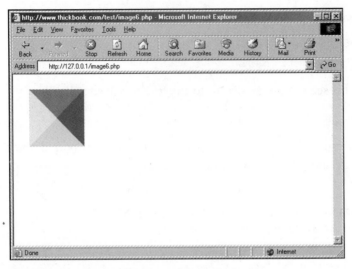

FIGURE 8-8 *Copying images with alpha blending*

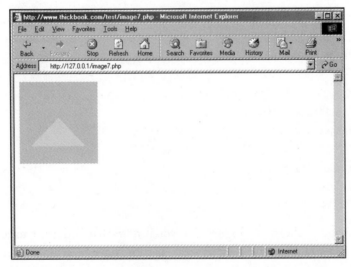

FIGURE 8.9 *Copying images without alpha blending*

Expanding Your Image-Related Knowledge

I cannot stress enough the importance of reading the Image Functions section of the PHP Manual, at http://www.php.net/manual/en/ref.image.php. This chapter has given you only a brief introduction to the basics of creating and manipulating images with PHP, and in no way has it taught you everything there is to know—far from it!

As with almost everything in programming, understanding the process is the first step in applying the methods. You've learned that you must have a drawing canvas—be it a blank canvas or a canvas consisting of an existing image. You've also learned that you must allocate colors to the image, and that all things image-related come in steps. Study the processes and do a lot of trial-and-error with creating things like pie charts, bar graphs, resized images, and so forth. That's really the best way to learn image creation—by practicing the small parts.

Additionally, you may find it interesting and useful to read the nuts and bolts information about the underlying libraries, such as the GD Graphics library and the JPEG and PNG libraries. Also, keep up on the browser support for image functions; for example, PNGs are not supported by all browsers, but are used to create much better images than GIFs and even JPEGs, in some instances. Such information is especially useful when determining the types of graphics you'll use PHP to create for your intended audience.

Chapter 9

This short chapter will introduce the basic concepts of working with XML and PHP, but in no way should this be considered a definitive guide on the subject! There are entire books written on XML, and, in fact, entire books written on the pairing of XML and PHP. Use this chapter as a primer for a subject you may decide to explore further on your own.

XML Overview

The name XML comes from the full name of the language, Extensible Markup Language. Although "markup" is in its name, do not think of XML like you do HTML, because aside from the fact that both languages are based on tag pairs, there are no similarities. At its core, XML is a method of data exchange, in that it holds well-defined content within its boundaries. HTML, on the other hand, couldn't care less what is contained in the content or how it is structured—its only purpose is to display the content to the browser. XML is used to define and carry the content, while HTML is used to make it "pretty."

This is not to say that XML data cannot be made pretty, or that you cannot display XML data in your Web browser. You can, in fact, do so, using Extensible Style Language (XSL) and Cascading Style Sheets (CSS) to transform the content into a browser-renderable format while still preserving the content categorization. For example, say you have an area on your Web site reserved for recent system messages, and those items each contain the following:

- title
- message
- author
- date of message

The HTML used to display this information may have the title in bold tags, the message inside paragraph containers, the author's name in italics and the date in a small font. XML, on the other hand, is more concerned with knowing that there are four distinct content elements. The categorization of content is crucial to data exchange—by separating the data and its structure from the presentation elements, you can use the content however you wish, and are not limited to the particular marked-up style that static HTML has forced on you.

Basic XML Document Structure

Before moving forward into working with XML documents, you need to know exactly how to create them! XML documents contain two major elements, the prolog and the body. The *prolog* contains the XML declaration statement (much like an HTML document type definition statement), and any processing instructions and comments you may want to add. In this example, you'll just use the declaration statement and a comment.

 NOTE

For a complete definition of XML documents, read the XML Specification at http://www.w3.org/TR/REC-xml.

Using the system message example from the previous section, you'll create a file called `messages.xml` and begin it with

```
<?xml version="1.0" ?>
<!--Sample XML document -->
```

In the declaration, only the version is required, but you can also add an `encoding` value and a `standalone` value. For example:

```
<?xml version="1.0" encoding="UTF-8" standalone="yes" ?>
```

All the fun begins in the body area of the document, where the content structure is contained. XML is hierarchical in nature. Think of it like a book—a book has a title, and it contains chapters, each of which contain paragraphs, and so forth. There is only one root element in an XML document—using the book example, the element may be called `Book` and the tags `<Book></Book>` surround all other information.

Using the system messages example, call the element `SystemMessage` and add an open tag to your messages.xml document:

```
<SystemMessage>
```

Next, add all subsequent elements—called *children*—to your document. In this example, you need title, body, author, and date information. Create children elements called `MessageTitle`, `MessageBody`, `MessageAuthor`, and `MessageDate`. But wait a minute—for the author information, what if you want both the name and an email address? Not a problem—you just create another set of child elements within your parent element (which just happens to be a child element of the root element):

```
<MessageAuthor>
<MessageAuthorName>Joe SystemGod</MessageAuthorName>
<MessageAuthorEmail>systemgod@someserver.com</MessageAuthorEmail>
</MessageAuthor>
```

All in all, your messages.xml document could look like this:

```
<?xml version="1.0" ?>
<!--Sample XML document -->
<SystemMessage>
        <MessageTitle>System Down for Maintenance</MessageTitle>
        <MessageBody>This system will be going down for maintenance between 3am
and 5am GMT on February 10th.</MessageBody>
        <MessageAuthor>
                <MessageAuthorName>Joe SystemGod</MessageAuthorName>

                <MessageAuthorEmail>systemgod@someserver.com</MessageAuthorEmail>
        </MessageAuthor>
        <MessageDate>Feb 8th, 2003</MessageDate>
</SystemMessage>
```

Here are two very important rules to keep in mind for creating valid XML documents:

◆ XML is case-sensitive. `<Book>` and `<book>` are different elements.

◆ All XML tags must be properly closed. XML tags must be properly nested, and no overlapping tags are allowed.

Put the messages.xml file (or one like it) on your Web server for use in later examples. As a side note, if you have the Microsoft Internet Explorer Web browser, you can actually view your XML document in a tree-like format. This browser uses an internal stylesheet to provide a default tree view of valid XML documents. Figures 9.1 and 9.2 show the original view (all elements opened), as well as a view with the `MessageAuthor` element collapsed.

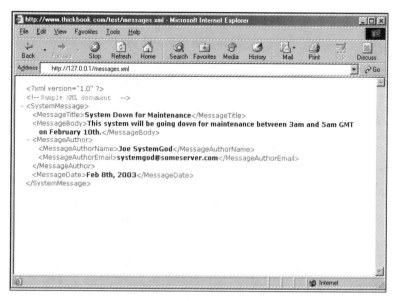

FIGURE 9.1 *All XML elements displayed*

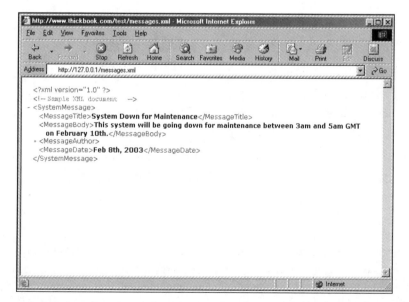

FIGURE 9.2 *One collapsed element*

XML and Traditional Databases

Based on the description of XML given so far, a natural question is, "Is XML a database?" This is a very good question indeed. The simple answer is "sort of," but that's not really a technical explanation. If a database is defined simply as a collection of data, then sure—XML is a database because it categorizes and holds information in a centralized place.

When compared to a database management system, such as MySQL, Oracle, Microsoft SQL Server, and so forth, the differences become obvious. XML stores categorized content, you can interface with it (as we will do in this chapter), and you can move it from location to location. However, as XML is simply a text file residing on your file system, it does not have the efficiency, security, and accessibility that the traditional database system has.

For more on XML and databases—the pros, cons, differences and so forth—go to http://www.rpbourret.com/xml/index.htm, where a man named Ronald Bourret has posted some exceptional introductory documents. For the remainder of this chapter, just focus on XML being used as a portable data container.

Preparing to Use XML with PHP

The XML extension for PHP uses the `expat` library to work with XML documents. XML functionality is enabled by default at the time of PHP configuration and installation; if you're using version of Apache greater than 1.3.9 (and you should be!), the bundled `expat` library will be used.

However, Linux/UNIX users who want to use a different version of `expat` can get it from http://sourceforge.net/projects/expat/ and then add the following to the PHP configure parameters:

```
--with-expat-dir=[path to expat directory]
```

After running the configure program again, go through the `make` and `make install` process as you did in Chapter 1. Then restart your Web server and look at the output of the `phpinfo()` function. You should see a section called "xml," and you're looking for something that says "xml support active."

Windows users, regardless of Web server software, have no changes to make, as XML support is built into the Windows version of PHP.

Once XML support is enabled, you can move on to parsing, transforming, and even generating XML using PHP. All of the examples used in this chapter are very basic, and again I recommend you do a great deal of reading on your own if you're interested in working with XML to any great extent.

Parsing XML

In this section, you'll see a few examples of how PHP can parse a valid XML document using the messages.xml file created earlier in this chapter. These examples do not provide earth-shattering functionality, and in fact are simply annotated versions of code found in the PHP Manual. However, these very basic scripts exemplify the stepwise methods used to parse XML files with PHP; for anything beyond this, please investigate on your own. As with everything in this book, it's all about gaining a foundation!

The first example script, called parse.php, will simply open an XML document, parse it, and display back the names of the entities. If your file is not a valid XML document, this script will throw an error, indicating the line number and reason.

First, assign the name of the file to a variable called $filename, because you'll use it more than once. Then, create an array called $depth. The $depth array is used to hold the parser's place as it goes through your XML file in a linear fashion.

```
$filename = "messages.xml";
$depth = array();
```

Next, create two functions called startElement() and endElement(). These functions can really be called anything you want, but they are used to find and display the beginning and end of the current element as the parser goes though the XML file, hence the suggested names.

```
function startElement($parser, $name, $attributes) {
    global $depth;
    for ($i = 0; $i < $depth[$parser]; $i++) {
        echo " ";
    }
    echo "$name<br>\n";
    $depth[$parser]++;
}
```

In the startElement() function above, the $depth array is listed as a global variable because its value is used in various places in the script, not just in that particular function. Next, a for loop goes through and, for each element start tag, echoes a bit of white space to the screen, followed by the name of the element. The index value of the $depth array is incremented as it moves on.

Next, the endElement() function simply decrements the index value of the $depth array, as the parser moves through the file:

```
function endElement($parser, $name) {
    global $depth;
    $depth[$parser]--;
}
```

Neither of these functions do anything on their own; they are set up at the beginning of the PHP script and used during the actual XML parsing process, which you will now write. First, call the xml_parser_create() function to create a new parser. In this case the reference is stored in a variable called $xml_parser.

```
$xml_parser = xml_parser_create();
```

Next, use the xml_set_element_handler() function to define the functions that will handle opening and closing tags in the XML document—not surprisingly, these are the startElement() and endElement() functions you just created:

```
xml_set_element_handler($xml_parser, "startElement", "endElement");
```

The next step is to open the XML file and start a while loop that reads the data from the XML file you just opened:

```
$fp = fopen("$filename", "r") or die("Couldn't open XML file.");
while ($data = fread($fp, filesize ($filename))) {
```

Inside the while loop, use the xml_parse() function to do the actual parsing of the data stream for the entire length of the file. The die() function uses a couple of XML-related functions to get useful information (the error and the line number) and display it back to you should an error occur.

```
//parse the data using the parser we opened above
xml_parse($xml_parser, $data, feof($fp)) or die(sprintf("XML error: %s at line
%d", xml_error_string(xml_get_error_code($xml_parser)),
xml_get_current_line_number($xml_parser)));
```

After closing the `while` loop, close the file that you opened for reading and free the memory used by the XML parser:

```
fclose($fp);
xml_parser_free($xml_parser);
```

The complete parse.php script looks something like this:

```
<?
$filename = "messages.xml";
$depth = array();


function startElement($parser, $name, $attributes) {
    global $depth;
    for ($i = 0; $i < $depth[$parser]; $i++) {
        echo " ";
    }
    echo "$name<br>\n";
    $depth[$parser]++;
}


function endElement($parser, $name) {
    global $depth;
    $depth[$parser]--;
}



//create a new parser
$xml_parser = xml_parser_create();
//tell php which functions handle opening and closing tags
xml_set_element_handler($xml_parser, "startElement", "endElement");
//open the XML file for reading
$fp = fopen("$filename", "r") or die("Couldn't open XML file.");
//read the XML file
while ($data = fread($fp, filesize ($filename))) {
    //parse the data using the parser we opened above
    xml_parse($xml_parser, $data, feof($fp)) or die(sprintf("XML error: %s at
line %d", xml_error_string(xml_get_error_code($xml_parser)),
xml_get_current_line_number($xml_parser)));
```

```
}
//close the XML file
fclose($fp);
//free up memory
xml_parser_free($xml_parser);
?>
```

If you place this file and the messages.xml document on your Web server and access it with your Web browser, you'll see something like Figure 9.3—all of your XML elements are displayed.

If you change something in messages.xml and break a rule for XML validity, you can invoke the error message in your script. If you do something like delete the ending tag for the MessageAuthor element, you will get a "mismatched tag" error, as shown in Figure 9.4.

The parse.php script shows the absolute basics of reading an XML document and determining the start and end tags for each element. To take this concept further, the next section shows you how to map XML elements to specific HTML markup, eventually displaying the information in presentation formation.

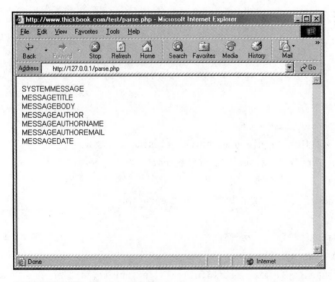

FIGURE 9.3 *All of the XML elements in messages.xml*

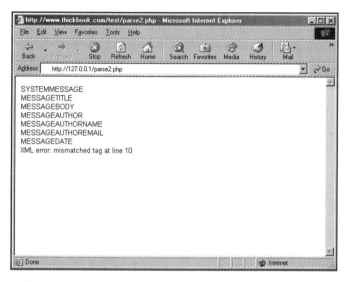

FIGURE 9.4 *Missing end tag error*

Parse and Display Content from XML Files

You've already seen much of the code for this section in the parse.php file. In this section, the markup.php script will read the messages.xml file and map HTML markup to XML elements, eventually displaying what you'd normally see in a Web browser. As such, we'll go through the new elements step by step, and assume you have a handle on the similar features.

After defining $filename as "messages.xml", set up two arrays which map specific XML elements to both opening and closing HTML markup tags.

```
$filename = "messages.xml";
$startTags = array(
"MESSAGETITLE" => "<P><strong>",
"MESSAGEBODY" => "<p>",
"MESSAGEAUTHOR" => "<p>Added by: ",
"MESSAGEAUTHORNAME" => "<em>",
"MESSAGEAUTHOREMAIL" => "<em>(",
"MESSAGEDATE" => "<font size=-1>on "
```

```
);

$endTags = array(
"MESSAGETITLE" => "</strong><br>",
"MESSAGEBODY" => "</p>",
"MESSAGEAUTHORNAME" => "</em>",
"MESSAGEAUTHOREMAIL" => ")</em>",
"MESSAGEDATE" => "</font>",
);
```

These two arrays are pretty self-explanatory; the $startTags array includes the HTML markup, which will be printed when the XML parser comes across an element whose name matches a key in the array. Similarly, the $endTags array will be used to close up the HTML markup for each mapped XML element. You can see this functionality in the startElement() and endElement() functions:

```
function startElement($parser, $name, $attrs) {
        global $startTags;
        // if XML element is a $startTags key, print its markup
        if ($startTags[$name]) {
                echo $startTags[$name];
        }
}


function endElement($parser, $name) {
        global $endTags;
        // if XML element is a $endTags key, print its markup
        if ($endTags[$name]) {
                echo $endTags[$name];
        }
}
```

For example, when the parser comes across the opening MESSAGETITLE XML element, it will print <P>, and when it comes across the ending MESSAGETITLE XML element, it will print <br>. But this leaves the important part—the MESSAGETITLE content itself—out of the equation! So, create a function called characterData(), which will print the XML content for that element:

```
function characterData($parser, $data) {
            echo $data;
}
```

Now comes the series of xml_* PHP functions that make this script work. You've seen these before:

```
$xml_parser = xml_parser_create();
xml_set_element_handler($xml_parser, "startElement", "endElement");
```

The next function is a new one, and it's used to interpret the content of the XML element, using the characterData() function you defined above:

```
xml_set_character_data_handler($xml_parser, "characterData");
```

The script wraps up with the reading/parsing code you've seen before, so that the entire markup.php script looks something like this:

```
<?
$filename = "messages.xml";
$startTags = array(
"MESSAGETITLE" => "<P><strong>",
"MESSAGEBODY" => "<p>",
"MESSAGEAUTHOR" => "<p>Added by: ",
"MESSAGEAUTHORNAME" => "<em>",
"MESSAGEAUTHOREMAIL" => "<em>(",
"MESSAGEDATE" => "<font size=-1>on "
);
$endTags = array(
"MESSAGETITLE" => "</strong><br>",
"MESSAGEBODY" => "</p>",
"MESSAGEAUTHORNAME" => "</em>",
"MESSAGEAUTHOREMAIL" => ")</em>",
"MESSAGEDATE" => "</font>",
);
function startElement($parser, $name, $attrs) {
          global $startTags;
          // if XML element is a $startTags key, print its markup
          if ($startTags[$name])  {
```

```
                echo $startTags[$name];
        }
}
function endElement($parser, $name) {
        global $endTags;
        // if XML element is a $endTags key, print its markup
        if ($endTags[$name])    {
                echo $endTags[$name];
        }
}
function characterData($parser, $data) {
        echo $data;
}
//create a new parser
$xml_parser = xml_parser_create();
//tell php which functions handle opening and closing tags
xml_set_element_handler($xml_parser, "startElement", "endElement");
//tell php which function handles the data inside the tags
xml_set_character_data_handler($xml_parser, "characterData");
//open the XML file for reading
$fp = fopen("$filename", "r") or die("Couldn't open XML file.");
//read the XML file
while ($data = fread($fp, filesize ($filename))) {
    //parse the data using the parser we opened above
    xml_parse($xml_parser, $data, feof($fp)) or die(sprintf("XML error: %s at
line %d", xml_error_string(xml_get_error_code($xml_parser)),
xml_get_current_line_number($xml_parser)));
}
//close the XML file
fclose($fp);
//free up memory
xml_parser_free($xml_parser);
?>
```

If you place this file and the messages.xml document on your Web server and access it with your Web browser, you'll see something like Figure 9.5, with each element marked up as mapped!

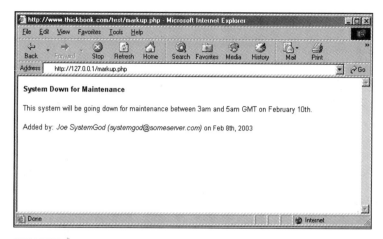

FIGURE 9.5 *Mapped XML content*

Both the parse.php and markup.php scripts show the absolute basics of reading an XML document and working with its content. To take this concept further, have a look at the examples in the PHP Manual, or at the numerous tutorials available at PHP-related developer Web sites.

Appendix A

Essential PHP Language Reference

This appendix is by no means a copy of the PHP Manual (found at http://www.php.net/manual/), which is absolutely huge and contains user-submitted comments and code samples. Instead, this appendix serves as an "essential" reference—it contains the elements of PHP which (in my opinion) you can't live without. The PHP Development Team and all of the documentation contributors have done a wonderful job with the entire PHP Manual, and there's no need to reinvent the wheel. However, since this appendix touches on only a small percentage of all there is to know about PHP, check the PHP Manual before asking a question on one of the PHP mailing lists.

PHP Syntax

To combine PHP code with HTML, the PHP code must be *escaped*, or set apart, from the HTML. The PHP engine will consider anything within the tag pairs shown in Table A.1 PHP code.

Table A.1 Basic PHP Syntax

Opening Tag	Closing Tag
`<?php`	`?>`
`<?`	`?>`
`<script language="php">`	`</script>`

Here's an example that uses all three in the same script, called `tagtest.php`:

```
<HTML>
<HEAD>
<TITLE>Tag Test</TITLE>
</HEAD>
<BODY>
<?php echo "I am using the first tag pair type.<br>"; ?>
```

```
<? echo "I am using the second tag pair type.<br>"; ?>
<script language="php">
echo "I am using the third tag pair type.<br>";
</script>
</BODY>
</HTML>
```

When accessed, the script displays this in your browser:

I am using the first tag pair type.

I am using the second tag pair type.

I am using the third tag pair type.

When you create PHP scripts, you're creating a series of instructions that are sent to the PHP engine. Each instruction must end with a semicolon (;), also known as an instruction separator.

These are examples of properly terminated instructions:

```
<?php
        echo "<P>Hello World! I'm using PHP!</P>\n";
        echo "<P>This is another message.</P>";
?>
```

One of these instructions is missing a semicolon:

```
<?php
        echo "<P>Hello World! I'm using PHP!</p>\n"
        echo "<P>This is another message.</p>";
?>
```

so it will produce a nasty error, such as this:

```
Parse error: parse error, expecting "," or ";" in /path/to/script on line 9
```

The last important bit of PHP syntax is the method of commenting inside code. Use double forward slashes (//) to indicate a comment:

```
<?php
        // The next statement prints a line of text
        echo "<P>Hello World! I'm using PHP!</P>\n"
?>
```

The comment "The next statement prints a line of text" is visible in your source code but is not printed in your HTML output.

For multi-line comments, you can surround your text with /* and */, like this:

```php
<?php
        /* This is a really long comment that
        will run onto multiple lines */
?>
```

Commenting code is a good habit to have, because it helps other programmers figure out what you're trying to do with a piece of code if they have to make changes or if they're trying to learn from your work.

Variables

You create variables to represent data. For instance, the following variable holds a value for sales tax:

```php
$sales_tax = 0.0875;
```

This variable holds a SQL statement:

```php
$sql = "SELECT * FROM MY_TABLE";
```

You can refer to the value of other variables when determining the value of a new variable:

```php
$tax_total = $sales_tax * $sub_total;
```

The following are true of variable names:

- They begin with a dollar sign ($).
- They cannot begin with a numeric character.
- They can contain numbers and the underscore character (_).
- They are case-sensitive.

Here are some common variable types:

- floats
- integers
- strings

These types are determined by PHP, based on the context in which they appear.

Floats

Each of the following variables is a float, or floating-point number. Floats are also known as "numbers with decimal points."

```
$a = 1.552;
$b = 0.964;
$sales_tax = 0.875;
```

Integers

Integers are positive or negative whole numbers, zero, or "numbers without decimal points." Each of the following variables is an integer.

```
$a = 15;
$b = -521;
```

Strings

A series of characters grouped within double quotes is considered a string:

```
$a = "I am a string.";
$b = "<P>This book is <strong>cool</strong>!";
```

You can also reference other variables within your string, which will be replaced when your script is executed. For example:

```
$num = 57; // an integer
$my_string = "I read this book $num times!"; // a string
```

When you run the script, $my_string will become "I read this book 57 times!"

Variables from HTML Forms

Depending on the method of your HTML form (GET or POST), the variables will be part of the $_POST or $_GET superglobal associative array. The name of the input field will become the name of the variable. For example, when a form is sent using the POST method, the following input field produces the variable $_POST[first_name]:

```
<input type="text" name="first_name" size="20">
```

If the method of this form were GET, this variable would be $_GET[first_name].

Variables from Cookies

Like variables from forms, variables from cookies are kept in a superglobal associative array called $_COOKIE. If you set a cookie called user with a value of Joe Smith, like so:

```
SetCookie ("user", "Joe Smith", time()+3600);
```

a variable called user is placed in $_COOKIE, with a value of Joe Smith. You then refer to $_COOKIE[user] to get that value.

Environment Variables

When a Web browser makes a request of a Web server, it sends along with the request a list of extra variables called *environment variables*. They can be very useful for displaying dynamic content or authorizing users.

By default, environment variables are available to PHP scripts as $VAR_NAME. However, to be absolutely sure that you're reading the correct value, you can use the getenv() function to assign a value to a variable of your choice. Following are some common environment variables:

REMOTE_ADDR gets the IP address of the machine making the request. For example:

```
<?php
        $remote_address = getenv("REMOTE_ADDR");
        echo "Your IP address is $remote_address.";
?>
```

HTTP_USER_AGENT gets the browser type, browser version, language encoding, and platform. For example:

```
<?php
        $browser_type = getenv("HTTP_USER_AGENT");
        echo "You are using $browser_type.";
?>
```

For a list of HTTP environment variables and their descriptions, visit http://hoohoo.ncsa.uiuc.edu/cgi/env.html.

Arrays

Simply put, arrays are sets of variables that are contained as a group. In the following example, $fave_colors is an array that contains strings representing array elements. In this case, the array elements (0 to 3) are names of colors.

```
$fave_colors[0] = "red";
$fave_colors[1] = "blue";
$fave_colors[2] = "black";
$fave_colors[3] = "white";
```

Array elements are counted with 0 as the first position in the numerical index.

Operators

An operator is a symbol that represents a specific action. For example, the + arithmetic operator adds two values, and the = assignment operator assigns a value to a variable.

Arithmetic Operators

Arithmetic operators bear a striking resemblance to simple math, as shown in Table A.2. In the examples, $a = 5 and $b = 4.

Table A.2 Arithmetic Operators

Operator	Name	Example
+	addition	$c = $a + $b; // $c = 9
−	subtraction	$c = $a - $b; // $c = 1
*	multiplication	$c = $a * $b; // $c = 20
/	division	$c = $a / $b; // $c = 1.25
%	modulus, or "remainder"	$c = $a % $b; // $c = 1

Assignment Operators

The = sign is the basic assignment operator:

```
$a = 124; // the value of $a is 124
```

Other assignment operators include +=, -=, and .=.

```
$ex += 1; // Assigns the value of ($ex + 1) to $ex.
          // If $ex = 2, then the value of ($ex += 1) is 3.
$ex -= 1; // Assigns the value of ($ex - 1) to $ex.
          // If $ex = 2, then the value of ($ex -= 1) is 1.
$ex .= "coffee";  // Concatenates (adds to) a string. If $ex = "I like "
// then the value of ($ex .= "coffee") is "I like coffee".
```

Comparison Operators

It should come as no surprise that comparison operators compare two values. A value of true or false is returned by the comparison, as shown in Table A.3.

Table A.3 Comparison Operators

Operator	Name	Example	Result (T/F)
==	equal to	$a == $b	TRUE if $a is equal to $b
!=	not equal to	$a != $b	TRUE if $a is not equal to $b
>	greater than	$a > $b	TRUE if $a is greater than $b
<	less than	$a < $b	TRUE if $a is less than $b
>=	greater than or equal to	$a >= $b	TRUE if $a is greater than or equal to $b
<=	less than or equal to	$a <= $b	TRUE if $a is less than or equal to $b

Increment/Decrement Operators

The increment/decrement operators do just what their name implies: add or subtract from a variable (see Table A.4).

Table A.4 Increment/Decrement Operators

Name	Usage	Result
++$a	Pre-increment	Increments by 1 and returns $a
$a++	Post-increment	Returns $a and then increments $a by 1
--$a	Pre-decrement	Decrements by 1 and returns $a
$a--	Post-decrement	Returns $a and then decrements $a by 1

Logical Operators

Logical operators allow your script to determine the status of conditions and, in the context of your if...else or while statements, execute certain code based on which conditions are true and which are false (see Table A.5).

Table A.5 Logical Operators

Operator	Name	Example	Result (T/F)
!	not	!$a	TRUE if $a is not true
&&	and	$a && $b	TRUE if both $a and $b are true
||	or	$a || $b	TRUE if either $a or $b is true

Control Structures

Programs are essentially a series of statements. Control structures, as their name implies, control how those statements are executed. Control structures are usually built around a series of conditions, such as "If the sky is blue, go outside and play." In this example, the condition is "If the sky is blue" and the statement is "go outside and play."

Control structures utilize curly braces ({ and }) to separate the groups of statements from the remainder of the program. Examples of common control structures follow; memorizing these will make your life much easier.

if...elseif...else

The if...elseif...else construct executes a statement based on the value of the expression being tested. In the following sample if statement, the expression being tested is "$a is equal to 10."

```
if ($a == "10") {
        // execute some code
}
```

After $a is evaluated, if it is found to have a value of 10 (that is, if the condition is true), the code inside the curly braces will execute. If $a is found to be something other than 10 (if the condition is false), the code will be ignored and the program will continue.

To offer an alternative series of statements should $a not have a value of 10, add an else statement to the structure, to execute a section of code when the condition is false:

```
if ($a == "10") {
        echo "a equals 10";
} else {
        echo "a does not equal 10";
}
```

The elseif statement can be added to the structure to evaluate an alternative expression before heading to the final else statement. For example, the following structure first evaluates whether $a is equal to 10. If that condition is false, the elseif statement is evaluated. If it is found to be true, the code within its curly braces executes. Otherwise, the program continues to the final else statement:

```
if ($a == "10") {
        echo "a equals 10";
} elseif ($b == "8") {
        echo "b equals 8";
} else {
```

```
        echo "a does not equal 10 and b does not equal 8.";
}
```

You can use if statements alone or as part of an if...else or if...elseif...else statement. Whichever you choose, you will find this structure to be an invaluable element in your programs!

while

Unlike the if...elseif...else structure, in which each expression is evaluated once and an action is performed based on its value of true or false, the while statement continues to loop until an expression is false. In other words, the while loop continues while the expression is true.

For example, in the following while loop, the value of $a is printed on the screen and is incremented by 1 as long as the value of $a is less than or equal to 5.

```
$a = 0 // set a starting point
while ($a <= "5") {
        echo "a equals $a<br>";
        $a++;
}
```

Here is the output of this loop:

> a equals 0
>
> a equals 1
>
> a equals 2
>
> a equals 3
>
> a equals 4
>
> a equals 5

for

Like while loops, for loops evaluate the set of conditional expressions at the beginning of each loop. Here is the syntax of the for loop:

```
for (expr1; expr2; expr3) {
        // code to execute
}
```

At the beginning of each loop, the first expression is evaluated, followed by the second expression. If the second expression is true, the loop continues by executing the code and then evaluating the third expression. If the second expression is false, the loop does not continue, and the third expression is never evaluated.

Take the counting example used in the while loop, and rewrite it using a for loop:

```
for ($a = 0; $a <= "5"; $a++) {
        echo "a equals $a<br>";
}
```

The output is the same as the while loop:

> a equals 0
>
> a equals 1
>
> a equals 2
>
> a equals 3
>
> a equals 4
>
> a equals 5

Built-In Functions

The functions to be described in the following sections are just a small sampling of the numerous functions that make up the PHP language; they are the ones I use on a regular basis. Depending on what you'll be doing with PHP, you may or may not need more functions, but do visit the PHP manual, at http://www.php.net/manual/, and familiarize yourself with what is available.

Array Functions

Numerous PHP functions are available for use with arrays. Noted here are only those that I find absolutely essential, and those that form a foundation of knowledge for working with arrays.

array()

The array() function allows you to manually assign values to an array. Here is the syntax of the array() function:

```
$array_name = array("val1", "val2", "val3", …);
```

For example, to create an array called $colors containing the values "blue", "black", "red", and "green", use the following:

```
$colors = array("blue", "black", "red", "green");
```

array_push()

The array_push() function allows you to add one or more elements to the end of an existing array.

The syntax of the array_push() function is

```
array_push($array_name, "element 1", "element 2", ...);
```

For example, say you have an array that contains the elements "1" and "2" and you want to add the elements "3", "4", "5", and "cool" to it. You would use this snippet of code:

```
$sample = array(1, 2);
array_push($sample, 3, 4, 5, "cool");
```

You can use the example script below to print the "Before" and "After" versions of the $sample array:

```
<?php
$sample = array(1, 2);
echo "BEFORE:<br>";
while (list($key,$value) = each($sample)) {
        echo "$key : $value<br>";
}
reset($sample);
array_push($sample, 3, 4, 5, "cool");
echo "<br>AFTER:<br>";
while (list($key,$value) = each($sample)) {
        echo "$key : $value<br>";
}
?>
```

The script will print the following:

BEFORE:

0 : 1

1 : 2

AFTER:

0 : 1

1 : 2

2 : 3

3 : 4

4 : 5

5 : cool

array_pop()

The array_pop() function allows you to take (pop) off the last element of an existing array.

The syntax of the array_pop() function is

```
array_pop($array_name);
```

For example, say you have an array that contains the elements "1", "2", "3", "4", "5" and "cool", and you want to pop off the "cool" element. You would use this snippet of code:

```
$sample = array(1, 2, 3, 4, 5, "cool");
$last = array_pop($sample);
```

You can use the example script below to print the "Before" and "After" versions of the $sample array and the value of $last:

```
<?php
$sample = array(1, 2, 3, 4, 5, "cool");

echo "BEFORE:<br>";
while (list($key,$value) = each($sample)) {
        echo "$key : $value<br>";
```

```
}
reset($sample);
$last = array_pop($sample);
echo "<br>AFTER:<br>";
while (list($key,$value) = each($sample)) {
        echo "$key : $value<br>";
}
echo "<br>and finally, in \$last: $last";
?>
```

The script will print the following:

> BEFORE:
>
> 0 : 1
>
> 1 : 2
>
> 2 : 3
>
> 3 : 4
>
> 4 : 5
>
> 5 : cool
>
> AFTER:
>
> 0 : 1
>
> 1 : 2
>
> 2 : 3
>
> 3 : 4
>
> 4 : 5

and finally, in $last: cool

array_unshift()

The `array_unshift()` function allows you to add elements to the beginning of an existing array.

The syntax of the `array_unshift()` function is:

```
array_unshift($array_name, "element 1", "element 2", ...);
```

For example, say you have an array that contains the elements "1" and "2", and you want to add the elements "3", "4", "5", and "cool". You would use this snippet of code:

```
$sample = array(1, 2);
array_unshift($sample, 3, 4, 5, "cool");
```

You can use the example script below to print the "Before" and "After" versions of the $sample array:

```
<?php
$sample = array(1, 2);
echo "BEFORE:<br>";
while (list($key,$value) = each($sample)) {
        echo "$key : $value<br>";
}
reset($sample);
array_unshift($sample, 3, 4, 5, "cool");
echo "<br>AFTER:<br>";
while (list($key,$value) = each($sample)) {
        echo "$key : $value<br>";
}
?>
```

The script will print the following:

    BEFORE:

    0 : 1

    1 : 2

    AFTER:

    0 : 3

    1 : 4

    2 : 5

    3 : cool

    4 : 1

    5 : 2

array_shift()

The `array_shift()` function allows you to take off the first element (shift the list back a step) of an existing array.

The syntax of the `array_shift()` function is:

```
array_shift($array_name);
```

For example, say you have an array that contains the elements "1", "2", "3", "4", "5", and "cool", and you want to pop off the "1" element. You would use this snippet of code:

```
$sample = array(1, 2, 3, 4, 5, "cool");
$first = array_shift($sample);
```

You can use the example script below to print the "Before" and "After" versions of the $sample array and the value of $first:

```
<?php
$sample = array(1, 2, 3, 4, 5, "cool");
echo "BEFORE:<br>";
while (list($key,$value) = each($sample)) {
        echo "$key : $value<br>";
}
reset($sample);

$first = array_shift($sample);
echo "<br>AFTER:<br>";
echo "in \$first: $first<br>";
while (list($key,$value) = each($sample)) {
        echo "$key : $value<br>";
}
?>
```

The script will print:

BEFORE:

0 : 1

1 : 2

2 : 3

3 : 4

4 : 5

5 : cool

AFTER:

in $first: 1

0 : 2

1 : 3

2 : 4

3 : 5

4 : cool

array_slice()

The `array_slice()` function allows you extract a chunk of an existing array.

The syntax of the `array_slice()` function is

```
array_slice($array_name, start_position, offset, length);
```

For example, say you have an array that contains the elements "1", "2", "3", "4", "5" and "cool", and you want to extract some portions of this array. Some examples are

```
$sample = array(1, 2, 3, 4, 5, "cool");

// start at 2nd position
$slice1 = array_slice($sample, 1);

// start at 2nd position, go to next to last
$slice2 = array_slice($sample, 1, -1);
```

```
// start 5th position
$slice3 = array_slice($sample, 4);

// start at 1st position, take 3 elements
$slice4 = array_slice($sample, 0, 3);
```

You can use the example script below to print the "Before" version of the $sample array and the value of the various "slices":

```php
<?php
$sample = array(1, 2, 3, 4, 5, "cool");
echo "BEFORE:<br>";
while (list($key,$value) = each($sample)) {
        echo "$key : $value<br>";
}
reset($sample);

$slice1 = array_slice($sample, 1);
$slice2 = array_slice($sample, 1, -1);
$slice3 = array_slice($sample, 4);
$slice4 = array_slice($sample, 0, 3);

echo "<br>slice1 (start at 2nd position) looks like:<br>";
while (list($key,$value) = each($slice1)) {
        echo "$key : $value<br>";
}

echo "<br>slice2 (start at 2nd pos, go to next to last) looks like:<br>";
while (list($key,$value) = each($slice2)) {
        echo "$key : $value<br>";
}

echo "<br>slice3 (start 5th pos) at looks like:<br>";
while (list($key,$value) = each($slice3)) {
        echo "$key : $value<br>";
}
```

```
echo "<br>slice4 (start at 1st pos, print 3 elements) looks like:<br>";
while (list($key,$value) = each($slice4)) {
        echo "$key : $value<br>";
}
?>
```

The script will print each of the slices in succession.

array_merge()

The `array_merge()` function allows you to combine two or more existing arrays.

The syntax of the `array_merge()` function is:

```
array_merge($array1, $array2, …);
```

For example, say you have an array that contains the elements "1", "2", "3", "4", "5", and "cool", and another array that contains the elements "a", "b", "c", "d", "e", and "cooler", and you want to combine the two. You would use this snippet of code:

```
$sample1 = array(1, 2, 3, 4, 5, "cool");
$sample2 = array(a, b, c, d, e, "cooler");
$merged = array_merge($sample1, $sample2);
```

You can use the example script below to print the "Before" and "After" versions of the arrays:

```
<?php
$sample1 = array(1, 2, 3, 4, 5, "cool");
echo "BEFORE - SAMPLE1:<br>";
while (list($key,$value) = each($sample1)) {
        echo "$key : $value<br>";
}
reset($sample1);
$sample2 = array(a, b, c, d, e, "cooler");
echo "<br>BEFORE - SAMPLE2:<br>";
while (list($key,$value) = each($sample2)) {
        echo "$key : $value<br>";
}
```

```
reset($sample2);
$merged = array_merge($sample1, $sample2);
echo "<br>AFTER:<br>";
while (list($key,$value) = each($merged)) {
        echo "$key : $value<br>";
}
?>
```

The script will print each sample array.

array_keys()

The array_keys() function will return an array of all the key names in an existing array.

The syntax of the array_keys() function is

```
array_keys($array_name);
```

Suppose you have an array that looks like this:

```
$sample = array("key0" => "1", "key1" => "2", "key2" => "3", "key3" => "4",
"key4" => "5", "key6" => "cool");
```

You can use the example script below to print all the keys in $sample:

```
<?php
$sample = array("key0" => "1", "key1" => "2", "key2" => "3", "key3" => "4",
"key4" => "5", "key6" => "cool");

echo "SAMPLE ARRAY:<br>";
while (list($key,$value) = each($sample)) {
        echo "$key : $value<br>";
}
$keys = array_keys($sample);
echo "<br>KEYS IN SAMPLE ARRAY:<br>";
while (list($key,$value) = each($keys)) {
        echo "$key : $value<br>";
}
?>
```

The script will print the following:

SAMPLE ARRAY:

key0 : 1

key1 : 2

key2 : 3

key3 : 4

key4 : 5

key6 : cool

KEYS IN SAMPLE ARRAY:

0 : key0

1 : key1

2 : key2

3 : key3

4 : key4

5 : key6

array_values()

The `array_values()` function will return an array of all the values in an existing array.

The syntax of the `array_values()` function is

```
array_values($array_name);
```

Suppose you have an array that looks like this:

```
$sample = array("key0" => "1", "key1" => "2", "key2" => "3", "key3" => "4",
"key4" => "5", "key6" => "cool");
```

You can use the example script below to print all the values in `$sample`:

```
<?php
$sample = array("key0" => "1", "key1" => "2", "key2" => "3", "key3" => "4",
"key4" => "5", "key6" => "cool");
echo "SAMPLE ARRAY:<br>";
```

```
while (list($key,$value) = each($sample)) {
        echo "$key : $value<br>";
}
$values = array_values($sample);
echo "<br>VALUES IN SAMPLE ARRAY:<br>";
while (list($key,$value) = each($values)) {
        echo "$key : $value<br>";
}
?>
```

The script will print the following:

> SAMPLE ARRAY:
>
> key0 : 1
>
> key1 : 2
>
> key2 : 3
>
> key3 : 4
>
> key4 : 5
>
> key6 : cool
>
> VALUES IN SAMPLE ARRAY:
>
> 0 : 1
>
> 1 : 2
>
> 2 : 3
>
> 3 : 4
>
> 4 : 5
>
> 5 : cool

count()

The count() function counts the number of elements in a variable. It's usually used to count the number of elements in an array, because any variable that is not an array will have only one element—itself.

In the following example, $a is assigned a value equal to the number of elements in the $colors array:

```
$a = count($colors);
```

If $colors contains the values "blue", "black", "red", and "green", $a will be assigned a value of 4.

You can create a for loop that will loop through an array and print its elements, using the result of the count() function as the second expression in the loop. For example:

```
$colors = array("blue", "black", "red", "green");
for ($i = 0; $i < count($colors); $i++) {
        echo "The current color is $colors[$i].<br>";
}
```

produces this result:

> The current color is blue.
>
> The current color is black.
>
> The current color is red.
>
> The current color is green.

In this example, the value of the count() function is used as the stopping point for the loop; the statement $i < count($colors) in this case is the equivalent of $i < 4.

each() and list()

The each() and list() functions usually appear together, in the context of stepping through an array and returning its keys and values. Here is the syntax for these functions:

```
each(arrayname);
list(val1, val2, val3, ...);
```

For example, when you submit an HTML form via the GET method, each key/value pair is placed in the global variable $_GET. If your form input fields are named first_name and last_name and the user enters values of Joe and Smith, the key/value pairs are first_name/Joe and last_name/Smith. In the $_GET array, these variables are represented as the following:

```
$_GET["first_name"] // value is "Joe"
$_GET["last_name"] // value is "Smith"
```

You can use the each() and list() functions to step through the array in this fashion, printing the key and value for each element in the array:

```
while (list($key, $val) = each($HTTP_GET_VARS)) {
    echo "$key has a value of $val<br>";
}
```

Continuing the example, this would produce the following results:

> first_name has a value of Joe.
>
> last_name has a value of Smith.

reset()

The reset() function rewinds the pointer to the beginning of the array. The syntax of the reset() function is

```
reset($array_name);
```

shuffle()

The shuffle() function will randomize the elements of a given array. The syntax of the shuffle() function is

```
shuffle($array_name);
```

For example, say you have an array that contains the numbers "1" through "10" and you want to randomize the elements. You can use the example script below to print the "Before" and "After" versions of the $sample array:

```
<?php
$sample = array(1, 2, 3, 4, 5, 6, 7, 8, 9, 10);
echo "BEFORE:<br>";
while (list($key,$value) = each($sample)) {
        echo "$key : $value<br>";
}

reset($sample);
srand(time());
shuffle($sample);
```

```
echo "<br>AFTER:<br>";
while (list($key,$value) = each($sample)) {
        echo "$key : $value<br>";
}
?>
```

The script will print the original, and then a randomly shuffled result.

sizeof()

The sizeof() function counts the number of elements in an array. In the following example, $a is assigned a value equal to the number of elements in the $colors array:

```
$a = sizeof($colors);
```

If $colors contains the values "blue", "black", "red", and "green", $a is assigned a value of 4.

You can create a for loop that will loop through an array and print its elements, using the sizeof() function as the second expression in the loop. For example:

```
$colors = array("blue", "black", "red", "green");
for ($i = 0; $i < sizeof($colors); $i++) {
        echo "The current color is $colors[$i].<br>";
}
```

Here is the result:

> The current color is blue.
>
> The current color is black.
>
> The current color is red.
>
> The current color is green.

In this example, the value of the sizeof() function is used as the stopping point for the loop. The statement $i < sizeof($colors) in this case is the equivalent of $i < 4.

Database Connectivity Functions

Database connectivity functions in PHP tend to follow the same patterns: connect to database, get results, close connection, and so on. However, several specific database types have their own set of functions, taking into consideration the nuances of the software. The following sections show the basic syntax of the database functions for select database types. Extended examples for select database can be found in Chapter 3, "Working with Databases." Additional information on the multitude of other database connectivity functions can be found in the PHP Manual, at http://www.php.net/manual/.

MySQL Functions

Numerous PHP functions exist for connecting to and querying a MySQL server. Following are some basic functions and their syntax. See the PHP Manual at http://www.php.net/manual/ref.mysql.php for a complete listing of MySQL functions.

mysql_connect()

This function opens a connection to MySQL. It requires a server name, username, and password.

```
$connection = mysql_connect("servername","username","password");
```

mysql_select_db()

This function selects a database on the MySQL server for use by subsequent queries; it requires that a valid connection has been established.

```
$db = mysql_select_db("myDB", $connection);
```

mysql_query()

This function issues the SQL statement. It requires an open connection to the database.

```
$sql_result = mysql_query("SELECT * FROM SOMETABLE",$connection);
```

mysql_fetch_array()

This function automatically places the SQL statement result row into an array.

```
$row = mysql_fetch_array($sql_result)
```

mysql_free_result()

This function frees the memory resources used by a database query.

```
mysql_free_result($sql_result);
```

mysql_close()

This function explicitly closes a database connection.

```
mysql_close($connection);
```

PostgreSQL Functions

Numerous PHP functions exist for connecting to and querying a PostgreSQL Server. Following are some basic functions and their syntax. See the PHP Manual at http://www.php.net/manual/ref.pgsql.php for a complete listing of PostgreSQL functions.

pg_connect()

this function opens a connection to a PostgreSQL database; it requires a hostname, database name, username, and password.

```
$connection = pg_connect("host=YourHostname dbname=YourDBName user=YourUsername
password=YourPassword");
```

pg_exec()

This function issues the SQL statement; it requires an open connection to the database.

```
$sql_result = pg_exec($connection,$sql);
```

pg_fetch_array()

This function automatically places the SQL statement result row into an array.

```
$row = pg_fetch_array($sql_result)
```

pg_freeresult()

This function frees the memory resources used by a database query.

```
pg_freeresult($sql_result);
```

pg_close()

This function explicitly closes a database connection.

```
pg_close($connection);
```

Oracle Functions

Numerous PHP functions exist for connecting to and querying an Oracle version 7, 8, or 9 database server. Following are some basic functions and their syntax. See the PHP Manual at http://www.php.net/manual/ref.oci8.php for a complete listing of Oracle functions.

OCILogon()

This function opens a connection to Oracle; it requires that the environment variable ORACLE_SID has been set and that you have a valid username and password.

```
$connection = OCILogon("username","password");
```

OCIParse()

This function parses a SQL statement; it requires an open database connection.

```
$sql_statement = OCIParse($connection,"SELECT * FROM TABLENAME");
```

OCIExecute()

This function executes a prepared SQL statement.

```
OCIExecute($sql_statement);
```

OCIFetch()

This function gets the next row in the result of a SQL statement and places it in a results buffer; it requires a valid result set.

```
OCIFetch($sql_statement);
```

OCIResult()

This function gets the value of the named column in the current result row; it requires a valid result set.

```
OCIResult($sql_statement,"COLUMN")
```

OCIFreeStatement()

This function frees the resources in use by the current statement.

```
OCIFreeStatement($sql_result);
```

OCILogoff()

This function explicitly closes a database connection.

```
OCILogoff($connection);
```

Microsoft SQL Server Functions

There are numerous PHP functions for connecting to and querying Microsoft SQL Server. Following are some basic functions and their syntax. See the PHP Manual at http://www.php.net/manual/ref.mssql.php for a complete listing of Microsoft SQL Server functions.

mssql_connect()

This function opens a connection to the Microsoft SQL Server; it requires a server name, username, and password.

```
$connection = mssql_connect("servername","username","password");
```

mssql_select_db()

This function selects a database on the Microsoft SQL Server for use by subsequent queries; it requires that a valid connection has been established.

```
$db = mssql_select_db("myDB", $connection);
```

mssql_query()

This function issues the SQL statement; it requires an open connection to the database.

```
$sql_result = mssql_query("SELECT * FROM SOMETABLE",$connection);
```

mssql_fetch_array()

This function automatically places the SQL statement result row into an array.

```
$row = mssql_fetch_array($sql_result)
```

mssql_free_result()

This function frees the memory resources used by a database query.

```
mssql_free_result($sql_result);
```

mssql_close()

This function explicitly closes a database connection.

```
mssql_close($connection);
```

ODBC Functions

PHP contains functions for making generic ODBC connections should your database type not have an explicit set of functions, or if you simply need to use ODBC connectivity. Following are some basic functions and their syntax. See the PHP Manual at http://www.php.net/manual/ref.odbc.php for a complete listing of ODBC functions.

odbc_connect()

This function opens an ODBC connection; it requires a server name, username, and password.

```
$connection = odbc_connect("DSN=YourDataSourceName","username","password");
```

odbc_prepare()

This function readies a SQL statement for execution by the ODBC datasource.

```
$sql_statement = odbc_prepare($connection,"SELECT * FROM TABLENAME");
```

odbc_execute()

This function executes a prepared SQL statement.

```
$sql_result = odbc_execute($sql_statement);
```

odbc_result_all()

This function automatically formats query results into an HTML table; it requires a query result and can optionally include HTML table attributes.

```
odbc_result_all($sql_result,"border=1");
```

odbc_free_result()

This function frees the memory resources used by a database query.

```
odbc_free_result($sql_result);
```

odbc_close()

This function explicitly closes a database connection.

```
odbc_close($connection);
```

Date and Time Functions

The basic PHP date and time functions let you easily format timestamps for use in database queries and calendar functions, as well as simply printing the date on an order form receipt.

date()

The date() function returns the current server timestamp, formatted according to a given a set of parameters. Here is the syntax of the date() function:

```
date(format, [timestamp]);
```

If the timestamp parameter is not provided, the current timestamp is assumed. Table A.6 shows the available formats.

Table A.6 date() Function Formats

Character	Meaning
a	Prints "am" or "pm"
A	Prints "AM" or "PM"
h	Hour, 12-hour format (01 to 12)
H	Hour, 24-hour format (00 to 23)
g	Hour, 12-hour format without leading zero (1 to 12)
G	Hour, 24-hour format without leading zero (0 to 23)
i	Minutes (00 to 59)
s	Seconds (00 to 59)
Z	Time zone offset in seconds (-43200 to 43200)
U	Seconds since the Epoch (January 1, 1970 00:00:00 GMT)
d	Day of month, two digits (01 to 31)
j	Day of month, two digits without leading zero (1 to 31)
D	Day of week, text (Mon to Sun)
l	Day of week, long text (Monday to Sunday)
w	Day of week, numeric, Sunday to Saturday (0 to 6)
F	Month, long text (January to December)
m	Month, two digits (01 to 12)
n	Month, two digits without leading zero (1 to 12)
M	Month, three-letter text (Jan to Dec)
Y	Year, four digits (2000)
y	Year, two digits (00)
z	Day of the year (0 to 365)
t	Number of days in the given month (28 to 31)
S	English ordinal suffix (th, nd, st)

For example, the following:

```
echo date ("F jS Y, h:iA.");
```

will print the current date in this format: December 16th 2002, 09:17AM.

checkdate()

The checkdate() function validates a given date. Successful validation means that the year is between 0 and 32767, the month is between 1 and 12, and the proper number of days are in each month (leap years are accounted for). Here's the syntax of checkdate():

```
checkdate(month, day, year);
```

For example, if you have a date such as "12/30/1973" (which happens to be my birthday so I'm pretty sure it's valid), you can use the following code to break apart the date and validate it, returning a response to the user:

```php
<?php
$orig_date = "12/30/1973";
$date = explode("/", "$orig_date");

$month = $date[0];
$day = $date[1];
$year = $date[2];

$res = checkdate($month, $day, $year);

if ($res == 1) {
        echo "$orig_date is a valid date!";
} else {
        echo "$orig_date is not valid.";
}
?>
```

The output of this script is

        12/30/1973 is a valid date!

mktime()

The mktime() function returns the UNIX timestamp as a long integer (in the format of seconds since the Epoch, which is January 1, 1970) for a given date. Thus, the primary use of mktime() is to format dates in preparation for mathematical functions and date validation. Here's the syntax of mktime():

```
mktime(hour, minute, second, month, day, year);
```

For example, if the month is December (12), the day of the month is 17, and the year is 2002:

```
echo mktime(0,0,0,12,17,2002);
the result is 1040112000.
```

time() and microtime()

The time() function returns the current system time, measured in seconds since the Epoch. The syntax of time() is simply

```
time();
```

For example, to print the current system timestamp, use

```
echo time();
```

You could get a result such as 1040112000. Well, actually you couldn't, because that moment has already passed, about 15 seconds before I wrote this sentence!

Using microtime() adds a count of microseconds, so instead of just 1040112000, I got 0.10026200 1040221299 at the exact moment I asked for the time since the Epoch, in both seconds and microseconds.

Filesystem Functions

The built-in filesystem functions can be very powerful tools—or weapons, if used incorrectly. Be very careful when using filesystem functions, especially if you have PHP configured to run as root or some other system-wide user. For example, using a PHP script to issue an rm -R command while at the root level of your directory would be a very bad thing.

chmod(), chgrp() and chown()

Like the shell commands of the same name, the chmod(), chgrp(), and chown() functions will modify the permissions, group, and owner of a directory or file. The syntax of these functions is

```
chmod("filename", mode);
chmgrp("filename", newgroup);
chown("filename", newowner);
```

For example, to change the permissions on a file called index.html in your home directory, use

```
chmod("/home/username/index.html", 0755);
```

To change to a new group, called users:

```
chmgrp("/home/username/index.html", users);
```

To change to a new owner, called joe:

```
chown("/home/username/index.html", joe);
```

In order to change permissions, groups, and owners, the PHP user must be the owner of the file, or the permissions must already be set to allow such changes by that user.

copy()

The copy() function works much like the cp shell command: it needs a file name and a destination in order to copy a file. The syntax of copy() is

```
copy("source filename", "destination");
```

For example, to make a backup copy of the file index.html in your home directory, use

```
copy("/home/username/index.html", "/home/username/index.html.bak");
```

The PHP user must have permission to write into the destination directory, or the copy function will fail.

diskfreespace()

The diskfreespace() function returns the total free space for a given directory, in bytes. The syntax of diskfreespace() is

```
diskfreespace(directory);
```

For example, to see the available space on your UNIX machine, use

```
$space = diskfreespace("/");
echo "$space";
```

On your Windows machine, you can use

```
$space = diskfreespace("C:\\");
echo "$space";
```

fopen()

The fopen() function opens a specified file or URL for reading and/or writing. The syntax of fopen() is

```
fopen("filename", "mode")
```

To open a URL, use http:// or ftp:// at the beginning of the file name string.

If the file name begins with anything else, then the file is opened from the filesystem and a file pointer to the opened file is returned. Otherwise, the file is assumed to reside on the local filesystem.

The specified mode determines whether the file is opened for reading, writing, or both. Table A.7 lists the valid modes.

Table A.7 fopen() Function Modes

Mode	Description
r	Read-only. The file pointer is at the beginning of the file.
r+	Reading and writing. The file pointer is at the beginning of the file.
w	Write-only. The file pointer is at the beginning of the file, and the file is truncated to zero length. If the file does not exist, attempt to create it.
w+	Reading and writing. The file pointer is at the beginning of the file, and the file is truncated to zero length. If the file does not exist, attempt to create it.
a	Write-only. The file pointer is at the end of the file (it appends content to the file). If the file does not exist, attempt to create it.
a+	Reading and writing. The file pointer is at the end of the file (it appends content to the file). If the file does not exist, attempt to create it.

For example, to open the file index.html in your home directory for reading only, use

```
$fp = fopen("/home/username/index.html", "r");
```

To open a nonexistent file called temp.txt in your home directory, use

```
$fp = fopen("/home/username/temp.txt", "w+");
```

fread()

Use the fread() function to read a specified number of bytes from an open file pointer. The syntax of fread() is

```
fread(filepointer, length);
```

For example, to read the first 1024 bytes of a file and assign the string as a value of a variable called $content, use this code:

```
$fp = fopen("/home/username/temp.txt", "r"); // open the file pointer
$content = fread($fp, 1024); // read 1024 bytes into a variable
```

fputs()

The fputs() function writes to an open file pointer. The syntax of fputs() is

```
fputs(filepointer, content, [length]);
```

The file pointer must be open in order to write to the file. The length parameter is optional. If it isn't specified, then all specified content is written to the file.

For example, to write "I love PHP" to an open file pointer, use

```
fputs($filepointer, "I love PHP");
```

Alternatively, you can place the content in a variable and then reference only the variable:

```
$content = "I love PHP";
fputs($filepointer, $content);
```

fclose()

Use the fclose() function to close an open file pointer. The syntax of fclose() is

```
fclose(filepointer);
```

For example, if you used the `fopen()` function to open a file pointer called `$new_file`, you would use the following code to close the file pointer:

```
fclose($new_file);
```

file_exists()

The `file_exists()` function checks to see if a file of the specified name already exists. The syntax of `file_exists()` is

```
file_exists("filename");
```

For example, the following code checks to see if the file index.html exists in a directory and then prints a message depending on the results:

```
if (!file_exists("/home/username/index.html")) {
        echo "The file index.html does not exist.";
} else {
        echo "Success! index.html exists.";
}
```

mkdir()

Like the `mkdir` shell command, the `mkdir()` function creates a new directory on the filesystem. The syntax of `mkdir()` is

```
mkdir("pathname", mode);
```

For example, to create a directory called `public_html` in your home directory, use

```
mkdir("/home/username/public_html", 0755);
```

The PHP user must have write permission in the specified directory.

rename()

As its name suggests, the `rename()` function attempts to give a new name to an existing file. The syntax of `rename()` is

```
rename("oldname", "newname");
```

For example, to rename a file in your home directory from index.html to temp1.html, use

```
rename("/home/username/index.html", "/home/username/temp1.html");
```

The PHP user must have permission to modify the file.

rmdir()

Like the rmdir shell command, the rmdir() function removes a directory from the filesystem. The syntax of rmdir() is

rmdir("pathname");

For example, to remove the directory public_html from your home directory, use

rmdir("/home/username/public_html");

The PHP user must have write permission in the specified directory.

symlink()

The symlink() function creates a symbolic link from an existing file or directory on the filesystem to a specified link name. The syntax of symlink() is

symlink("targetname", "linkname");

For example, to create a symbolic link called index.phtml to an existing file called index.html, use

symlink("index.html", "index.phtml");

unlink()

The unlink() function deletes a file from the filesystem. The syntax of unlink() is

unlink("filename");

For example, to delete a file called index.html in your home directory, use

unlink("/home/username/index.html");

The PHP user must have write permission for this file.

HTTP Functions

The built-in functions for sending specific HTTP headers and cookie data are crucial to developing large Web-based applications in PHP. Luckily, the syntax for these functions is quite easy to understand and implement.

header()

The header() function outputs an HTTP header string, such as a location redirection. This output must occur before any other data is sent to the browser, including HTML tags.

NOTE

This information bears repeating over and over again: Do not attempt to send information of any sort to the browser before sending a header(). You can perform any sort of database manipulations or other calculations before the header(), but you cannot print anything to the screen—not even a new line character.

For example, to use the header() function to redirect a user to a new location, use this code:

```
header("Location: http://www.newlocation.com");
exit;
```

TIP

Follow a header statement with the exit command. Doing so ensures that the code does not continue to execute.

setcookie()

The setcookie() function sends a cookie to the user. Cookies must be sent before any other header information is sent to the Web browser. The syntax for set-cookie() is

```
setcookie("name", "value", "expire", "path", "domain", "secure");
```

For example, you would use the following code to send a cookie called username with a value of joe that is valid for one hour within all directories on the test-company.com domain:

```
setcookie("username","joe", time()+3600, "/", ".testcompany.com");
```

Mail Function

The PHP mail function makes the interface between your HTML forms and your server's mail program a snap!

mail()

If your server has access to sendmail or an external SMTP server, you can use the `mail()` function to send mail to a specified recipient. Its syntax is

```
mail("recipient", "subject", "message", "mail headers");
```

For example, the following code sends mail to julie@thickbook.com, with a subject of "I'm sending mail!" and a message body saying "PHP is cool!" The "From:" line is part of the additional mail headers:

```
mail("julie@thickbook.com", "I'm sending mail!", "PHP is cool!", "From: youre-mail@yourdomain.com\n");
```

Mathematical Functions

As I have very little aptitude for mathematics, I find PHP's built-in mathematical functions to be of utmost importance! In addition to all the functions, the value of pi (calculated as 3.14159265358979323846) is already defined as a constant in PHP (`M_PI`).

ceil()

The `ceil()` function rounds a fraction up to the next higher integer. The syntax of `ceil()` is

```
ceil(number);
```

For example:

```
ceil(2.56); // result is "3";
ceil(1.22); // result is "2";
```

decbin() and bindec()

The `decbin()` and `bindec()` functions convert decimal numbers to binary numbers and binary numbers to decimal numbers, respectively. The syntax of these functions is

```
decbin(number);
bindec(number);
```

For example, the following code takes a decimal number, converts it to binary, and converts it back to decimal:

```php
<?php
$orig_dec = 66251125;
$dec2bin = decbin($orig_dec);
$bin2dec = bindec($dec2bin);

echo "original decimal number: $orig_dec <br>";
echo "new binary number: $dec2bin <br>";
echo "back to decimal: $bin2dec <br>";
?>
```

The output of this script is

> original decimal number: 66251125
>
> new binary number: 11111100101110100101110101
>
> back to decimal: 66251125

dechex() and hexdec()

The dechex() and hexdec() functions convert decimal numbers to hexadecimal numbers and hexadecimal numbers to decimal numbers, respectively. The syntax of these functions is

```
dechex(number);
hexdec(number);
```

For example, the following code takes a decimal number, converts it to hexadecimal, and converts it back to decimal:

```php
<?php
$orig_dec = 255;
$dec2hex = dechex($orig_dec);
$hex2dec = hexdec($dec2hex);
echo "original decimal number: $orig_dec <br>";
echo "new hexadecimal number: $dec2hex <br>";
echo "back to decimal: $hex2dec <br>";
?>
```

The output of this script is

> original decimal number: 255
>
> new hexadecimal number: ff
>
> back to decimal: 255

decoct() and octdec()

The decoct() and octdec() functions convert decimal numbers to octal numbers and octal numbers to decimal numbers, respectively. The syntax of these functions is

```
decoct(number);
octdec(number);
```

For example, the following code takes a decimal number, converts it to octal, and converts it back to decimal:

```php
<?php
$orig_dec = 34672;
$dec2oct = decoct($orig_dec);
$oct2dec = octdec($dec2oct);
echo "original decimal number: $orig_dec <br>";
echo "new octal number: $dec2oct <br>";
echo "back to decimal: $oct2dec <br>";
?>
```

The output of this script is

> original decimal number: 34672
>
> new octal number: 103560
>
> back to decimal: 34672

floor()

The floor() function rounds a fraction down to the next-lowest integer. The syntax of floor() is

```
floor(number);
```

For example:

```
floor(2.56); // result is "2";
floor(1.22); // result is "1";
```

number_format()

The `number_format()` function returns the formatted version of a specified number. The syntax of `number_format()` is

```
number_format("number", "decimals", "dec_point", "thousands_sep");
```

For example, to return a formatted version of the number 12156688, with two decimal places and a comma separating each group of thousands, use

```
echo number_format("12156688","2",".",",");
```

The result is 12,156,688.00.

If only a number is provided, the default formatting does not use a decimal point and has a comma between every group of thousands.

pow()

The `pow()` function returns the value of a given number, raised to the power of a given exponent. The syntax of `pow()` is

```
pow(number, exponent);
```

For example, this code raises 19 to the fifth power:

```
echo pow(19, 5);
```

The result is 2476099.

rand()

The `rand()` function generates a random value from a specific range of numbers. The syntax of `rand()` is

```
rand(min, max);
```

For example, to return a random value between 0 and 576, use

```
echo rand(0,576);
```

round()

The round() function rounds a fraction to the next higher or next lower integer. The syntax of the round() function is

```
round(number);
```

For example:

```
round(2.56);    // returns "3"
round(1.22);    // returns "1"
round(55.22);   // returns "55"
```

sqrt()

The sqrt() function returns the square root of a given number. The syntax of sqrt() is

```
sqrt(number);
```

For example, to find the square root of 5561, use

```
echo sqrt(5561);
```

The result is 74.572112750009.

srand()

The srand() function provides the random number generator with a set of possible values. The syntax of srand() is

```
srand(seed);
```

A common practice is to seed the random number generator by using a number of microseconds:

```
srand((double)microtime()*1000000);
```

Miscellaneous Functions

The die() and exit functions provide useful control over the execution of your script, offering an "escape route" for programming errors.

die()

The `die()` function outputs a given message and terminates the script when a returned value is false. The syntax of `die()` is

```
die("message");
```

For example, you would use the following code to print a message and stop the execution of your script upon failure to connect to your database:

```
$connection = mysql_connect("servername", "username", "password") or die ("Can't
connect to database.");
```

exit

The `exit` function terminates the execution of the current script at the point where the `exit` function is called.

For example, to exit the script after a location redirection header has been sent, use

```
header("Location: http://www.newlocation.com/");
exit;
```

sleep() and usleep()

The `sleep()` and `usleep()` functions put a pause, or a delay, at a given point in the execution of your PHP code. The syntax of these functions is

```
sleep(seconds);
usleep(microseconds);
```

The only difference between `sleep()` and `usleep()` is that the given wait period for `sleep()` is in seconds, and the wait period for `usleep()` is in microseconds.

uniqid()

The `uniqid()` function generates a unique identifier, with a prefix if you so desire. The basic syntax of `uniqid()` is

```
uniqid("prefix");
```

That's boring, though. Suppose you want a unique id with a prefix of "phpuser", so you use

```
$id = uniqid("phpuser");
echo "$id";
```

and get something like phpuser38b320a6b5482.

But if you use something really cool like

```
$id = md5(uniqid(rand()));
echo "$id";
```

Then you get an id like 999d8971461bedfc7caadcab33e65866.

Network Functions

There are several network functions available. Some are for opening and reading from sockets, and some are FTP functions. The two network functions that I use most often are the IP and name resolution functions.

gethostbyaddr() and gethostbyname()

The gethostbyaddr() and gethostbyname() functions will return the hostname or IP address of a given machine, respectively. The syntax of these commands is

```
gethostbyaddr(IP);
gethostbyname(hostname);
```

The sample code below shows both of these functions in action:

```php
<?php
// assign some variables
$ip = "204.71.200.75";
$host = "www.yahoo.com";

$verify_ip = gethostbyaddr($ip);
$verify_name = gethostbyname($host);

echo "$ip resolves to $verify_ip<br>";
echo "$host resolves to $verify_name<br>";
?>
```

The output of this script is:

> 204.71.200.75 resolves to www10.yahoo.com
>
> www.yahoo.com resolves to 204.71.200.74

PHP Version and Related Information

Sometimes you'll need to get a quick snapshot of your operating environment, especially if you're like me and can't remember what you've loaded on which Web server! PHP has a few functions that make environment information very easy to discover and modify.

phpinfo()

Calling the `phpinfo()` function will output a template containing PHP version information, extensions information, and numerous other environment variables. Simply create a file with one line in it:

```
<? phpinfo(); ?>
```

Access that file with your Web browser. You'll see more information than you ever needed to know!

phpversion()

If `phpinfo()` provides more information than you want, you can use the `phpversion()` function to return just the version number currently in use. For example, on one of my systems, this snippet of code

```
echo "Current version is: ".phpversion();
```

shows

> Current version is: 4.0b3

Program Execution Functions

You can use PHP's built-in program execution functions to use programs residing on your system, such as encryption programs, third-party image manipulation programs, and so forth. For all program execution functions, the PHP user must have permission to execute the given program.

exec()

The exec() function executes an external program. Its syntax is

```
exec(command, [array], [return_var]);
```

If an array is specified, the output of the exec() function will append to the array. If return_var is specified, it will be assigned a value of the program's return status.

For example, you would use the following code to perform a "ping" of a server five times and print the output:

```
$command = "ping -c5 www.thickbook.com";
exec($command, $result, $rval);
for ($i = 0; $i < sizeof($result); $i++) {
echo "$result[$i]<br>";
}
```

passthru()

Like the exec() function, the passthru() function executes an external program. The difference between the two is that passthru() returns the raw output of the action. The syntax of passthru() is

```
passthru(command, return_var);
```

If return_var is specified, it will be assigned a value of the program's return status.

system()

The system() function executes an external program and displays output as the command is being executed. Its syntax is

```
system(command, [return_var]);
```

If return_var is specified, it will be assigned a value of the program's return status.

For example, you would use the following code to perform a "ping" of a server five times and print the raw output:

```
$command = "ping -c5 www.thickbook.com";
system($command);
```

Regular Expression Functions

Regular expressions are used during string manipulation and vary in complexity. PHP has several built-in functions that utilize a powerful, bundled regular expression library.

ereg_replace() and eregi_replace()

The `ereg_replace()` and `eregi_replace()` functions replace instances of a pattern within a string and return the new string. The `ereg_replace()` function performs a case-sensitive match, and `eregi_replace()` performs a case-insensitive match. Here is the syntax for both functions:

```
ereg_replace(pattern, replacement, string);
eregi_replace(pattern, replacement, string);
```

For example, you would use the following code to replace "ASP" with "PHP" in the string "I really love programming in ASP!"

```
<?
$old_string = "I really love programming in ASP!";
$new_string = ereg_replace("ASP", "PHP", $old_string);
echo "$new_string";
?>
```

If "ASP" is mixed case, such as "aSp", use the `eregi_replace()` function:

```
<?
$old_string = "I really love programming in aSp!";
$new_string = eregi_replace("ASP", "PHP", $old_string);
echo "$new_string";
?>
```

split()

The `split()` function splits a string into an array using a certain separator (comma, colon, semicolon, and so on). Its syntax is

```
split(pattern, string, [limit]);
```

If a limit is specified, the `split()` function stops at the named position—for example, at the tenth value in a comma-delimited list.

Session-Handling Functions

Session handling is a way of holding onto data as a user navigates your Web site. Data can be variables or entire objects. These simple functions are just a few of the session-related functions in PHP; see the PHP manual at http://www.php.net/manual/ for more.

session_start()

The session_start() function starts a session if one has not already been started, or it resumes a session if the session ID is present for the user. This function takes no arguments and is called simply by placing the following at the beginning of your code:

```
session_start();
```

session_destroy()

The session_destroy() function effectively destroys all the variables and values registered for the current session. This function takes no arguments and is called simply by placing the following in your code:

```
session_destroy();
```

String Functions

This section will only scratch the surface of PHP's built-in string manipulation functions, but if you understand these common functions, your programming life will be quite a bit easier!

addslashes() and stripslashes()

The addslashes() and stripslashes() functions are very important when inserting and retrieving data from a database. Often, text inserted into a database will contain special characters (single quotes, double quotes, backslashes, NULL) that must be "escaped" before being inserted. The addslashes() function does just that, using the syntax

```
addslashes(string);
```

Similarly, the stripslashes() function will return a string with the slashes taken away, using the syntax

```
stripslashes(string);
```

chop(), ltrim() and trim()

All three of these functions remove errant white space from a string. The chop() function removes white space from the end of a string, while ltrim() removes white space from the beginning of a string. The trim() function removes both leading and trailing white space from a string. The syntax of these functions is

```
chop(string);
ltrim(string);
trim(string);
```

echo()

The echo() function returns output. The syntax of echo() is

```
echo (parameter1, parameter 2, ...)
```

For example:

```
echo "I'm using PHP!";    // output is: I'm using PHP!
echo 2+6; // output is: 8
```

The parentheses are not required when using echo.

explode() and implode()

The explode() function splits a string, using a given separator, and returns the values in an array. The syntax of explode() is

```
explode("separator", "string");
```

For example, the following code takes a string called $color_list, containing a comma-separated list of colors, and places each color into an array called $my_colors:

```
$color_list = "blue,black,red,green,yellow,orange";
$mycolors = explode(",", $color_list);
```

Conversely, the `implode()` function takes an array and makes it into a string, using a given separator. The syntax of `implode()` is

```
implode("separator", "string");
```

For example, the following code takes an array called `$color_list`, then creates a string called `$mycolors`, containing the values of the `$color_list` array, separated by commas:

```
$mycolors = implode(",", $color_list);
```

htmlspecialchars() and htmlentities()

The `htmlspecialchars()` and `htmlentities()` functions convert special characters and HTML entities within strings into their acceptable entity representations. The `htmlspecialchars()` function only converts the less-than sign (< becomes <), greater-than sign (> becomes >), double quotes ("" becomes ") and the ampersand (& becomes &). The `htmlentities()` function will convert the characters in the ISO-8859-1 character set to the proper HTML entity. The syntax of these functions is

```
htmlspecialchars(string);
htmlentities(string);
```

nl2br()

The `nl2br()` function will replace all ASCII newlines with the XHTML-compliant line break (`<BR/>`). The syntax of the `nl2br()` function is

```
nl2br(string);
```

sprintf()

The `sprintf()` function returns a string that has been formatted according to a set of directives. The syntax of `sprintf()` is

```
sprintf(directives, string);
```

Table A.8 lists the formatting directives.

Table A.8 sprintf() Function Formatting Directives

Directive	Result
%	Adds a percent sign.
b	Considers the string an integer and formats it as a binary number.
c	Considers the string an integer and formats it with that ASCII value.
d	Considers the string an integer and formats it as a decimal number.
f	Considers the string a double and formats it as a floating-point number.
o	Considers the string an integer and formats it as an octal number.
s	Considers and formats the string as a string.
x	Considers the string an integer and formats it as a hexadecimal number (lowercase letters).
X	Considers the string an integer and formats it as a hexadecimal number (uppercase letters).

For example, to format currency using `sprintf()`, use this code:

```
<?
$tax = 1.06;
$subtotal = 10.94;
$total = $tax + $subtotal;
$fmt_total = sprintf ("%0.2f", $total);
echo "$fmt_total";
?>
```

The value of `$fmt_total` is 12.00 instead of simply 12.

strlen()

The `strlen()` function returns the length of a given string. The syntax of the `strlen()` function is

```
strlen(string);
```

strtolower()

The `strtolower()` function returns a given string with all alphabetic characters in lowercase. The syntax of `strtolower()` is

```
strtolower(str);
```

For example, to return ABGH 10023 as lowercase, use

```
echo strtolower("ABGH 10023");
```

The result is abgh 10023.

strtoupper()

The `strtoupper()` function returns a given string with all alphabetic characters in uppercase. The syntax of `strtoupper()` is

```
strtoupper (str);
```

For example, to return abgh 10023 as uppercase, use

```
<? echo strtoupper ("abgh 10023"); ?>
```

The result is ABGH 10023.

substr()

The `substr()` function returns a portion of a string, given a starting position and optional ultimate length. The syntax of `substr()` is

```
substr(string, start, [length]);
```

If the start position is a positive number, the starting position is counted from the beginning of the string. If the start position is negative, the starting position is counted from the end of the string.

Similarly, if the optional length parameter is used and is a positive number, then the length is counted from the beginning of the string. If the length parameter is used and is a negative number, the length is counted from the end of the string.

For example:

```
<?
$new_string = substr("PHP is great!", 1); // returns "HP is great!"
$new_string = substr("PHP is great!", 0, 7); // returns "PHP is"
$new_string = substr("PHP is great!", -1); // returns "!"
$new_string = substr("PHP is great!", -6, 5); // returns "great"
?>
```

ucfirst()

The ucfirst() function changes the first alphabetic character in a string to an uppercase character. The syntax of ucfirst() is

```
ucfirst(string);
```

For example, if your string is "i love PHP", the following code returns "I love PHP":

```
ucfirst("i love PHP");
```

ucwords()

The ucwords() function changes the first letter of each word in a string to upper-case. The syntax of ucwords() is

```
ucwords(string);
```

For example, if your string is "i love PHP", the following code will return "I Love PHP":

```
ucwords("i love PHP");
```

Variable Functions

The two basic variable functions, isset() and unset(), help you manage your variables within the scope of an application.

isset() and unset()

The isset() function determines whether a variable exists. The unset() function explicitly destroys the named variable. Here is the syntax of each:

```
isset(var);
unset(var);
```

The isset() function returns true if the variable exists and false if it does not. For example, if you have a variable called $foo with a value of "bar", the following returns true:

```
$foo = "bar";
echo isset($foo);
```

Now, if you use the unset() function on $foo, like this:

```
unset($foo);
```

The value of isset($foo) will now be false:

```
echo isset($foo); // FALSE!
```

Appendix B

Getting Support

One of the greatest benefits of the Open Source community is that people are eager to help you learn as much as you can, so that you can become an advocate as well. However, you probably should attempt to find answers to your questions before posing them to the community at large. Doing so includes reading available manuals and FAQs, searching through mailing list archives, and visiting PHP-related Web sites. Chances are very good that someone else has had the same question you have.

Web Sites

The Web sites listed below are only a sampling of the sites that are out there for PHP developers. The majority of these sites are maintained by people on their own time, so if you use any of their resources, try to give back to the community by helping others out with their questions, when you can, and contributing code snippets to code repositories, and so forth.

www.php.net

Start at the home of PHP. The on-line manual is here, as well as links to ISPs that offer access to PHP, the PHP FAQ, news articles, a calendar of PHP-related events, and much more!

www.thickbook.com

I created this Web site as a supplement for my books. You will find links to other Web sites, additional code samples and tutorials, code fixes for examples in this book, and the code used in this book (downloadable so you don't have to type).

www.zend.com

Zend Technologies, the folks behind the Zend engine of PHP, have created a portal site for PHP developers. This personalized site not only showcases how you can build a high-traffic, dynamic site using PHP, it provides pointers, resources, and lessons on how to maximize the potential of PHP in all your on-line applications. You can also learn about their product offerings, such as the Zend Optimizer.

Webmonkey (hotwired.lycos.com/webmonkey/)

The company that brings us *Wired Magazine* also brings us HotWired, which spawned Webmonkey, a developer's resource site with a section devoted to PHP. Don't limit yourself just to the PHP section of Webmonkey, because there's much information to be had in other sections as well.

WeberDev (www.weberdev.com)

A longtime favorite of PHP developers, this site contains development tricks and tips for many programming languages (just to be fair) as well as a content management system for everyone to add their own code snippets, tutorials, and more! Great weekly newsletter, and high traffic. Go contribute!

PHPBuilder (www.phpbuilder.com)

A very good tutorial site for intermediate and advanced PHP developers, containing weekly "How To" columns for real-world applications, such as "Building Dynamic Pages with Search Engines in Mind," "Generating Pronounceable Passwords," and tons more. Highly recommended!

DevShed (www.devshed.com)

Many user-submitted tutorials, news articles, interviews, and competitive analyses of server-side programming languages. Covers PHP as well as many other topics of interest to developers, such as servers and databases.

px.sklar.com

A bare-bones code repository, but who needs graphics when all you're looking for are code snippets? Borrowing from the "take a penny, leave a penny" mentality, grab a code snippet to start with, then add your own when you feel confident in sharing.

Mailing Lists

There are several high-traffic mailing lists available for PHP discussion. Please remember your netiquette when asking a question: be polite, offer as many examples you can (if you're describing a problem), provide your system information (if looking for a solution), and did I mention to say please and thank you?

A comprehensive mailing list subscription management tool for the PHP-related mailing lists can be found at http://www.php.net/mailing-lists.php. The English PHP mailing lists are archived and available for searching at http://marc.theaimsgroup.com/. Just look for the PHP-related lists under the "WWW" heading. An invaluable resource, which archives the MySQL mailing list as well as quite a few others!

Index

Symbols

+ (addition operator), 38, 255
&& (AND operator), 40, 257
* (asterisk), 28
(\) backslash, 33, 43, 87
[ ] (brackets), 29
{ } (curly braces), 258
/ (division operator), 38, 255
$ (dollar sign), 34, 252
== (double equals sign), 38, 256
// (double slashes), 33, 251
= (equals sign), 15, 34, 38
% (modulus operator), 38, 255
* (multiplication operator), 38, 255
\n (newline character), 67
!= (not equal to), 256
! (NOT operator), 40, 257
|| (OR operator), 40, 257
" " (quotation marks), 33, 35
; (semicolon), 32, 251
- (subtraction operator), 38, 255
\t (tab character), 67
_ (underscore character), 34, 252

A

A format, date function, 281
a format, date function, 281
a mode, writing data files, 70, 285
a+ mode, writing data files, 70
ACTION attribute, 30
activating extensions, 17
Add Record button, 124
additional operator (+), 38, 255
addresses, IP, authentication, 149–150
addslashes() function, 300
align-center attribute, 23
ALTER command, 86
American National Standards Institute (ANSI), 84
AND operator (&&), 40, 257
ANSI (American National Standards Institute), 84
Apache
    Apache Software Foundation, 2
    installing and configuring
        Installer Welcome screen, 8
        on Linux/Unix, 3–7
        on Windows, 8–10
    licensing, 9
    overview, 2
    start page, 7
apachectl utility, 6–7
arithmetic operators, 38–39, 255
array() function, 45–46, 261
array_keys() function, 269–270
array_merge() function, 268–269
array_pop() function, 262–263

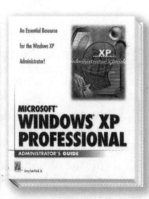